Newcomer
English Language Development
Teacher's Guide

Program Authors

Dr. Diane August
Managing Director,
American Institutes for Research
Washington, D.C.

Dr. Jana Echevarria
California State University, Long Beach
Long Beach, California

Dr. Josefina V. Tinajero
University of Texas at El Paso
El Paso, Texas

Cover: Nathan Love

www.mheonline.com/readingwonders

Send all inquiries to:
McGraw-Hill Education
2 Penn Plaza
New York, New York 10121

ISBN: 978-0-02-132644-0
MHID: 0-02-132644-4

Printed in the United States of America.

6 7 8 9 LOV 22

A

TABLE OF CONTENTS

UNIT 3: Community

UNIT 4: The World

INTRODUCTION

The *Wonders for English Learners* Newcomer components are designed to help your students build their listening, speaking, reading, and writing skills in English.

These components will help newcomers develop oral language by creating frequent opportunities for students to engage in conversations with their classmates.

Ken Karp/McGraw-Hill Education

Teaching Strategies for Newcomers: Building Oral Language

To progress academically, newcomers must have access to basic, high-utility vocabulary from which they can build English language skills. Much of this vocabulary will become a part of their everyday speech when they are given opportunities to converse with their classmates.

Here are some general strategies to keep in mind as you build a classroom environment that encourages conversation:

- Provide enough time for students to answer questions.
- Allow responses in the native language.
- Utilize nonverbal cues, such as pointing, acting out, or drawing.
- Use corrective feedback to model correct form for a response.
- Repeat correct answers to validate and motivate students.
- Elaborate on answers to model fluent speaking and grammatical patterns.
- Elicit more detailed responses by asking follow-up questions.
- Remind students that listening is as important as speaking.

USING THE *WONDERS FOR ENGLISH LEARNERS* NEWCOMER COMPONENTS

Teacher's Guide

The Teacher's Guide provides instruction with three lessons for each conversation topic.

Set Purpose

Prepare students for the lesson purpose and objective.

Teach/Model Vocabulary

Sing the song/chant before teaching new vocabulary and language structures.

Practice/Apply

Pair students to engage in collaborative conversations and apply what they've learned.

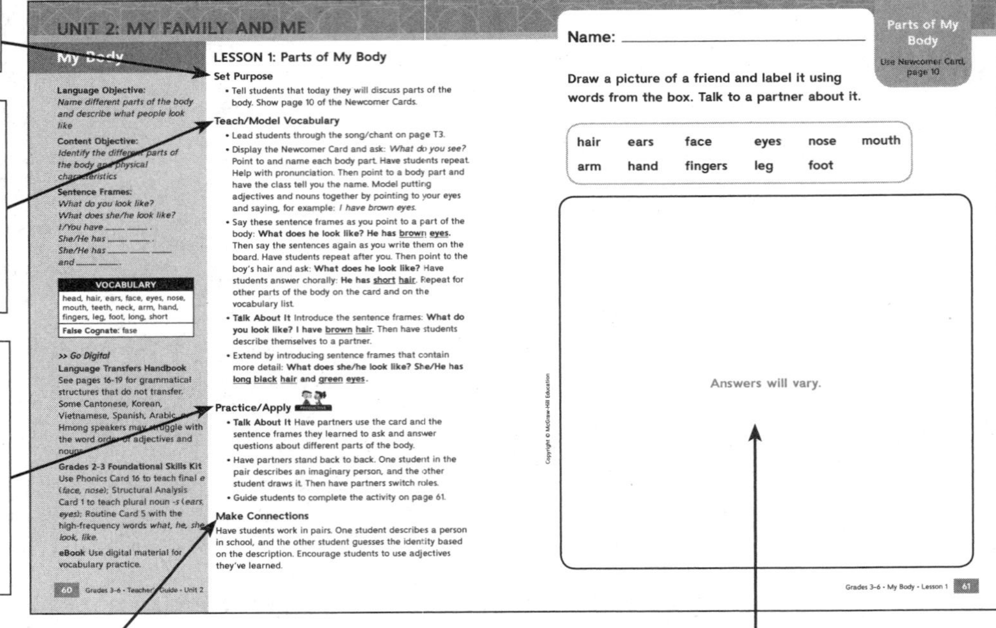

UNIT 2: MY FAMILY AND ME

My Body

Language Objective: *Name different parts of the body and describe what people look like*

Content Objective: *Identify the different parts of the body and physical characteristics*

Sentence Frames:
What do you look like?
What does she/he look like?
I/You have ___ ___.
She/He has ___ ___.
She/He has ___ ___ and ___ ___.

VOCABULARY
head, hair, ears, face, eyes, nose, mouth, teeth, neck, arm, hand, fingers, leg, foot, long, short

False Cognate: fase

>> Go Digital
Language Transfers Handbook
See pages 16–19 for grammatical structures that do not transfer. Some Cantonese, Korean, Vietnamese, Spanish, Arabic, and Hmong speakers may struggle with the word order of adjectives and nouns.

Grades 2–3 Foundational Skills Kit
Use Phonics Card 16 to teach final e (*face, nose*); Structural Analysis Card 1 to teach plural noun -s (*ears, eyes*); Routine Card 5 with the high-frequency words *what, he, she, look, like.*

eBook Use digital material for vocabulary practice.

LESSON 1: Parts of My Body

Set Purpose
- Tell students that today they will discuss parts of the body. Show page 10 of the Newcomer Cards.

Teach/Model Vocabulary
- Lead students through the song/chant on page T3.
- Display the Newcomer Card and ask: *What do you see?* Point to and name each body part. Have students repeat. Help with pronunciation. Then point to a body part and have the class tell you the name. Model putting adjectives and nouns together by pointing to your eyes and saying, for example: *I have brown eyes.*
- Say these sentence frames as you point to a part of the body: **What does he look like? He has brown eyes.** Then say the sentences again as you write them on the board. Have students repeat after you. Then point to the boy's hair and ask: **What does he look like?** Have students answer chorally: **He has short hair.** Repeat for other parts of the body on the card and on the vocabulary list.
- **Talk About It** Introduce the sentence frames: **What do you look like? I have brown hair.** Then have students describe themselves to a partner.
- Extend by introducing sentence frames that contain more detail: **What does she/he look like? She/He has long black hair and green eyes.**

Practice/Apply
- **Talk About It** Have partners use the card and the sentence frames they learned to ask and answer questions about different parts of the body.
- Have partners stand back to back. One student in the pair describes an imaginary person, and the other student draws it. Then have partners switch roles.
- Guide students to complete the activity on page 61.

Make Connections
Have students work in pairs. One student describes a person in school, and the other student guesses the identity based on the description. Encourage students to use adjectives they've learned.

60 Grades 3–6 • Teacher's Guide • Unit 2

Name: ___

Parts of My Body
Use Newcomer Card, page 10

Draw a picture of a friend and label it using words from the box. Talk to a partner about it.

hair	ears	face	eyes	nose	mouth
arm	hand	fingers	leg	foot	

Answers will vary.

Copyright © McGraw-Hill Education

Grades 3–6 • My Body • Lesson 1 61

Make Connections

Extend learning beyond the lesson and connect to students' personal lives.

Provide opportunities to practice and write about what they've learned.

Unit Overview

Each unit overview provides a snapshot of the content.

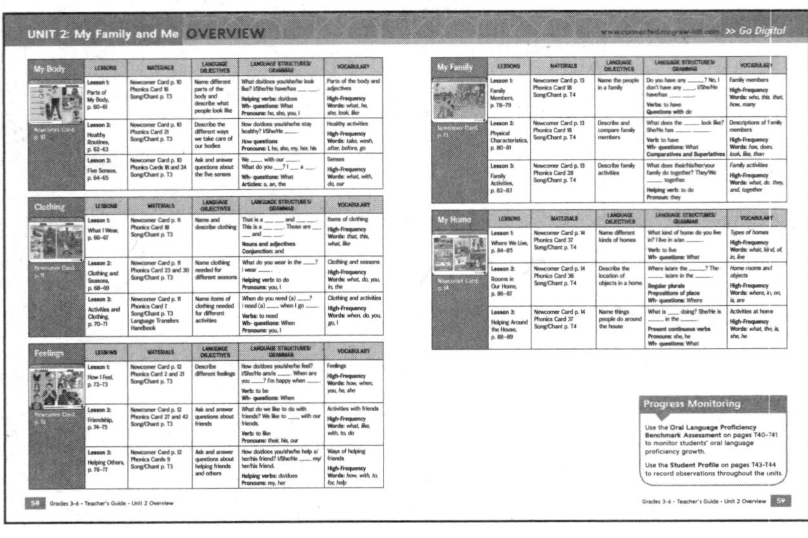

UNIT 2: My Family and Me OVERVIEW

www.connected.mcgraw-hill.com >> Go Digital

Progress Monitoring

Use the Oral Language Proficiency Benchmark Assessment on pages T40–T41 to monitor students' oral language proficiency growth.

Use the Student Profile on pages T43–T44 to record observations throughout the units.

58 Grades 3–6 • Teacher's Guide • Unit 2 Overview

Grades 3–6 • Teacher's Guide • Unit 2 Overview 59

Teacher Support

Includes Games, Songs/Chants, Answer Key, and Progress Monitoring.

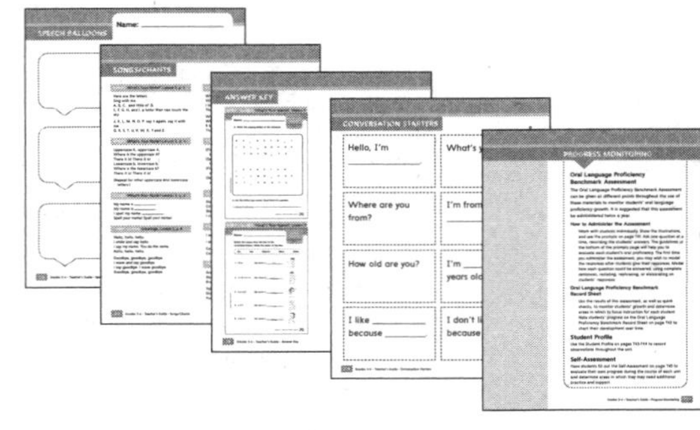

Newcomer Cards

Newcomer cards include colorful illustrations and photographs to stimulate conversations. Each card presents a topic supported in the Teacher's Guide over three lessons.

>> Go Digital
www.connected.mcgraw-hill.com

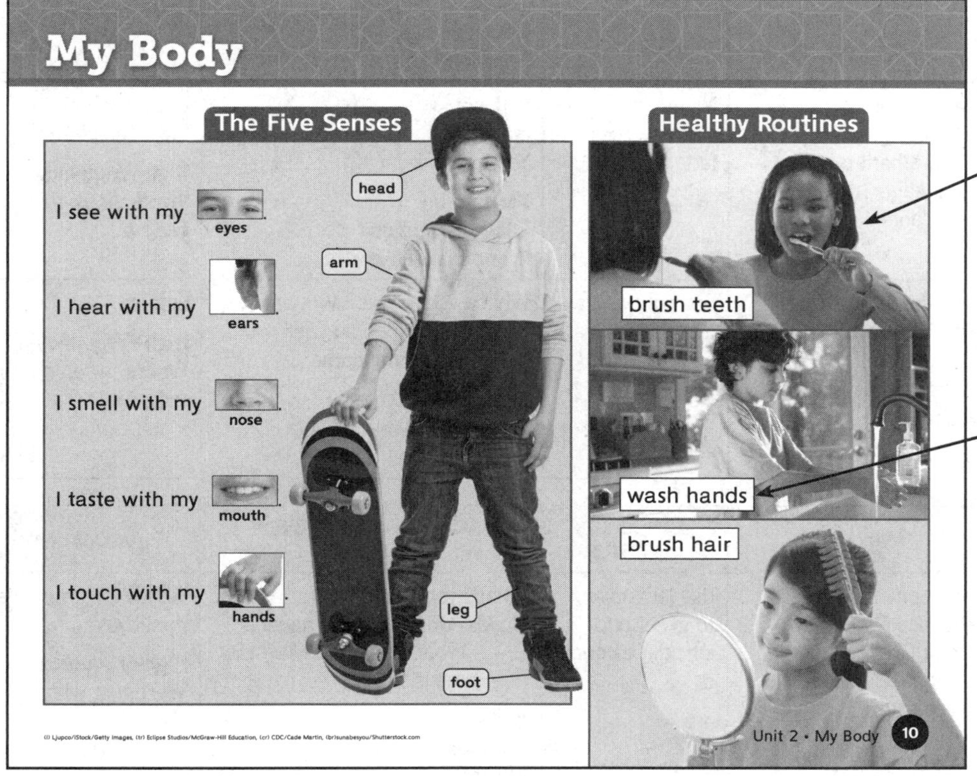

Colorful images provide context for new content.

Labels indicate lesson vocabulary.

Digital

eBook

Presents Newcomer Cards in a student-friendly eBook with additional activities that include audio support and recording features.

Online Games

Offer additional interaction and practice with the vocabulary.

Online Visuals

Offer additional images for each topic to extend students' collaborative conversations.

Components (Grades 3-6)

- Newcomer Teacher's Guide
- Newcomer Cards
- eBook of Newcomer Cards
- Online Games
- Online Visuals

Wonders Materials also referenced:

- Language Transfers Handbook
- Foundational Skills Kit
  - Phonemic Awareness
  - Phonological Awareness
  - Structural Analysis
  - Fluency

What's Your Name?	LESSONS	MATERIALS	LANGUAGE OBJECTIVES	LANGUAGE STRUCTURES/ GRAMMAR	VOCABULARY
Newcomer Card, p. 1	**Lesson 1:** Letters of the Alphabet, p. 2–3	Newcomer Card p. 1 Song/Chant p. 154 Language Transfers Handbook	Name the letters of the alphabet	Is this the letter ____? Yes, it is. No, it isn't the letter ____. It's the letter ____. **Verb:** to be **Yes/No questions** **Contractions:** isn't, it's **Pronouns**: this, it	Letters of the alphabet **High-Frequency Words:** *is, it, yes, no*
	Lesson 2: Uppercase and Lowercase, p. 4–5	Newcomer Card p. 1 Phonics Card 7 Song/Chant p. 154 Language Transfers Handbook	Name uppercase and lowercase letters	Is this a lowercase ____? Is this an uppercase ____? Yes, it is. No, it's a(n) ____. **Verb:** to be **Yes/No questions** **Pronouns**: this, it	Uppercase and lowercase letters **High-Frequency Words:** *it, is, this, yes, no*
	Lesson 3: Spelling My Name, p. 6–7	Newcomer Card p. 1 Phonics Card 5 Song/Chant p. 154 Language Transfers Handbook	Say your name and the letters of your name	What's your name? My name is ____. How do you spell your name? I spell my name ____. **Helping verb:** to do **Pronouns**: I, you, my, your **Wh- questions**: What	Letters **High-Frequency Words:** *what, how, is, your, my*

Greetings	LESSONS	MATERIALS	LANGUAGE OBJECTIVES	LANGUAGE STRUCTURES/ GRAMMAR	VOCABULARY
Newcomer Card, p. 2	**Lesson 1:** Hello and Goodbye, p. 8–9	Newcomer Card p. 2 Phonics Card 37 Song/Chant p. 154 Language Transfers Handbook	Use language to greet and introduce people	What's your name? I'm ____. I'm Mr./Ms./Mrs. ____. My name is ____. What's his/her name? His/ Her name is ____. **Verb:** to be **Pronouns**: his, her **Wh- questions**: Who, What **Contractions**: I'm, What's	Words for greetings and goodbyes **High-Frequency Words:** *is, who, this, what*
	Lesson 2: Talking About You and Me, p. 10–11	Newcomer Card p. 2 Phonics Card 7 Song/Chant p. 154 Language Transfers Handbook	Ask and answer questions about yourself and others	Where do you live? What's your/ their address? I/We/They live in/on/at ____. What's your phone number? My phone number is ____. **Verbs:** to be **Pronouns:** I, my, you, we, your, their **Prepositions of place** **Wh- questions:** Where, What	Personal information **High-Frequency Words:** *where, is, in, on*
	Lesson 3: Likes and Dislikes, p. 12–13	Newcomer Card p. 2 Phonics Card 9 Song/Chant p. 154 Language Transfers Handbook	Use language to express and explain likes and dislikes	I like/don't like ____. I like ____ and ____. Do you like ____? Why do/don't you like ____? I like/don't like ____ because ____. **Verb**: to like Questions with *do* **Negatives**: don't, doesn't **Wh- questions:** Why	Likes and dislikes **High-Frequency Words:** *like, because, I, why, they, it*

Geometric Shapes

Newcomer Card, p. 3

LESSONS	MATERIALS	LANGUAGE OBJECTIVES	LANGUAGE STRUCTURES/ GRAMMAR	VOCABULARY
Lesson 1: Shapes, p. 14–15	Newcomer Card p. 3 Phonics Cards 18 and 28 Song/Chant p. 154 Language Transfers Handbook	Name shapes	What shape is this? It's a ____. This is/That's a ____. These/ Those are ____. **Verb:** to be **Wh- questions:** What **Pronouns:** this, these, that, those **Regular plurals**	Shapes **High-Frequency Words:** *what, is, these, those*
Lesson 2: Colors, p. 16–17	Newcomer Card p. 3 Phonics Card 8 Song/Chant p. 154 Language Transfers Handbook	Name colors and shapes	What color is the ____? The __ is __. Point to a __ __ in the classroom. What do you see? It's a ____ ____. **Nouns and adjectives** **Imperatives**	Colors **High-Frequency Words:** *red, blue, green, brown, black, white*
Lesson 3: Shapes and Colors Around Us, p. 18–19	Newcomer Card p. 3 Phonics Card 43 Song/Chant p. 154 Language Transfers Handbook	Use language to identify shapes and colors around us	What shape is this/that? This/ That ___ ___ is a ____. What shape are these/those? These/ Those ____ ____ are ____. **Regular plurals** **Nouns and adjectives**	Shapes and colors of objects **High-Frequency Words:** *this, that, these, those, is, are*

Numbers

Newcomer Card, p. 4

PROGRESS MONITORING
Use pages T40–T41 to monitor oral language proficiency.

Use pages T43–T44 to record observations throughout the units.

LESSONS	MATERIALS	LANGUAGE OBJECTIVES	LANGUAGE STRUCTURES/ GRAMMAR	VOCABULARY
Lesson 1: Numbers 1–100, p. 20–21	Newcomer Card p. 4 Phonics Card 35 Song/Chant p. T1 Language Transfers Handbook	Name and sequence numbers 1–100	What number is this? This is number ____. Point to the number ____. Count from ____ to ____. **Wh- questions:** What **Imperatives**	Numbers **High-Frequency Words:** *from, to,* numbers one through ten
Lesson 2: How Old Are You?, p. 22–23	Newcomer Card p. 4 Phonics Card 32 Song/Chant p. T1 Language Transfers Handbook	Ask and answer questions about age	How old is she/he? She/He is ____ years old. How old are you? I'm ____ years old. ***How* questions** **Pronouns:** I, you, he, she **Contraction:** I'm	Ages **High-Frequency Words:** *he, she, is, years, old*
Lesson 3: How Many?, p. 24–25	Newcomer Card p. 4 Phonics Card 3 Song/Chant p. T1 Language Transfers Handbook	Name the number of objects	How many do they/we/you have? They/We/I have ____ ____. How many does she/ he have? She/He has ___ ___. I have ___ ___ and ___ ___. **Verb:** to have **Conjunction:** and ***How* questions**	Numbers of Objects **High-Frequency Words:** *they, she, he, we, I*

What's Your Name?

Language Objective:
Name the letters of the alphabet

Content Objective:
Identify the letters of the alphabet

Sentence Frames:
Is this the letter ____?
Yes, it is.
No, it isn't the letter ____.
It's the letter ____.

VOCABULARY						
A	B	C	D	E	F	G
H	I	J	K	L	M	N
O	P	Q	R	S	T	
U	V	W	X	Y	Z	

>> Go Digital

Language Transfers Handbook
See pages 10-14 to identify letters of the alphabet that have a sound and symbol match in Spanish, Vietnamese, and Hmong. A newcomer whose first language does not use the Latin alphabet may need more practice to master the letter names.

Grades 2-3 Foundational Skills Kit
Use Routine Card 1 to provide support with spelling words; Routine Card 5 with the high-frequency words *is, it, yes,* and *no*; Structural Analysis Card 17 for support with contractions with *not* (*isn't*).

eBook Use digital material to practice vocabulary.

LESSON 1: Letters of the Alphabet

Set Purpose

- Tell students that today they will discuss the letters of the alphabet. Show page 1 of the Newcomer Cards.

Teach/Model Vocabulary

- Lead students through the song/chant on page 154.
- Display the Newcomer Card. Have students point to and name letters they know. Help with pronunciation.
- Say these sentence frames as you point to a letter: **Is this the letter _C_? Yes, it is** *or* **No, it isn't the letter _C_. It's the letter _M_.** Then say the sentences again as you write them on the board, completing them with the letter. Have students repeat after you. Explain the difference between sentences and questions, using punctuation and intonation to demonstrate the difference. Then point to the letter *S* and ask: **Is this the letter _P_ ?** Have students answer chorally: **Yes, it is** *or* **No, it isn't the letter _P_. It's the letter _S_.** Provide support as needed. Repeat for other letters.
- **Talk About It** Have partners practice asking and answering each other's questions about different letters.

Practice/Apply COLLABORATIVE

- **Talk About It** Have partners use the Newcomer Card and sentence frames to name letters around the room.
- Guide students to complete the activity on page 3. They can create a similar practice page for a partner with different letters missing.
- In pairs, one student uses gestures to give clues about a letter and the partner guesses it. Then students switch roles. Model the activity: Stand straight with both arms out to the sides to form letter *T*. Ask: *Is this the letter _T_?* or *Is this the letter _M_?* Students can respond using the sentence frames they learned.

Make Connections

Each student can make a set of alphabet flashcards and then shuffle them. Partners can play a game where they race to put the cards in the correct order. Once the cards are in the correct order, students can read the letters to each other.

Name: ______________________________

Use Newcomer Card, page 1

A. Write the missing letters of the alphabet.

A B D E F G I

J K L N O P Q R

T U V W Y Z

B C D E F G H

J L M N P Q R

S T V W X Y Z

B. List the letters you wrote. Read them to a partner.

____

What's Your Name?

Language Objective:
Name uppercase and lowercase letters

Content Objective:
Identify uppercase and lowercase letters

Sentence Frames:
Is this an uppercase ____?
Is this a lowercase ____?
Yes, it is./No, it's a ____.

VOCABULARY					
Aa	Bb	Cc	Dd	Ee	
Ff	Gg	Hh	Ii	Jj	Kk
Ll	Mm	Nn	Oo	Pp	
Qq	Rr	Ss	Tt	Uu	Vv
Ww	Xx	Yy	Zz		
uppercase, lowercase					

>> Go Digital
Language Transfers Handbook
See pages 16-19 for grammatical structures that do not transfer. Hmong, Vietnamese, Korean, Arabic, Tagalog, or Cantonese speakers may mistake the article *one* for *a* or *an*.

Grades 2-3 Foundational Skills Kit
Use Phonics Card 7 to teach short *a, e, i, o,* and *u* sounds; Phonics Card 16 for final *e* (*uppercase*); Routine Card 5 with the high-frequency words *it, is, this, yes,* and *no.*

eBook Use digital material to practice vocabulary.

LESSON 2: Uppercase and Lowercase

Set Purpose

- Tell students that today they will discuss uppercase and lowercase letters. Show page 1 of the Newcomer Cards.

Teach/Model Vocabulary

- Elicit letters from Lesson 1.
- Lead students through the song/chant on page 154.
- Display the Newcomer Card. Have students take turns pointing to and identifying uppercase and lowercase letters. Help with pronunciation.
- Say these sentence frames as you point to lowercase letters: **Is this a lowercase _t_? Yes, it is** *or* **Is this a lowercase _l_? No, it's a lowercase _t_.** Then say the sentences again as you write them on the board, completing the sentences with the letter. Have students repeat after you. Then point to a lowercase *r* and ask: **Is this a lowercase _m_?** Have students answer chorally: **No, it's a lowercase _r_.** Repeat for other lowercase letters on the Newcomer Card.
- Expand by reusing the sentence frames with uppercase letters.
- **Talk About It** Have partners point to and identify different uppercase and lowercase letters around the room.

Practice/Apply

INTERPRETIVE

- **Talk About It** Have partners use the Newcomer Card and the sentence frames they learned to ask and answer questions about uppercase and lowercase letters.
- Have partners work together. One student in the pair indicates a letter somewhere in the room. Then the partner says and writes the uppercase or lowercase version of that letter. Partners can switch roles.
- Guide students to complete the activity on page 5.

Make Connections

Provide magazines. Students can cut out different uppercase and lowercase letters and glue them on paper so that all *A*s are together, all *B*s are together, and so on. Students can put the pages in order to make an alphabet book that partners read aloud to each other and keep as a reference.

Name: ____________________

Use Newcomer Card, page 1

A. Match the uppercase letter to its lowercase letter.

B	d
P	a
D	m
A	b
M	p

B. Write the pairs of letters you matched.

____

What's Your Name?

Language Objective:
Say your name and the letters of your name

Content Objective:
Say your name and the letters of your name

Sentence Frames:
What's your name?
My name is ____.
How do you spell your name?
I spell my name ____.

VOCABULARY						
A	B	C	D	E	F	G
H	I	J	K	L	M	N
O	P	Q	R	S	T	
U	V	W	X	Y	Z	
spell, name						

>> Go Digital

Language Transfers Handbook
See pages 16-19 for grammatical structures that do not transfer. Cantonese, Hmong, or Vietnamese speakers may struggle with possessive forms of pronouns.

Grades 2-3 Foundational Skills Kit
Use Phonics Card 5 in the Grade 2-3 Kit to teach short *e* (*spell*); Routine Card 5 with the high-frequency words *what, how, is, your,* and *my*.

eBook and Games Provide audio support, interaction, and practice with the vocabulary.

LESSON 3: Spelling My Name

Set Purpose

- Tell students that today they will discuss saying their name and the letters in their name. Show page 1 of the Newcomer Cards.

Teach/Model Vocabulary

- Elicit letters and have students take turns writing letters on the board.
- Lead students through the song/chant on page 154.
- Display the Newcomer Card. Point to the people speaking. Ask: *What do you think they're saying?*
- Say and write down the sentence frames: **My name is Mr./Mrs./Ms. ____. I spell my last name ____.** Introduce yourself to students and spell your last name.
- Read aloud the text in the speech balloons, modeling their conversation: **Hello! What's your name? Hi! My name is <u>Sharif</u>. How do you spell your name? I spell my name <u>S-h-a-r-i-f</u>.** Play the role of the girl or Sharif as you repeat the conversation a few times with individual students.
- **Talk About It** Have partners practice saying hello to each other and asking each other to spell their names.
- Expand by telling students that names begin with an uppercase letter, followed by lowercase letters. Students can practice saying and writing their first, middle, and last names.

Practice/Apply

- **Talk About It** Have partners use the Newcomer Card and the sentence frames they learned to practice spelling another classmate's name.
- Have partners take turns saying their first, middle, or last name using the sentence frame *I spell my name ____*. One student guesses if it is a first, middle, or last name. Then partners switch roles.
- Guide students to complete the activity on page 7.

Make Cultural Connections

Have students discuss the following prompt with a partner: *Name a friend from your home country and then spell his or her first and last name.*

Name: ______________________________

Spelling My Name

Use Newcomer Card, page 1

Match the names from the box to the scrambled letters. Write the name on the line.

Kai	Ted	Roberto	Mina	Aisha

1. i k a My name is ______________ .

2. o r b t e r o My name is ______________ .

3. a a s h i My name is ______________ .

4. e d t My name is ______________ .

5. a m n i My name is ______________ .

Greetings

Language Objective:
Use language to greet and introduce people

Content Objective:
Demonstrate understanding of greetings and introductions

Sentence Frames:
What's your name?
I'm ____.
I'm Mr./Ms./Mrs. ____.
My name is ____.
What's his/her name?
His/Her name is ____.

VOCABULARY
hello, goodbye, hi, bye, name, good morning, good night, see you tomorrow

>> Go Digital

Language Transfers Handbook
See pages 16-19 for grammatical structures that do not transfer. Korean or Vietnamese speakers may confuse subject pronouns with object pronouns.

Grades 2–3 Foundational Skills Kit
Use Phonics Card 37 to teach the variant vowel /ü/ in *good*; Routine Card 5 with the high-frequency words *is, who, this,* and *what.*

eBook Use digital material for vocabulary practice.

LESSON 1: Hello and Goodbye

Set Purpose

- Tell students that today they will discuss greeting people. Show page 2 of the Newcomer Cards.

Teach/Model Vocabulary

- Lead students through the song/chant on page 154.
- Display the card. Ask: *What do you see?*
- Say and write the sentence frames: **Hello. I'm Mr./Ms./Mrs. ____, I'm ____,** and **My name is ____.** Introduce yourself to students using the first sentence frame. Explain that we say *hello* to a new friend or adult, and *hi* to a good friend. Then students can say *hello* to you and to a friend.
- Read aloud the text in the speech balloons in box 1, modeling their conversation: **Hello. I'm Roberto. Good morning. My name is Lily.** Explain *good morning.*
- **Talk About It** Partners can greet each other using the sentence frames Roberto and Lily used.
- Repeat the instruction with the "goodbye" scene in box 4. Explain the different "goodbye" words and phrases listed in the sidebar. Partners can practice saying goodbye to each other.
- Extend the lesson by having partners ask and answer questions about the names of their classmates: **What is his/her name? His/Her name is ____.**

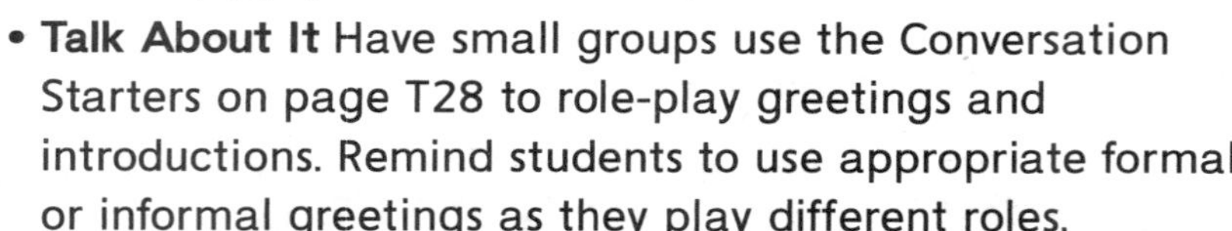

Practice/Apply

- **Talk About It** Have small groups use the Conversation Starters on page T28 to role-play greetings and introductions. Remind students to use appropriate formal or informal greetings as they play different roles.
- Have partners use the Speech Balloons on pages T26–T27 to write a dialogue. Have another group read the dialogue and guess who is who in the conversation.
- Guide students to complete the activity on page 9.

Make Connections

Students practice "hello" and "goodbye" gestures, such as shaking hands and waving. Have partners use these gestures as they present the dialogues they created in Practice/Apply.

Name: ______________________

Write other words in the chart that mean "hello" and "goodbye." Tell a partner when we use "hi" and when we use "hello."

hello	goodbye
______________	______________
______________	______________

Greetings

Language Objective:
Ask and answer questions about yourself and others

Content Objective:
Determine a person's address and phone number

Sentence Frames:
Where do you live?
What's your/their address?
I/We/They live in/on/at ____.
What's your phone number?
My (phone) number is ____.
Where does he/she live?
What's his/her address?
My address is ____.

VOCABULARY
live, address, phone number, street, lane, avenue
Cognates: avenida

>> Go Digital

Language Transfers Handbook
See pages 16-19 for grammatical structures that do not transfer. Korean, Spanish, or Arabic speakers may confuse the phrasal verbs *live in* and *live on.*

Grades 2–3 Foundational Skills Kit
Use Phonics Card 7 to teach short *a* (*address, avenue*); Routine Card 5 with the high-frequency words *where, is, in,* and *on*; Phonological Awareness Card 7 to teach syllable blending.

eBook Use digital material for vocabulary practice.

LESSON 2: Talking About You and Me

Set Purpose

- Tell students that today they will discuss addresses and phone numbers. Show page 2 of the Newcomer Cards.

Teach/Model Vocabulary

- Elicit vocabulary from Lesson 1.
- Lead students through the song/chant on page 154.
- Display the Newcomer Card. Point to box 2 and ask: *What do you see?* Then say and write these sentence frames, filling them in with information about yourself: **I live in/on/at ____. My phone number is ____.** Explain that **I live in/on/at ____** provides the same information as **My address is ____.** Then have students take turns asking and answering the question: *Where do you live?*
- Read aloud the text in the speech balloons in box 2, modeling their conversation: **I live on First Street. Where do you live? I live at 123 North Avenue. What's your phone number? My number is 555-6789.**
- **Talk About It** Have partners use the sentence frames to exchange addresses again and phone numbers.
- Extend the lesson by teaching the rest of the sentence frames listed in the sidebar, explaining the different pronouns and when to use them. Note the difference between *live on, live in,* and *live at.*

Practice/Apply

- **Talk About It** Have partners use the Newcomer Card and the sentence frames they learned to tell one thing they learned about Roberto and Lily.
- Have students pretend they are calling a new friend to discuss getting together. Partners can role-play making the phone call, greeting each other, and exchanging addresses and phone numbers using sentence frames they learned and the Conversation Starters on page T29. Model for students as needed.
- Guide students to complete the activity on page 11.

Make Connections

Have partners tell each other where their friends live. Have partners present to the class. Encourage other students to ask a follow up question.

Name: ______________________________

Talking About You and Me

Use Newcomer Card, page 2

Draw a picture of the street you live on. Then write your address.

I live ______________________________.

Greetings

Language Objective:
Use language to express and explain likes and dislikes

Content Objective:
Identify and explain likes and dislikes

Sentence Frames:
I like/don't like ____.
I like ____ and ____.
Do you like ____?
Does he/she like ____?
Yes/No, she/he likes/doesn't like ____.
Why do you like ____?
I like ____ because ____.
Why don't you like ____?
I don't like ____ because ____
Let's have a snack.

VOCABULARY
like, because, fruit, grapes, apples, bananas, books, cats, dogs
Cognates: fruta, bananas

>> Go Digital

Language Transfers Handbook See pages 16-19 for grammatical structures that do not transfer. Cantonese, Korean, Spanish, or Arabic speakers may omit helping verbs in negative statements.

Grades 2–3 Foundational Skills Kit Use Phonics Card 9 to teach *r* blends *(fruit, grapes);* Routine Card 5 with the high-frequency words *like, because, I, why, they,* and *it.*

eBook and Games Provide audio support, interaction, and practice with the vocabulary.

LESSON 3: Likes and Dislikes

Set Purpose

- Tell students that today they will discuss likes and dislikes. Show page 2 of the Newcomer Cards.

Teach/Model Vocabulary

- Elicit vocabulary from Lessons 1 and 2.
- Lead students through the song/chant on page 154.
- Display the Newcomer Card and point to box 3. Say and write these sentence frames: **I like ___** and **I don't like ___**, filling them in with information about yourself. Then have students take turns asking and answering the questions: *What do you like? What don't you like?*
- Read aloud the text in the speech balloons in box 3: **Let's have a snack. I like grapes. I like apples and bananas.** Repeat the instruction for *books, cats,* and *dogs* from the vocabulary list, and any other items students want to discuss. Then reuse the sentence frames for students to talk about dislikes.
- **Talk About It** Have partners compare their own likes and dislikes.
- Extend by introducing the conjunction *and*. Then expand further by introducing the sentence frames: **Why do/don't you like ____? I like/don't like ____ because ____.** Model as needed.

Practice/Apply

- **Talk About It** Have partners use the Conversation Starters on page T30 to express and explain their likes and dislikes.
- Provide partners with magazines showing items listed in the vocabulary and other items they know. Have one student hold up a picture while the partner uses the sentence frame: **I like/don't like ____ because ____.** Then they switch roles.
- Guide students to complete the activity on page 13.

Make Cultural Connections

Have partners describe fruits from their home countries. Have them explain why they like or don't like each of them.

Name: ___________________________

Likes and Dislikes

Use Newcomer Card, page 2

Write six things you like.

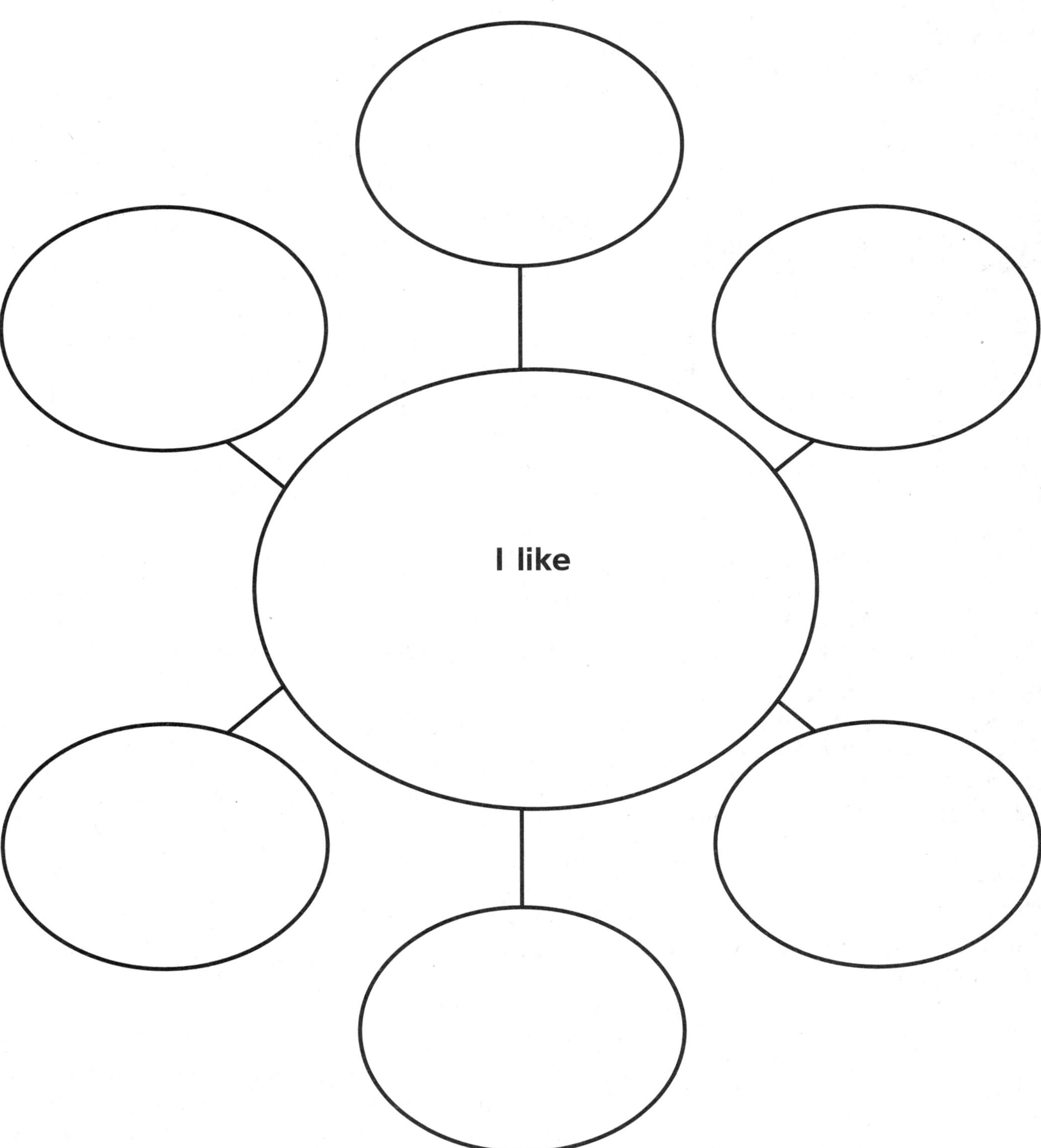

Geometric Shapes

Language Objective:
Name shapes

Content Objective:
Identify shapes

Sentence Frames:
What shape is this?
It's a ____.
This is/That's a(n) ____.
These/Those are ____.

VOCABULARY
circle, triangle, rectangle, square, star, diamond, shape, oval
Cognates: círculo, triángulo, rectángulo

>> Go Digital

Language Transfers Handbook
See pages 16-19 for grammatical structures that do not transfer. Cantonese, Hmong, Korean, Arabic, or Tagalog speakers may struggle with irregular subject-verb agreement (*is, are*).

Grades 2-3 Foundational Skills Kit
Use Phonics Card 18 to teach the consonant digraph *sh* in *shape*; Phonics Card 28 to teach the *r*-controlled vowel /är/ in *star* and *are*; Routine Card 5 with high-frequency words *what, is, these,* and *those*.

eBook Use digital material to practice vocabulary.

LESSON 1: Shapes

Set Purpose

- Tell students that today they will discuss shapes. Show page 3 of the Newcomer Cards.

Teach/Model Vocabulary

- Lead students through the song/chant on page 154.
- Display the Newcomer Card and ask: *What do you see?* Then point to and name each shape at the top. Have students repeat. Help with pronunciation.
- Say these sentence frames as you point to a shape: **What shape is this? It's a <u>square</u>.** Then say the sentences again as you write them on the board, completing the second sentence with the name of the shape. Have students repeat after you. Then point to the circle and ask: **What shape is this?** Have students answer chorally: **It's a <u>circle</u>**, filling in the name of the shape. Repeat for the other shapes on the Newcomer Card, listed in the vocabulary list, and in the classroom.
- **Talk About It** Have partners talk about the different shapes on the card and around the classroom.
- Expand by introducing the sentence frames **This is/That's a(n) ____** and **These/Those are ____.** Provide support with plural forms of shapes. Explain that the words *this* and *these* are used for objects up close while *that* and *those* are used for objects farther away.

Practice/Apply

INTERPRETIVE

- **Talk About It** Have partners use the Newcomer Card and the sentence frames they learned to ask and answer questions about different shapes on each other's clothes.
- Have students create a tally chart listing the shapes they have learned. Then have partners walk around the room to check off and talk about each shape they find.
- Guide students to complete the activity on page 15.

Make Connections

In pairs, have one student draw a picture of a shape she or he saw in the room and checked on the tally chart. Have the partner guess and name the shape. For example: a student can draw a square and the partner says: *That's a square*. Then they can switch roles.

Name: ______________________________

Shapes

Use Newcomer Card, page 3

Write the names of the black shapes.
Use the words from the box.

circles	squares	triangle	stars	rectangle

1. 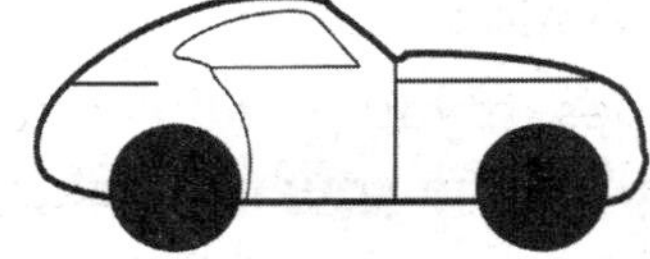

1. These are ____________________ .

2. 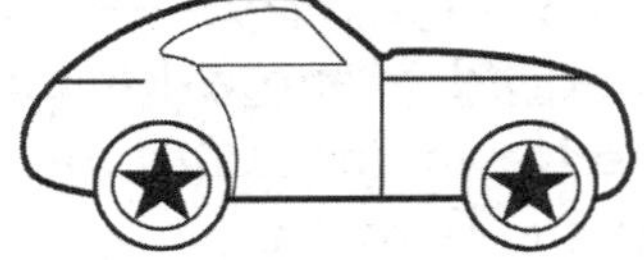

2. These are ____________________ .

3. 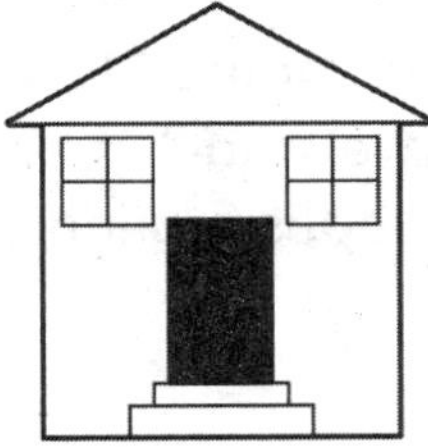

3. This is a ____________________ .

4. 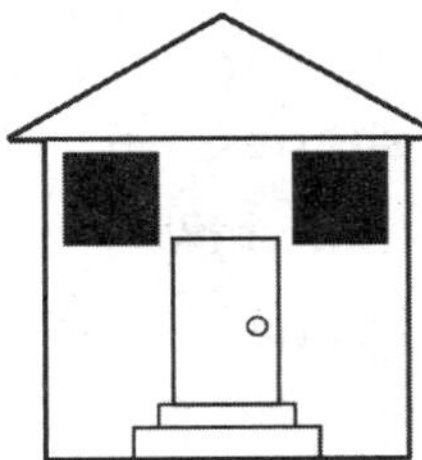

4. These are ____________________ .

5. 

5. That's a ____________________ .

Geometric Shapes

Language Objective:
Name colors and shapes

Content Objective:
Identify colors and shapes

Sentence Frames:
What color is the ____?
The ____ is ____.
What do you see?
It's a(n) ____ ____.
Point to a ____ ____ in the classroom.

VOCABULARY
red, orange, yellow, green, blue, purple, white, black, brown, color
Cognates: color

>> Go Digital

Language Transfers Handbook
See pages 16-19 for grammatical structures that do not transfer. Cantonese, Hmong, Korean, Spanish, Arabic, or Vietnamese speakers may struggle with the word order of nouns and adjectives.

Grades 2-3 Foundational Skills Kit
Use Phonics Card 8 to teach the *l* blend in *black* and *blue;* Routine Card 5 with the high-frequency words *red, blue, green, brown, black,* and *white.*

eBook Use digital material to practice vocabulary.

LESSON 2: Colors

Set Purpose

- Tell students that today they will discuss colors and shapes. Show page 3 of the Newcomer Cards.

Teach/Model Vocabulary

- Elicit the names of shapes discussed in Lesson 1.
- Lead students through the song/chant on page 154.
- Display the Newcomer Card and ask: *What colors do you see?* Then point to and name each color. Have students repeat. Help with pronunciation.
- Say these sentence frames as you point to a shape: **What color is the square? The square is blue. What do you see? It's a blue square.** Say the sentences again as you write them on the board. Have students repeat after you. Then point to the red triangle and ask: **What color is the triangle?** Have students answer chorally: **The triangle is red. It's a red triangle.** Repeat for other colors and shapes on the Newcomer Card, on the vocabulary list, and in the classroom.
- **Talk About It** Have partners talk about different colors and shapes on their clothes and around the classroom.
- Expand by introducing the command **Point to a blue circle in the classroom.** Have students ask each other to point to different colored shapes around the room.

Practice/Apply

INTERPRETIVE

- **Talk About It** Have partners use the Newcomer Card and the sentence frames they learned to ask and answer questions about colors and shapes.
- Guide students to complete the activity on page 17.
- In pairs, have one student dictate the name of a color and shape while the other student draws and colors it. Then they switch roles. Afterwards have partners describe their pictures to each other.

Make Connections

Have partners discuss their favorite color using the sentence frame **I like ____.** Students can name the color and things that have that color, such as **I like blue. The flower is blue.** Then ask students to share why they like a certain color using the sentence frame **I like ____ because ____.**

Name: ______________________________

Use Newcomer Card, page 3

A. Color each shape a different color listed in the box. Then use the words from the box to complete each sentence.

Colors	red	yellow	green	blue	orange	black	brown
Shapes	circle	square	triangle	rectangle			

1.  This is a __________ __________.

2.  This is a __________ __________.

3.  This is a __________ __________.

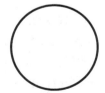

4.  This is a __________ __________.

B. Draw more than one square on the back of your paper and color them. Then write a sentence starting with the word *These*.

____

Geometric Shapes

Language Objective:
Use language to identify shapes and colors around us

Content Objective:
Identify shapes and colors around us

Sentence Frames:
What shape is this ____ ____?
What shape is that ____ ____?
What shapes are these/those ____ ____?
This/That ____ ____ is a ____.
These/Those ____ ____ are ____.

VOCABULARY
calendar, door, clock, book, window, garbage can, map, rug, shelf
Cognates: calendario

>> Go Digital

Language Transfers Handbook
See pages 16-19 for grammatical structures that do not transfer. Cantonese, Hmong, Korean, Vietnamese, Arabic, or Spanish speakers may struggle with the plural marker *-s.*

Grades 2-3 Foundational Skills Kit
Use Phonics Card 43 to teach closed syllables (*window, clock*); Routine Card 5 with the high-frequency words *this, that, these, those, is,* and *are.*

eBook and Games Provide audio support, interaction, and practice with the vocabulary.

LESSON 3: Shapes and Colors Around Us

Set Purpose

- Tell students that today they will discuss shapes and colors around us. Show page 3 of the Newcomer Cards.

Teach/Model Vocabulary

- Elicit the shapes and colors discussed in Lessons 1 and 2.
- Lead students through the song/chant on page 154.
- Display the Newcomer Card and ask: *What do you see in the classroom?* Then point to and name each object. Have students repeat. Help with pronunciation.
- Say these sentence frames as you point to an object: **What shape is this red clock? This red clock is a circle.** Then say the sentences again as you write them on the board. Have students repeat after you. (You can also use the clock to begin a discussion about the basics of telling time in English.) Then point to the window and ask: **What shape is that green window?** Have students answer chorally: **That green window is a square.** Repeat for other objects on the Newcomer Card and in the classroom.
- **Talk About It** Have partners talk about the shape and color of different objects outside their classroom window.
- Expand by introducing sentence frames that review plural demonstrative pronouns *these* and *those*: **What shapes are these/those yellow books? These/Those yellow books are rectangles.**

Practice/Apply

- **Talk About It** Have partners use the Newcomer Card and the sentence frames they learned to ask and answer questions about shapes and colors around them.
- Guide students to complete the activity on page 19.
- In pairs, one student tells the information in his/her graphic organizer while the other student draws what he/she hears. Then they switch roles. Afterwards, have students compare their drawings with their partner's graphic organizer. Model the activity if necessary.

Make Cultural Connections

Have partners talk about the colors and shapes of objects in their home countries. Then have them share with you.

Name: ______________________________

Write the shapes and colors of objects around you. Then tell your partner about them.

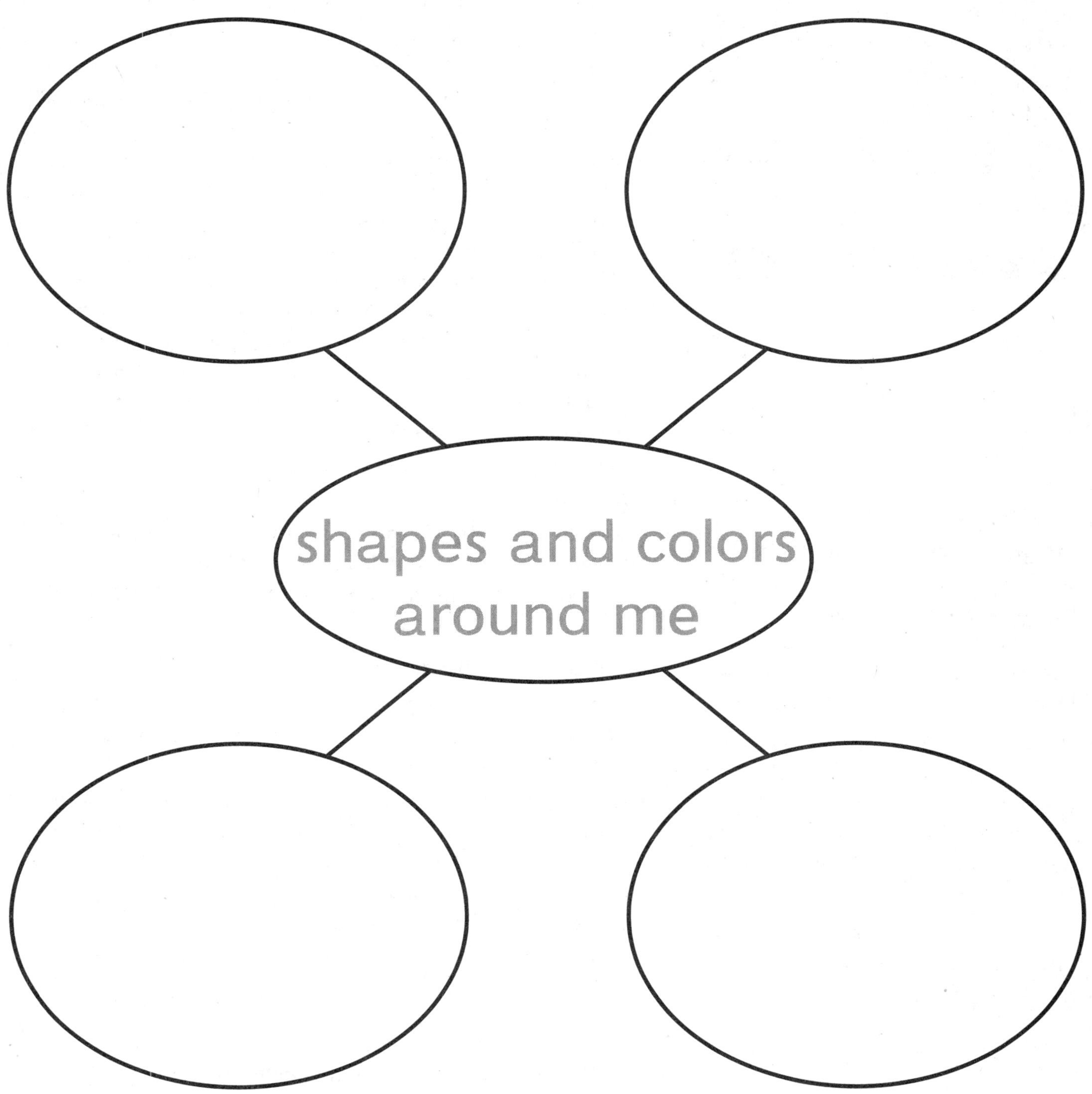

Numbers

Language Objective:
Name and sequence numbers 1–100

Content Objective:
Identify and sequence numbers 1–100

Sentence Frames:
What number is this?
This is number ____.
Point to the number ____.
Count from ____ to ____.

VOCABULARY
1, 2, 3, 4, 5, 6, 7, 8, 9, 10, 11, 12, 13, 14, 15, 16, 17, 18, 19, 20, 21, 22, 23, 24, 25, 26, 27, 28, 29, 30, 40, 50, 60, 70, 80, 90, 100, count, point to
Cognates: contar

>> Go Digital

Language Transfers Handbook See pages 16-19 for sounds that do not transfer. Cantonese, Vietnamese, Hmong, or Tagalog speakers may struggle with the letter *x* and sound /ks/ in *six* and *sixteen.*

Grades 2-3 Foundational Skills Kit Use Phonics Card 35 to teach the diphthong *ou* in *count;* Routine Card 5 for the high-frequency words *from* and *to,* and numbers one through ten.

eBook Use digital materials to practice vocabulary.

LESSON 1: Numbers 1–100

Set Purpose

- Tell students that today they will discuss numbers 1–100. Show page 4 of the Newcomer Cards.

Teach/Model Vocabulary

- Lead students through the song/chant on page T1.
- Display the Newcomer Card. Ask students what they see. Have students take turns pointing to and naming each number in order on the card. Continue counting from 30 to 100 by tens. Then repeat and have students echo you.
- Say these sentence frames as you point to a number: **What number is this? This is number 5**. Then say the sentences again as you write them on the board. Have students repeat after you. Next to the numeral 5, write the word "five" so that students begin to connect the numeral with the word. Then point to the number 18 and ask: **What number is this?** Have students answer chorally: **This is number 18**. Again, write the word "eighteen" next to the numeral. Repeat for other numbers on the Newcomer Card.
- **Talk About It** Have students discuss numbers they see around the classroom.
- Extend instruction using commands: **Point to the number 25** and **Count from 20 to 30** and completing the sentences with numbers on the card or in the room.

Practice/Apply PRODUCTIVE

- **Talk About It** Have partners use the Newcomer Card and the sentence frames they learned to name and sequence numbers.
- Have students work with a partner. Provide sets of index cards numbered from 1 to 30, one set for each student. Have partners play Go Fish, taking turns asking for a number to make a pair. Students put their pairs aside. The student who pairs all cards first wins the game.
- Guide students to complete the activity on page 21.

Make Connections

Provide magazines. Have students cut out numbers to form their telephone number. Students paste the numbers on paper and read their phone number aloud to a partner.

Name: ______________________________

Use Newcomer Card, Page 4

A. Read each number in the first box. Find the numbers and circle them in the second box.

1	62	99	50	25	18

45	1	16
28	82	25
50	11	99
72	4	51
14	43	8
65	95	62
18	37	28
21	81	20
30	96	15

B. Choose a number. Write a sentence that names the number.

____

Numbers

Language Objective:
Ask and answer questions about age

Content Objective:
Understand which numbers make up a person's age

Sentence Frames:
How old are you?
I'm ____ years old.
How old is she/he?
She's/He's ____ years old.

VOCABULARY
1, 2, 3, 4, 5, 6, 7, 8, 9, 10, 11, 12, 13, 14, 15, 16, 17, 18, 19, 20, years old

>> Go Digital

Language Transfers Handbook
See pages 16-19 for grammatical structures that do not transfer. Korean, Spanish, or Vietnamese speakers may omit subject pronouns.

Grades 2-3 Foundational Skills Kit
Use Phonics Card 32 to teach long *a* (*eight*); Structural Analysis Card 14 to teach compound words (*fourteen*); Routine Card 5 for high-frequency words *he, she, is, years,* and *old.*

eBook Use digital material to practice vocabulary.

LESSON 2: How Old Are You?

Set Purpose

- Tell students that today they will discuss numbers we use to say age. Show page 4 of the Newcomer Cards.

Teach/Model Vocabulary

- Elicit the numbers discussed in Lesson 1.
- Lead students through the song/chant on page T1.
- Display the Newcomer Card and say: *Tell me about the boy.* Students can say what they know. Then point to the card he's holding and the number on the card.
- Say these sentence frames as you point to the boy and the card: **How old is he? He's 10 years old.** Then say the sentences again as you write them on the board. Have students repeat after you. Then, indicate a student whose age you know and ask the class: **How old is she/he?** Provide the age and have the students answer chorally: **She's/He's 12 years old.**
- **Talk About It** Have partners guess and talk about the ages of other people on the card and in the classroom.
- Expand by introducing the sentence frames **How old are you? I'm 11 years old.** Have partners take turns asking each other about their age.

Practice/Apply COLLABORATIVE

- **Talk About It** Have partners use the Newcomer Card, the Conversation Starters on page T28, and the sentence frames they learned to ask and answer questions about the ages of people they know.
- Students stand in a circle. Give one student a ball. The student tosses the ball to another student and asks *How old are you?* The student that catches the ball says *I'm ____*, then tosses the ball to another student. Play several rounds to make sure all students have asked and answered. Encourage students to do it faster each time.
- Guide students to complete the activity on page 23.

Make Connections

Have partners talk about their last birthday by drawing pictures and using the vocabulary from Lessons 1 and 2. Encourage students to tell their age and how they celebrated.

Name: ______________________________

How Old Are You?

Use Newcomer Card, Page 4

A. Circle the number or numbers that make up your age.

0 1 2 3 4 5 6 7 8 9

B. Write the number in the box. Add colors or shapes to decorate your number. Share your number with a partner.

C. Write a sentence telling your age.

____

Numbers

Language Objective:
Name the number of objects

Content Objective:
Identify the number of objects

Sentence Frames:
How many do you/we/they have?
I/We/They have ____ ____.
How many does she/he have?
She/He has ____ ____.
I have ____ ____ and ____ ____.

VOCABULARY
bananas, kittens, apples, forks, muffins, gifts, plant
Cognates: banana

>> Go Digital

Language Transfers Handbook
See pages 16-19 for grammatical structures that do not transfer. Korean, Cantonese, or Arabic speakers may struggle with pronouns and number agreement.

Grades 2-3 Foundational Skills Kit
Use Phonics Card 3 to teach short *i* in *kittens* and *gifts*; Routine Card 5 with high-frequency words *they, she, he, we,* and *I*.

eBook and Games Provide audio support, interaction, and practice with the vocabulary.

LESSON 3: How Many?

Set Purpose

- Tell students that today they will discuss counting objects. Show page 4 of the Newcomer Cards.

Teach/Model Vocabulary

- Elicit numbers and ages discussed in Lessons 1 and 2.
- Lead students through the song/chant on page T1.
- Display the Newcomer Card and ask: *What do you see at the party?* Then have students take turns pointing to, naming, and counting objects, as they are able. Help with pronunciation.
- Say this sentence frame as you point to the bananas: **How many do they have? They have 4 bananas.** Then say the sentences again as you write them on the board. Have students repeat after you. Then point to the forks and ask: **How many do they have?** Have students answer chorally: **They have 3 forks**. Repeat for other objects on the Newcomer Card and in the classroom.
- **Talk About It** Have partners count and discuss the number of objects on or in their desks.
- Extend by reusing the frames with pronouns *I, you,* and *we*. Then, expand by introducing **How many does she/he have? She/He has 2 gifts** and **I have 4 bananas and 5 apples.**

Practice/Apply

- **Talk About It** Have students use the Newcomer Card and the sentence frames they learned to count and discuss the total number of things to eat at the party.
- Give pairs of students several random numbers from 1–10. Have the pairs search the room to find amounts of objects that match the numbers they were given. For example, a pair might find two pencils and nine paperclips. They should then present their findings to you and use the sentence frame **We have** ____ ____ to describe what they found.
- Guide students to complete the activity on page 25.

Make Cultural Connections

Have students describe number games they played in their home country, similar to games like hopscotch or bingo. Students can describe the game or show others how to play.

Name: ______________________________

Count the objects. Complete each sentence with a numeral and a word from the box.

kittens	apples	forks	bananas	gifts	muffins

1.  I have ______________________ .

2.  We have ______________________ .

3. 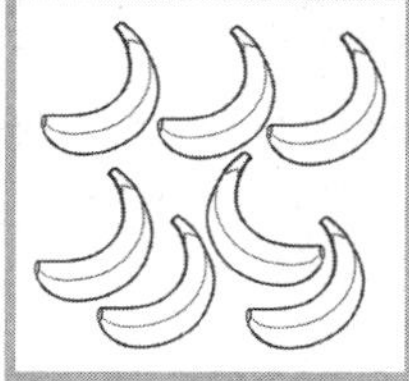 She has ______________________ .

4.  You have ______________________ .

5.  He has ______________________ .

6.  They have ______________________ .

In the Classroom

Newcomer Card, p. 5

LESSONS	MATERIALS	LANGUAGE OBJECTIVES	LANGUAGE STRUCTURES/ GRAMMAR	VOCABULARY
Lesson 1: Classroom Objects, p. 28–29	Newcomer Card p. 5 Phonics Card 27 Song/Chant p. T1	Name classroom objects	What color is her/his____? It's ____. She/He has ____. She/He has a ____ ____ and a ____ ____. I/You/We/They have ____. **Verbs:** to be, to have **Regular plurals**	Classroom objects **High-Frequency Words:** *they, he, she, you, we, I*
Lesson 2: Classroom Activities, p. 30–31	Newcomer Card p. 5 Phonics Card 18 Song/Chant p. T1	Name classroom activities	What is she/he doing? She/He is ____. What are you doing? **Verb:** present continuous of *do* **Wh- questions:** What	Classroom activities **High-Frequency Words:** *is, are, we, they, he, she*
Lesson 3: Classroom Commands, p. 32–33	Newcomer Card p. 5 Phonics Card 33 Song/Chant p. T1	Understand commands heard in the classroom	Please ____. Listen to me. Raise your hand. Stop! Ask questions. Write your name. **Imperatives** **Pronouns:** me, your	Classroom commands **High-Frequency Words:** *your, please, is, are*

Computers

Newcomer Card, p. 6

LESSONS	MATERIALS	LANGUAGE OBJECTIVES	LANGUAGE STRUCTURES/ GRAMMAR	VOCABULARY
Lesson 1: Location of Objects, p. 34–35	Newcomer Card p. 6 Phonics Card 19 Song/Chant p. T1	Describe location of objects	Where is/are the ____? The ____ is/are ____ the ____. **Verb:** to be **Prepositions of place** ***Wh-* questions:** Where	Locations **High-Frequency Words:** *where, they, the, is, are*
Lesson 2: Asking for Help, p. 36–37	Newcomer Card p. 6 Phonics Card 33 Song/Chant p. T1	Use language to ask for help	Can you help me? Is this correct? I don't ____. I have a question. **Modal verb:** can **Verb:** to have	Help and clarification **High-Frequency Words:** *can, help, you, me, I*
Lesson 3: Using Computers, p. 38–39	Newcomer Card p. 6 Phonics Cards 20 and 35 Song/Chant p. T2	Describe the order of tasks when using a computer	How do you ____? First, ____. Then, ____. Next, ____. Finally, ____. ***How* questions** **Sequence words**	Computer terms **High-Frequency Words:** *first, then, on, use*

A Day at School

Newcomer Card, p. 7

LESSONS	MATERIALS	LANGUAGE OBJECTIVES	LANGUAGE STRUCTURES/ GRAMMAR	VOCABULARY
Lesson 1: Places at School, p. 40–41	Newcomer Card p. 7 Phonics Card 3 Song/Chant p. T2	Name places in school	What is this? This is a ____. **Verb:** to be ***Wh-* questions:** What **Irregular plurals**	Places in school **High-Frequency Words:** *is, this, a*
Lesson 2: What We Do in School, p. 42–43	Newcomer Card p. 7 Phonics Card 8 Song/Chant p. T2	Name what we do in school	Where do we____? We ____ in the ____. ***Wh-* questions:** Where **Pronouns:** we, he, she, I	Action words **High-Frequency Words:** *we, the, in*
Lesson 3: People in School, p. 44–45	Newcomer Card p. 7 Phonics Card 27 Song/Chant p. T2	Name people we see in school	Who is in the ____? The ____ is in the ____. **Verb:** to be ***Wh-* questions:** Who	People in school **High-Frequency Words:** *who, in, is, the*

Calendar	LESSONS	MATERIALS	LANGUAGE OBJECTIVES	LANGUAGE STRUCTURES/ GRAMMAR	VOCABULARY
Newcomer Card, p. 8	**Lesson 1:** Days and Months p. 46–47	Newcomer Card p. 8 Phonics Card 21 Song/Chant p. T2	Name the days of the week and months of the year	What day/month is/was ___? Today/Tomorrow is ____. Yesterday was ____. **Simple past tense** ***Wh-* questions:** What	Days and months **High-Frequency Words:** *is, what, the, after*
	Lesson 2: School-Day Routine, p. 48–49	Newcomer Card p. 8 Phonics Cards 5 and 24 Song/Chant p. T2	Recount school-day events	What do you do on a school day? What does she/he do on a school day? First/Then/ Next/Finally, I/She/He ___. **Pronouns:** I, she, he **Sequence words**	School-day events **High-Frequency Words:** *get, go, have, often, sleep*
	Lesson 3: Times of the Day, p. 50–51	Newcomer Card p. 8 Phonics Cards 2 and 29 Song/Chant p. T2	Name different times of day to do things	When do we/you ____? We/I ____ in the ____. ***Wh-* questions:** When **Pronoun:** we, I	Times of day **High-Frequency Words:** *when, do, we, go, at*

Weather	LESSONS	MATERIALS	LANGUAGE OBJECTIVES	LANGUAGE STRUCTURES/ GRAMMAR	VOCABULARY
Newcomer Card, p. 9	**Lesson 1:** Weather Conditions, p. 52–53	Newcomer Card p. 9 Phonics Card 25 Song/Chant p. T2	Describe the weather outside	How's the weather? It's ____ and ____ outside. **Contractions:** it's, how's ***How* questions**	Weather conditions **High-Frequency Words:** *the, not, and*
	Lesson 2: Seasons, p. 54–55	Newcomer Card p. 9 Phonics Cards 23 and 35 Song/Chant p. T2	Name the seasons	What season is it? The ____ are growing. There is ____. It is ____. **Present Continuous Verbs** **Pronoun:** it	Seasons **High-Frequency Words:** *what, and, it, there*
	Lesson 3: Up in the Sky, p. 56–57	Newcomer Card p. 9 Phonics Card 10 Song/Chant p. T2	Name objects in the sky	What can you/we see in the sky? I/We can see the ___. When can you/we see the ___? I/We can see the ____ at night/ during the day. **Modal verb:** can ***Wh-* questions:** What, Where **Prepositions of time**	Objects in the sky **High-Frequency Words:** *what, can, we, sun, see*

Progress Monitoring

Use the **Oral Language Proficiency Benchmark Assessment** on pages T40–T41 to monitor students' oral language proficiency growth.

Use the **Student Profile** on pages T43–T44 to record observations throughout the units.

In the Classroom

Language Objective:
Name classroom objects

Content Objective:
Identify classroom objects

Sentence Frames:
What color is her/his ____?
It's ____.
She/He has a(n) ____.
She/He has a(n) ____ and a(n) ____.
What color is your/their ____?
I/You/We/They have ____.
I/You/We/They have ____ and ____.

VOCABULARY
book, pencil, pen, notebook, backpack, calculator, ruler, desk, folder, eraser, we, they, have, two, three

>> Go Digital

Language Transfers Handbook
See pages 16-19 for grammatical structures that do not transfer. Cantonese, Hmong, Korean, Vietnamese, Arabic, or Spanish speakers may omit plural marker *-s*.

Grades 2-3 Foundational Skills Kit
Use Phonics Card 27 to teach the *r*-controlled vowel /ûr/ (*her, calculator*); Routine Card 5 to teach high-frequency words *they, he, she, you, we,* and *I;* Structural Analysis Card 15 to teach the contraction *it's*.

eBook Use digital material for vocabulary practice.

LESSON 1: Classroom Objects

Set Purpose

- Tell students that today they will discuss classroom objects. Show page 5 of the Newcomer Cards.

Teach/Model Vocabulary

- Lead students through the song/chant on page T1.
- Display the Newcomer Card and ask: *What do you see?* Point to and name the classroom objects. Elicit other objects in your classroom and on the vocabulary list. Have students repeat. Help with pronunciation.
- Say these sentence frames as you point to the girl writing: **What color is her <u>pen</u>? It's <u>black</u>. She has a <u>black</u> <u>pen</u>.** Then say the sentences again as you write them on the board. Have students repeat after you. Then, point to the book on the teacher's desk and ask: **What color is his <u>book</u>?** Have students chorally answer: **It's <u>blue</u>. He has a <u>blue</u> <u>book</u>**. Repeat for other objects on the card, in the vocabulary list, and in the classroom. For multiple objects, use: **She/He has a <u>blue</u> <u>notebook</u> and a <u>yellow</u> <u>pencil</u>**.
- **Talk About It** Partners can describe objects in their favorite class.
- Extend by introducing: **What color is your/their ____? I/You/We/They have ____.** Have students ask each other about the color of their classroom objects. Expand the sentence frames with numbers and plural ending *-s*.

Practice/Apply INTERPRETIVE

- **Talk About It** Have partners use the Newcomer Card and the sentence frames they learned to ask and answer questions about classroom objects.
- In pairs, have one student describe objects in the classroom, telling the shape, color, and amount. The partner guesses which object is being described. Then they switch roles. For example: *We have four brown rectangles.* (*Those are desks.*)
- Guide students to complete the activity on page 29.

Make Connections

Have students draw a classroom object and write a sentence to describe it. Then they share with the class.

Name: ______________________________

Classroom Objects

Use Newcomer Card, page 5

A. Match each sentence to the correct picture.

1. He has a backpack.

2. They have notebooks and pens.

3. He has a calculator.

4. She has pens and pencils.

d.

B. Write a sentence about the classroom objects you have.

____

In the Classroom

Language Objective:
Name classroom activities

Content Objective:
Demonstrate understanding of classroom activities

Sentence Frames:
What are you/they doing?
I'm ____.
We are ____ and ____.
They are ____ and ____.
What is she/he doing?
She's/He's ____.

VOCABULARY
doing, writing, drawing, reading, listening, talking, counting, asking questions, matching, teaching

>> Go Digital

Language Transfers Handbook
See pages 16–19 for grammatical structures that do not transfer. Cantonese, Hmong, Korean, or Vietnamese speakers may struggle with inflectional endings on verbs.

Grades 2–3 Foundational Skills Kit
Use Phonics Card 18 to teach consonant digraph *ng*; Routine Card 5 to teach the high-frequency words *is, are, we, they, he,* and *she*; Structural Analysis Card 17 to teach contractions (*she's* and *he's*).

eBook Use digital material for vocabulary practice.

LESSON 2: Classroom Activities

Set Purpose

- Tell students that today they will discuss classroom activities. Show page 5 of the Newcomer Cards.

Teach/Model Vocabulary

- Elicit names of classroom objects to review Lesson 1.
- Lead students through the song/chant on page T1.
- Display the Newcomer Card and ask: *What are the students doing?* Then point to, name, and pantomime each classroom activity on the card. Have students repeat. Help with pronunciation.
- Say these sentence frames as you point to the boy reading: **What is he doing? He's reading.** Then say the sentences again for the other activities and write them on the board, completing the second sentence with the name of the activity. Have students repeat after you. Then, point to the girl writing and ask: **What is she doing?** Have students answer chorally: **She's writing.** Repeat for other activities on the Newcomer Card and the vocabulary list.
- **Talk About It** Have partners discuss their favorite classroom activity. Then, extend by introducing the sentence frames: **What are you/they doing? I'm ____. We/They are ____ and ____.**

Practice/Apply COLLABORATIVE

- **Talk About It** Have partners use the sentence frames they learned and vocabulary they know to explain to each other why they like their favorite classroom activity so much.
- Guide students to complete the activity on page 31.
- Have students work in small groups. Provide old magazines. Each group gets the name of an activity, such as writing, reading, or talking. The groups look for pictures that show people doing that activity, then they describe the picture to the class. Have the class ask follow-up questions.

Make Connections

Have students draw pictures of themselves doing a classroom activity, then describe it to a partner.

Name: ___________________________

Use Newcomer Card, page 5

Choose words from the box to write sentences.

reading	writing	talking
asking questions	counting	listening

1.  ___________________________

2.  ___________________________

3.  ___________________________

4.  ___________________________

5.  ___________________________

6.  ___________________________

In the Classroom

Language Objective:
Understand commands heard in the classroom

Content Objective:
Demonstrate understanding of classroom commands

Sentence Frames:
Please come here/sit down.
Please give me ____.
Listen to me.
Raise your hand.
Stop!
Write your name.
Ask questions.
Look at page ____.

VOCABULARY
please, raise your hand, stop, come here, sit down, listen to me, write your name, ask questions, look at page ____, give
False Cognates: *come*

>> Go Digital

Language Transfers Handbook
See pages 16-19 for grammar structures that do not transfer. Cantonese, Hmong, Korean, or Vietnamese speakers may struggle with object pronouns.

Grades 2–3 Foundational Skills Kit
Use Phonics Card 33 to teach silent letters *wr (write)*; Routine Card 5 with the high-frequency words *your, please, is,* and *are.*

eBook and Games Provide audio support, interaction, and practice with the vocabulary.

LESSON 3: Classroom Commands

Set Purpose

- Tell students that today they will discuss classroom commands. Show page 5 of the Newcomer Cards.

Teach/Model Vocabulary

- Elicit the names of classroom objects and activities discussed in Lessons 1 and 2.
- Lead students through the song/chant on page T1.
- Display the Newcomer Card and ask: *What do you see written on the blackboard?* Point to and read the classroom commands as you use gestures. Then use gestures and say the rest of the commands in the sidebar. Have students repeat. Help with pronunciation.
- **Talk About It** Have volunteers take turns giving commands as the class responds.
- **Talk About It** Pretend you are a student and one of the students is the teacher. Have the "teacher" give a command, which you respond to incorrectly (looking at a book instead of raising your hand). Have students say what your action was and show what your response should have been. Phase yourself out of the game and let the students play on their own.

Practice/Apply COLLABORATIVE

- **Talk About It** Have partners use the Newcomer Card and the commands they learned to talk about all of the classroom commands they know.
- Play "Simon Says" using the commands from the vocabulary list and sentence frames. Once all of the commands have been used, invite a student to be "Simon" with the option of adding his or her own command.
- Guide students to complete the activity on page 33.

Make Cultural Connections

Have partners talk about the different commands they heard in their home country's school. Have the students explain why the commands were different in their home country. Elicit descriptive words. Then have students share with the class.

Name: ____________________

A. Circle the picture that shows a student following the command.

1. Please sit down.

2. Raise your hand.

3. Write your name.

B. Write a command you hear in your classroom.

____

Computers

Language Objective:
Describe location of objects

Content Objective:
Identify location of objects

Sentence Frames:
Where is the ____?
The ____ is ____ the ____.
The ____ is between the ____ and the ____.
Where are the ____ and ____?
They are ____ the ____ and ____.

VOCABULARY
under, above, next to, behind, in, by, near, on, between, computer
Cognates: computadora

>> Go Digital

Language Transfers Handbook See pages 16-19 for grammatical structures that do not transfer. Cantonese, Hmong, Korean, Vietnamese, Arabic, and Tagalog speakers may omit articles.

Grades 2–3 Foundational Skills Kit Use Phonics Card 19 to teach consonant digraph *wh* (*where*); Routine Card 5 to teach high-frequency words *where, they, the, is,* and *are*; Structural Analysis Card 13B to teach phrasing with prepositions.

eBook Use digital material for vocabulary practice.

LESSON 1: Location of Objects

Set Purpose

- Tell students that today they will discuss the location of objects. Show page 6 of the Newcomer Cards.

Teach/Model Vocabulary

- Lead students through the song/chant on page T1.
- Display the Newcomer Card. Ask students to describe what they see. Then point to and name the objects and describe their locations using the prepostions in the sidebar. Have students repeat. Help with pronunciation.
- Say these sentence frames as you point to the book: **Where is the book? The book is next to the ruler.** Then say the sentences again as you write them on the board, completing the sentences with the objects on the card and their location. Have students repeat after you. Then, point to the pen and ask: **Where is the pen?** Have students answer chorally: **The pen is under the table.** Repeat for other objects on the Newcomer Card and in your classroom.
- Extend by introducing the sentence frames: **The book is between the ruler and the computer. Where are the ruler and book? They are between the computers.**

Practice/Apply

- **Talk About It** Have partners use sentence frames they learned to ask and answer questions about the location of objects in your classroom.
- In pairs, have students take turns placing classroom objects in the classroom in different locations. Then have them ask and answer questions about the location.
- Guide students to complete the activity on page 35.

Make Connections

Toss a ball to a student and ask: *Where is the ____?* Have the student answer the question in a complete sentence with the name and location of the object. Then have that student toss the ball to another student and ask: *Where is the ____?* Repeat until every student has had a turn asking for the location of an object.

Name: ______________________________

A. Match each sentence to the correct picture.

1. The pen is under the notebook. a. 

2. The ruler is above the book and the pen. b. 

3. The pencil is between the book and tape. c. 

4. The mouse is next to the computer. d. 

B. Put two classroom objects on your desk. Write a sentence about their locations.

____

Computers

Language Objective:
Use language to ask for help

Content Objective:
Understand how to ask for help

Sentence Frames:
Can you help me?
I need help.
I don't know/understand.
Please explain/repeat that.
Is this correct?
I have a question.

VOCABULARY
help, know, understand, explain, repeat, correct, question, need,
Cognates: explica, repite, correcto

>> Go Digital

Language Transfers Handbook
See pages 16-19 for grammatical structures that do not transfer. Korean, Spanish, or Vietnamese speakers may omit subject pronouns.

Grades 2–3 Foundational Skills Kit
Use Phonics Card 33 to teach silent letters *kn* in *know;* Routine Card 5 with the high-frequency words *can, help, you, me,* and *I;* Structural Analysis Card 17 to teach contractions with *not* (*don't*).

eBook Use digital material for or further practice.

LESSON 2: Asking for Help

Set Purpose

- Tell students that today they will discuss how to ask for help in school. Show page 6 of the Newcomer Cards.

Teach/Model Vocabulary

- Elicit locations of objects discussed in Lesson 1.
- Lead students through the song/chant on page T1.
- Display the Newcomer Card and ask: *What is the student asking?* Point to and read each of her questions: **Can you help me? Is this correct?** Have students repeat. Help with pronunciation. Explain the meaning of these questions.
- Say these sentences again as you write them on the board; mime the actions. Repeat and have students join. Introduce the other requests listed in the sidebar and repeat the instruction.
- **Talk About It** Expand by introducing simple responses to requests for help, such as "Of course!" and "Sure!" Then have partners take turns role-playing asking for help and responding to requests for help.

Practice/Apply COLLABORATIVE

- **Talk About It** Have partners discuss the different things they would say to a teacher if they didn't understand something.
- Provide pairs with different scenarios that require the students to asks for help. Have partners talk turns role playing as the "student" and as the "teacher." The "student" raises his/her hand. The "teacher" comes to help. The student uses the sentence frames learned in this lesson and then the "teacher" explains. Then they switch roles. Model as necessary.
- Guide students to complete the activity on page 37.

Make Connections

Provide the following prompt: *Think about a time you didn't understand something. What did you do? What did you say? Now what would you say?* Have students discuss their answers with a partner and then share with the class. Have students explain why these new sentence frames can help them.

Name: ______________________________

Asking for Help

Use Newcomer Card, page 6

Say and trace the words in the box. Then, use the words to complete the sentences.

understand me

correct repeat need

1. Can you help ______________ ?

2. I ______________ help.

3. Is this ______________ ?

4. Please ______________ that.

5. I don't ______________ .

Computers

Language Objective:
Describe the order of tasks when using a computer

Content Objective:
Understand sequence of events when using a computer

Sentence Frames:
How do you ____ ?
First, ____.
Then, ____.
Next, ____ a word in the ____.
Finally, click ____.

VOCABULARY
computer, keyboard, mouse, click, Internet, open, scroll up/down, use, turn on, search, search bar, type, screen
Cognates: computadora, Internet

>> Go Digital

Language Transfers Handbook
See pages 16-19 for grammatical structures that do not tranfer. Cantonese, Hmong, Korean, Vietnamese, Arabic, or Tagalog speakers may consistently omit articles.

Grades 2–3 Foundational Skills Kit
Use Phonics Card 20 to teach three-letter blend *scr* (*screen*); Phonics Card 35 to teach diphthong *ou* (*mouse*); Routine Card 5 to teach high-frequency words *first, then, on,* and *use.*

eBook and Games Provide audio support, interaction, and practice with the vocabulary.

LESSON 3: Using Computers

Set Purpose

- Tell students that today they will discuss using a computer. Show page 6 of the Newcomer Cards.

Teach/Model Vocabulary

- Elicit vocabulary from Lessons 1 and 2.
- Lead students through the song/chant on page T2.
- Display the Newcomer Card and say: *Look at the computers. What do you see?* Point to and name the computer parts shown on the card and in the vocabulary list. Have students repeat. Help with pronunciation.
- Say these sentences as you point to the students using the computers: **How do you search on the Internet? First, turn on the computer. Then, click on the mouse. Next, type a word in the search bar. Finally, click "search."** Then say the sentences again as you write them on the board. Have students repeat after you. Then, gesture each sentence as students chorally read them.
- **Talk About It** Extend by using the question and sequence words to talk about other tasks related to the computer. Then students can talk about what they use the computer for in school.

Practice/Apply INTERPRETIVE

- **Talk About It** Have partners talk about their favorite thing to do on a computer, tablet, or smart phone. Have students explain to their partner the steps for using a smart phone or tablet.
- Have students play charades in pairs. One student in the pair acts out doing something on the computer, and the other student uses complete sentences to name the action. Make the game more difficult by having students do multiple computer-related activities and then let the other student guess all of them, using the sentence frames. Have students switch roles.
- Guide students to complete the activity on page 39.

Make Cultural Connections

Have students draw a picture of a web page that uses words in their home language. Then have students describe the page to partner.

Name: ____________________

Write the commands in the correct order.

turn on the computer	type a word
click "search"	click on the mouse

A Day at School

Language Objective:
Name places in school

Content Objective:
Identify places in school

Sentence Frames:
What is this?
This is a ____.

VOCABULARY
library, gym, restroom, nurse's office, cafeteria, main office, classroom, hallway
Cognates: cafetería, oficina

>> Go Digital

Language Transfers Handbook
See pages 16-19 for grammatical structures that do not transfer. Hmong, Spanish, Vietnamese, or Arabic speakers may use prepositions to describe possessives.

Grades 2-3 Foundational Skills Kit
Use Phonics Card 3 to teach short *i* (*is, this*); Routine Card 5 with high-frequency words *is, this,* and *a;* Structural Analysis Card 8 to teach possessives (*nurse's office*).

eBook Use digital material to practice vocabulary.

LESSON 1: Places at School

Set Purpose

- Tell students that today they will discuss places in school. Show page 7 of the Newcomer Cards.

Teach/Model Vocabulary

- Lead students through the song/chant on page T2.
- Display the Newcomer Card and ask: *What places do you see inside the school?* Point to and name each place. Have students repeat. Help with pronunciation.
- Say these sentence frames as you point to a place in the school: **What is this? This is a gym.** Then say the sentences again as you write them on the board, completing the second sentence with the name of each place. Have students repeat after you. Then, point to the hallway and ask: **What is this?** Have students answer chorally **This is a hallway,** filling in the name of the place. Repeat for other places on the Newcomer Card and in your school.
- **Talk About It** Have partners talk about different places on the card and in their school.
- Extend by reusing the sentence frames **How many cafeterias do we have? We have one cafeteria.** Teach irregular plurals, as needed.

Practice/Apply COLLABORATIVE

- **Talk About It** Have partners use the Newcomer Card and the sentence frames they learned to ask and answer questions about places in school.
- Guide students to complete the activity on page 41.
- Have pairs create sentences to describe a place on the Newcomer Card using previously learned vocabulary, and let others guess which place is being described. Model for the students. For example: *It is next to the cafeteria. It is square. It is red.*

Make Connections

Have students make a blueprint of their school. Have them ask a partner: **What is this?** Their partner will answer with **This is a ____** as they label the places in school. Then have partners ask and answer questions about their drawings.

Name: ______________________________

Places at School

Use Newcomer Card, page 7

A. Complete each sentence. Use a word from the box.

1. 

a. 

2. Restroom

b. 

3. Cafeteria

c. 

4. 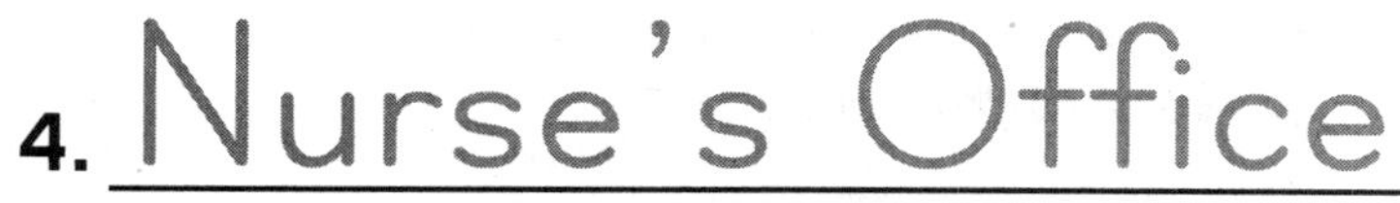

d. 

5. Gym

e. 

6. Classroom

f. 

A Day at School

Language Objective:
Name what we do in school

Content Objective:
Identify what we do in school

Sentence Frames:
Where do we ____?
We ____ in the ____.
I like/don't like to ____ in the ____.
She/He likes/doesn't like to ____ in the ____.

VOCABULARY
eat, play, walk, read, write, work, learn, throw
False cognates: playa

>> Go Digital

Language Transfers Handbook
See pages 16-19 for grammatical structures that do not transfer. Cantonese, Hmong, Korean, Vietnamese, Arabic, or Tagalog speakers may struggle with present tense verb ending *-s* (*likes*)

Grades 2-3 Foundational Skills Kit
Use Phonics Card 8 to teach blends (*play*); Routine Card 5 with high-frequency words *in, the,* and *we.*

eBook Use digital material to practice vocabulary.

LESSON 2: What We Do in School

Set Purpose

- Tell students that today they will discuss things we do in school. Show page 7 of the Newcomer Cards.

Teach/Model Vocabulary

- To review, elicit names of places in school.
- Lead students through the song/chant on page T2.
- Display the Newcomer Card and say: *Let's look at what we do in school. What are people doing?* Students can name the actions they know. Then point to, name, and pantomime each action on the card. Have students repeat your words and actions. Help with pronunciation.
- Say these sentence frames as you point to an action: **Where do we eat? We eat in the cafeteria.** Then say the sentences again as you write them on the board, completing the sentences with the action and place. Have students repeat after you. Then, point to the gym and ask: **Where do we play?** Have students answer chorally: **We play in the gym**, filling in the name of the action and place. Repeat for other actions in the vocabulary list and places on the card.
- **Talk About It** Have partners discuss other things they do in school.
- **Expand** by introducing the sentence frames **I like/don't like to write in the cafeteria** and **She/He likes/doesn't like to work in the hallway**.

Practice/Apply

COLLABORATIVE

- **Talk About It** Have partners use the Newcomer Card and the sentence frames they learned to ask and answer questions about places and actions in school.
- Guide students to complete the activity on page 43.
- In pairs, one student tells the information in his/her graphic organizer while the other student draws what she/he hears. Then they switch roles. Afterwards, have students compare their drawings with their partner's graphic organizer. Model the activity before beginning.

Make Connections

Have partners use vocabulary from Lessons 1 and 2 to play charades. One student acts out what she/he likes to do in each setting while the other student guesses the action and setting. Then partners can discuss what they like to do in school.

Name: ____________________

Write what you like or don't like to do in school.

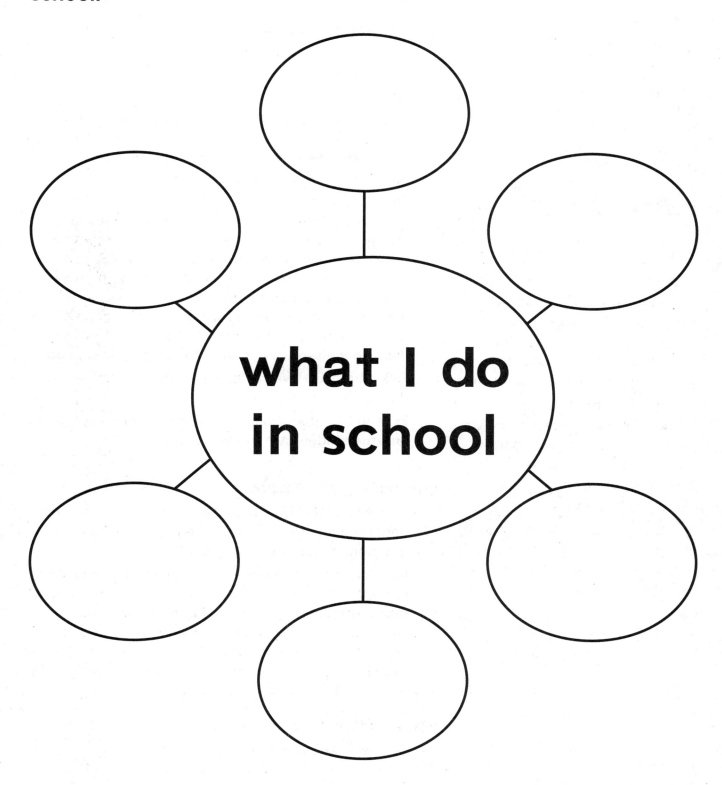

what I do in school

A Day at School

Language Objective:
Name people we see in school

Content Objective:
Identify where we see certain people in school

Sentence Frames:
Who's in the ____ ?
The ____ is in the ____ .
The ____ and the ____ are in the ____ .

VOCABULARY

nurse, principal, cafeteria worker, teacher, gym teacher, student

>> Go Digital

Language Transfers Handbook See pages 16-19 for grammatical structures that do not transfer. Spanish or Tagalog speakers may struggle with countable and uncountable nouns.

Grades 2-3 Foundational Skills Kit Use Phonics Card 27 to teach *r*-controlled vowels (*nurse*); Routine Card 5 with high-frequency words *is, who,* and *the.*

eBook and Games Provide audio support, interaction, and practice with the vocabulary.

LESSON 3: People in School

Set Purpose

- Tell students that today they will discuss people in school. Show page 7 of the Newcomer Cards.

Teach/Model Vocabulary

- Elicit the places and actions in school that were discussed in Lessons 1 and 2.
- Lead students through the song/chant on page T2.
- Display the card and say: *Look at the people inside the school. Who do you see?* Students can name the people they know. Then point to and name each person in the school. Have students repeat. Help with pronunciation.
- Say these sentence frames as you point to a person in the school. **Who is in the gym? The gym teacher is in the gym.** Then say the sentences again as you write them on the board, completing the sentences with the name of the person and place. Have students repeat after you. Then, point to the nurse's office and ask: **Who is in the nurse's office?** Have students chorally answer: **The nurse is in the nurse's office,** filling in the sentence frames. Repeat for other people.
- **Talk About It** Have partners talk about other people they see in school.
- Expand by introducing the sentence frame **The teacher and the student are in the classroom.**

Practice/Apply

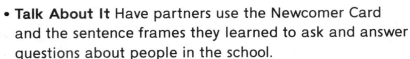

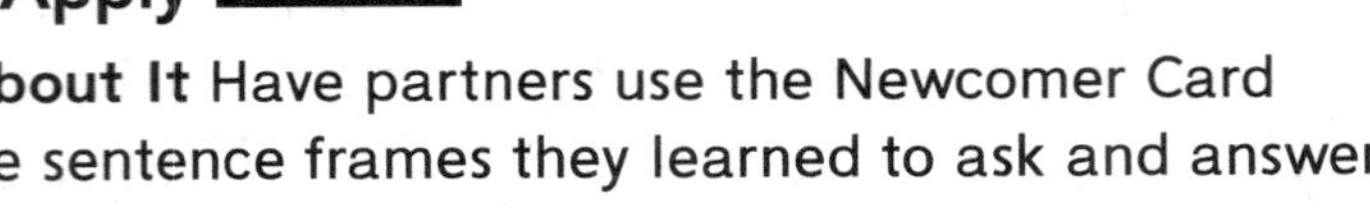

- **Talk About It** Have partners use the Newcomer Card and the sentence frames they learned to ask and answer questions about people in the school.
- Have partners copy this lesson's vocabulary onto slips of paper and put the slips in a pile. Then have students take turns choosing a slip and using the word in a sentence, incorporating the vocabulary learned in Lessons 1 and 2. Model the activity before beginning. For example, say: *The gym teacher likes to run in the gym.*
- Guide students to complete the activity on page 45.

Make Cultural Connections

Have students tell about the school in their home country. After each telling, have students ask a follow-up question.

Name: ______________________________

People in School

Use Newcomer Card, page 7

A. Draw a picture of someone working in school. Then write your own sentences.

B. Write two sentences about a person who works in your school.

____

____

Calendar

Language Objective:
Name the days of the week and months of the year

Content Objective:
Identify the days of the week and the months of the year

Sentence Frames:
What day/month is/was ____?
Today/Tomorrow is ____.
Yesterday was ____.
Today is ____ and tomorrow is ____.
Yesterday was ____ and today is ____.
The day/month after ____ is ____.

VOCABULARY

January, February, March, April, May, June, July, August, September, October, November, December, Monday, Tuesday, Wednesday, Thursday, Friday, Saturday, Sunday, today, yesterday, tomorrow, month, year, day, week, after, last

>> Go Digital

Language Transfers Handbook
See pages 16-19 for grammatical structures that do not transfer. Cantonese, Hmong, Korean, and Vietnamese speakers may omit tense markers.

Grades 2–3 Foundational Skills Kit
Use Phonics Card 21 to teach the long *a* in *day* and *yesterday*; Routine Card 5 to teach the high-frequency words *what, is, the,* and *after*.

eBook Use digital material for vocabulary practice.

LESSON 1: Days and Months

Set Purpose

- Tell students that today they will discuss days and months. Show page 8 of the Newcomer Cards.

Teach/Model Vocabulary

- Lead students through the song/chant on page T2.
- Display the Newcomer Card and ask: *What do you see?* Point to and name the days of the week and the month. Then display a yearly calendar and point to and name each month. Have students repeat.
- Say these sentence frames as you point to today: **What day is today? Today is ____. What day is tomorrow? Tomorrow is ____. What day was yesterday? Yesterday was ____.** Then say the sentences again as you write them on the board, completing the sentences with the correct days. Have students repeat after you. Then, point to the days again and say: **Today is ____. What day is tomorrow?** Have students answer chorally: **Tomorrow is ____.** Repeat for the months of the year.
- Explain that students can now talk in the past tense using the word *was* with *yesterday*. Then explain how to create the simple past tense of verbs students have already learned (adding *-ed*), and have students practice with *talk, listen, play,* and so on.
- Extend instruction using the other sentence frames in the sidebar.

Practice/Apply

- **Talk About It** Have partners use the sentence frames and the other vocabulary they know to talk about what happens at school during different days of the week.
- Have partners describe their past week, using descriptive words to tell about each day, and then have them describe what has happened so far today.
- Guide students to complete the activity on page 47.

Make Connections

Ask students: *What was your favorite day last week? Why?* Have students explain their answer to a partner. Then have individual students share with the class.

Name: ______________________________

Use Newcomer Card, page 8

Say and trace the days. Then complete the sentences with the correct day.

Sunday Monday Tuesday

Wednesday Thursday

Friday Saturday

1. Today is ______________________________.

2. Yesterday was ______________________________.

3. Tomorrow is ______________________________.

4. The day after tomorrow is ______________________________.

Calendar

Language Objective:
Recount school day events

Content Objective:
Identify events during a school day

Sentence Frames:
What do you do on a school day?
What does he/she do on a school day?
First I/he/she ____.
Then I/he/she ____.
Next I/he/she ____.
Finally I/he/she ____ and ____.

VOCABULARY

get up, brush my teeth, brush my hair, make my bed, get dressed, eat breakfast, go to school, go home, do homework, eat dinner, take a bath/shower, go to sleep, always, usually, never, sometimes, rarely.

>> Go Digital

Language Transfers Handbook
See pages 16-19 for grammatical structures that do not transfer. Korean, Spanish, or Vietnamese speakers may omit subject pronouns.

Grades 2–3 Kit Foundational Skills Kit
Use Phonics Card 5 to teach the short *e* sound (*bed, dressed*); Phonics Card 24 to teach the long *e* sound (*sleep, teeth*); Routine Card 5 to teach high-frequency words *get, go, have, often,* and *sleep.*

eBook Use digital material for vocabulary practice.

LESSON 2: School-Day Routine

Set Purpose

- Tell students that today they will discuss things we do on a school day. Show page 8 of the Newcomer Cards.

Teach/Model Vocabulary

- Elicit names of days and months from Lesson 1.
- Lead students through the song/chant on page T2.
- Display the Newcomer Card and ask: *What is she doing?* Students can name things they know. Then point to, name, and pantomime each activity. Have students repeat and copy your actions. Help with pronunciation.
- Say these sentence frames as you point to the morning activities: **What does she do on a school day? First she gets up. Then she brushes her teeth.** Then say the sentences again as you write them on the board. Have students repeat after you. Then point to the afternoon and evening activities and ask: **What does she do on a school day?** Have students answer chorally **First she does her homework after school. Then she eats dinner.** Repeat for the last event on the card and for other events in the vocabulary list.
- **Talk About It** Have partners ask each other about their daily routines using the sentence frame **What do you do on a school day?** and answer using sequence words.
- Extend by naming multiple events with the conjunction *and.* Expand by using frequency words in the sentence frames: *usually, often, sometimes, never, rarely, always.*

Practice/Apply COLLABORATIVE

- **Talk About It** Have partners discuss their routine on Mondays using frequency and sequence words.
- Have partners take turns acting out events they do on a school day. While one student acts out, his/her partner names the activity using the sentence frame: **First, you ____.** And so on.
- Guide students to complete the activity on page 49.

Make Connections

Have students draw pictures of themselves doing their favorite daily activity. Have them explain to a partner why it is their favorite daily activity. Individuals present to the class.

Name: ______________________________

School-Day Routine

Use Newcomer Card, page 8

Write the activities in the correct order.

I brush my teeth.

I go to school.

I get up.

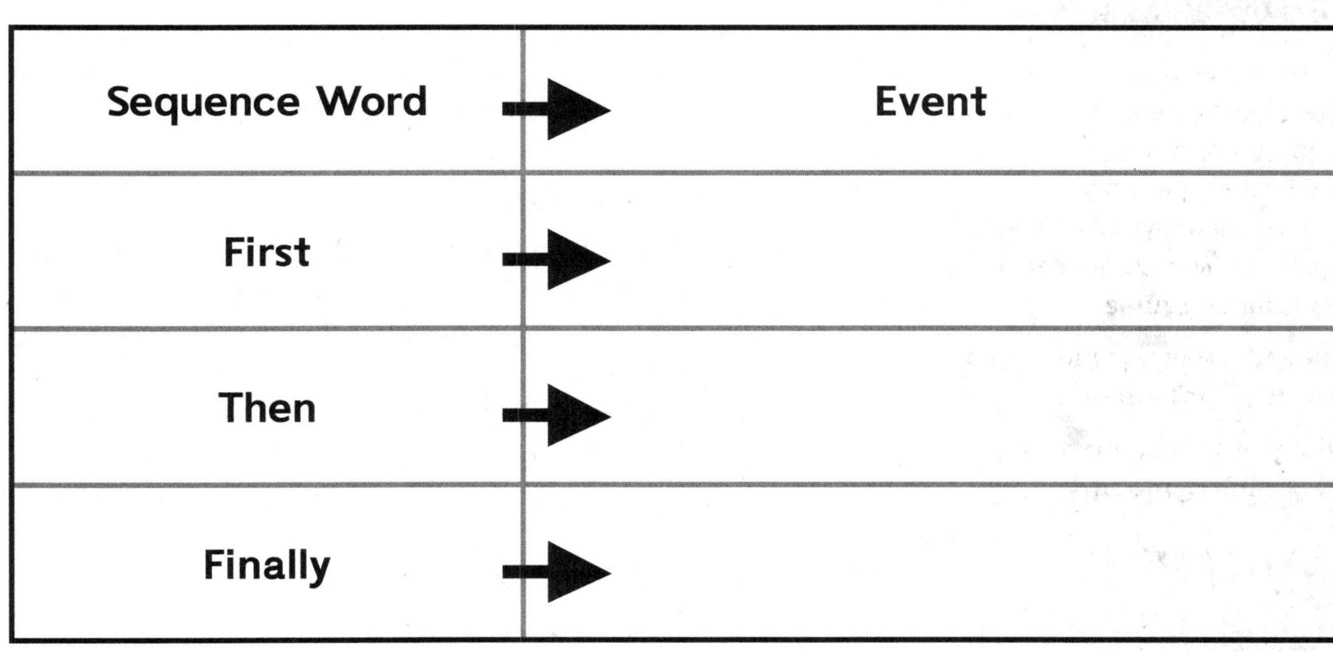

Sequence Word	→	Event
First	→	
Then	→	
Finally	→	

Calendar

Language Objective:
Name different times of day to do things

Content Objective:
Understand what happens during different times of the day

Sentence Frames:
When do we/you ____ ?
We/I ____ in the/at ____ .
We/I ____ early/late.

VOCABULARY
morning, afternoon, evening, night, early, late

>> Go Digital

Language Transfers Handbook
See pages 16-19 for grammatical structures that do not transfer. Cantonese or Hmong speakers may omit prepositions.

Grades 2–3 Foundational Skills Kit
Use Phonics Card 2 to teach short *a* sounds (*afternoon*); Phonics Card 29 to teach the *r*-controlled /ôr/ in *morning*; Routine Card 5 to teach high-frequency words *when, do, we, go,* and *at*.

eBook and Games Provide audio support, interaction, and practice with the language.

LESSON 3: Times of the Day

Set Purpose

- Tell students that today they will discuss times of the day. Show page 8 of the Newcomer Cards.

Teach/Model Vocabulary

- Elicit days, months, and routines from Lessons 1 and 2.
- Lead students through the song/chant on page T2.
- Display the Newcomer Card and ask students what they see. Then point to and name each time of day: morning, afternoon, night. Have students repeat. Help with pronunciation.
- Say these sentence frames as you point to the morning label: **When do we get up? We get up in the morning.** Then say the sentences again as you write them on the board, completing them with the activity and time of day. Have students repeat after you. Then, point to the evening label and ask: **When do we eat dinner?** Have students answer chorally: **We eat dinner at night.** Repeat for other events on the card.
- Talk About It Have partners talk about things they do at different times of the day.
- Extend by introducing the sentence frames: **We/I go to school early/late. We/I go to sleep at night**. Explain the terms "early" and "late." Give an example.

Practice/Apply INTERPRETIVE

- **Talk About It** Have partners use the sentence frames they learned to ask and answer questions about the different times of the day that their partner does things.
- Have pairs use previously learned vocabulary to create two sentences telling daily activities that occur at the same time of day. Let others guess the time of day. Model first: *I get up. I get dressed and go to school.* (morning)
- Guide students to complete the activity on page 51.

Make Cultural Connections

Have students tell what people do in the morning, afternoon, evening, and at night in their home countries. Elicit descriptive words and action words. Encourage students to use the past tense.

Times of the Day

Use Newcomer Card, page 8

Name: ______________________________

A. Use words from the box to complete the sentences about the time of day.

eat breakfast	do homework
go to sleep	brush our teeth

1. We ______________________________ in the morning.

2. We ______________________________ in the morning.

3. We ______________________________ in the afternoon.

4. We ______________________________ at night.

B. Write a sentence about something you do in the afternoon.

____

Weather

Language Objective:
Describe the weather outside

Content Objective:
Identify different kinds of weather

Sentence Frames:
How's the weather?
It's ____ and ____ outside.
It's not ____. It's ____.

VOCABULARY
sunny, rainy, snowy, cloudy, foggy, cold, warm, hot, cool

>> Go Digital

Language Transfers Handbook
See pages 16-19 for grammatical structures that do not transfer. Spanish, Vietnamese, or Hmong speakers may struggle with the gender-neutral pronoun *it*.

Grades 2-3 Foundational Skills Kit
Use Phonics Cards 25 to teach the long *e* sound (*sunny*); Routine Card 5 with high-frequency words *the*, *and*, and *not*; Structural Analysis Card 15 to teach contractions (*how's, it's*).

eBook Use digital materials to practice vocabulary.

LESSON 1: Weather Conditions

Set Purpose

- Tell students that today they will discuss weather conditions. Show page 9 of the Newcomer Cards.

Teach/Model Vocabulary

- Lead students through the song/chant on page T2.
- Display the Newcomer Card and ask: *What can you tell me about these pictures?* Then point to and name the different weather conditions. Have students repeat. Help with pronunciation.
- Say these sentence frames as you point to a picture: **How's the weather? It's hot and sunny outside.** Then say the sentences again as you write them on the board, completing the second sentence with the weather conditions. Have students repeat after you. Then, point to the spring scene and ask: **How's the weather?** Have students answer chorally: **It's rainy and warm outside,** filling in the weather conditions. Repeat for other weather conditions from the card and vocabulary list.
- **Talk About It** Have partners talk about the current weather outside.
- Expand by introducing the sentence frames **It's not sunny. It's foggy.**

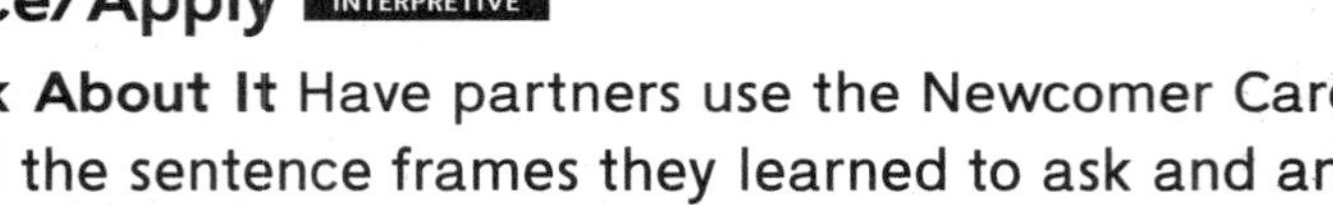

Practice/Apply

INTERPRETIVE

- **Talk About It** Have partners use the Newcomer Card and the sentence frames they learned to ask and answer questions about the weather conditions.
- Guide students to complete the activity on page 53.
- Have students play a guessing game. Partners take turns acting out how they feel in different weather conditions while the other partner guesses the weather. For example, one student pantomimes fanning his/her face and the guesser says: **It's hot and sunny outside**.

Make Connections

Have partners talk about the weather they like or don't like and why using the sentence frame **I like/don't like when it's ____ outside because ____.**

Name: ______________________________

Read the words in the box. Then write two words that describe the weather in the picture.

sunny	rainy	snowy	hot
cloudy	cold	windy	warm

1.  It's ____________ and ____________.

2.  It's ____________ and ____________.

3.  It's ____________ and ____________.

4.  It's ____________ and ____________.

Weather

Language Objective:
Name the seasons

Content Objective:
Demonstrate understanding of different seasons

Sentence Frames:
What season is it?
It is ____ .
The leaves on the trees are ____ .
There is ____ .
The ____ are growing.
It's ____ and ____ .

VOCABULARY
fall, summer, winter, spring, leaves, snow, flowers, growing
Cognates: flores

>> Go Digital

Language Transfers Handbook See pages 16-19 for grammatical structures that do not transfer. Korean, Spanish, or Vietnamese speakers may omit the subject pronoun *it*.

Grades 2-3 Foundational Skills Kit Use Phonics Card 23 to teach the long *o* sound *(snow* and *grow);* Phonics Card 35 to teach the diphthong *ow (flowers)*; Routine Card 5 with high-frequency words *what, and, it,* and *there*.

eBook Use digital materials to practice vocabulary.

LESSON 2: Seasons

Set Purpose

- Tell students that today they will discuss seasons. Show page 9 of the Newcomer Cards.

Teach/Model Vocabulary

- Elicit names of weather conditions discussed in Lesson 1.
- Lead students through the song/chant on page T2.
- Display the Newcomer Card and ask: *What can you tell me about the pictures? What do you see?* Students can name things they know. Then point to and name each season. Have students repeat. Help with pronunciation.
- Say these sentence frames as you point to a season: **What season is it? The flowers are growing. It is spring**. Then say the sentences again as you write them on the board. Have students repeat after you. Then, point to the winter scene and ask: **What season is it?** Have students answer chorally: **There is snow. It is winter**. Repeat for the other seasons and other things we see during different seasons.
- **Talk About It** Have partners talk about the seasons on the card. Then explain that not all places in the world experience seasons as shown on the card. Have students describe the seasons in their home country.
- Extend with the sentence frame **It's hot and sunny** to discuss multiple weather conditions during a season.

Practice/Apply

- **Talk About It** Have partners use the Newcomer Card and the sentence frames they learned to ask and answer questions about what they see during different seasons.
- Guide students to complete the activity on page 55.
- Have partners work together. One student in the pair describes a scene using the vocabulary and language structures from Lessons 1 and 2. The partner guesses which season it is. Then students switch roles.

Make Connections

Have students use the vocabulary from Lessons 1 and 2 to answer the question: *What is your favorite season? Why?* Have students share their answers with a partner and then with the class.

Name: ______________________________

A. Circle the season that matches the picture.

1.

summer

winter

2.

winter

spring

3.

summer

fall

4.

fall

summer

B. Write a sentence that describes the weather in one season.

____

Weather

Language Objective:
Name objects in the sky

Content Objective:
Identify objects in the sky

Sentence Frames:
What can you see in the sky?
I can see the _____.
I can see the _____ and the _____.
When can we see the _____?
We can see the _____ and _____ during the day/at night.

VOCABULARY
sky, stars, moon, sun, planets, Earth, day, night
Cognates: planetas, día

>> Go Digital

Language Transfers Handbook See pages 16-19 for grammatical structures that do not transfer. Some newcomers may omit the article *the*.

Grades 2-3 Foundational Skills Kit Use Phonics Card 10 to teach the *s*-blends in *sky* and *stars*; Routine Card 5 with high-frequency words *what, we, can, sun,* and *see;* Structural Analysis Card 1 to teach the plural ending *-s* (*planets*).

eBook and Games Provide audio support, interaction, and practice with the vocabulary.

LESSON 3: Up in the Sky

Set Purpose

- Tell students that today they will discuss objects in the sky. Show the page 9 of the Newcomer Cards.

Teach/Model Vocabulary

- Elicit vocabulary from Lessons 1 and 2.
- Lead students through the song/chant on page T2.
- Display the Newcomer Card and ask: *What do you see?* Students can name things they know. Then point to and name objects in the sky and identify if the scene is day or night. Have students repeat. Help with pronunciation.
- Say these sentence frames as you point to the winter scene: **What can you see in the sky? I can see the <u>moon</u>.** Then say the sentences again as you write them on the board, completing the second sentence with the name of the object in the sky. Have students repeat after you. Then, point to the stars in the night scene and ask: **What can you see in the sky?** Have students chorally answer: **We can see the <u>stars</u>,** filling in the objects. Repeat for other objects on the vocabulary list.
- **Talk About It** Have partners discuss objects in the sky.
- Extend by introducing the sentence frames **I can see the <u>moon</u> and <u>stars</u>** for multiple objects and **When can we see the <u>moon</u>? We can see the <u>moon</u> at night** for discussing the different times of day we can see objects in the sky.

Practice/Apply 

- **Talk About It** Have partners use the Newcomer Card and sentence frames to ask and answer questions about the sky and different objects we see there.
- Guide students to complete the activity on page 57.
- Have partners work together to describe a scene incorporating vocabulary from Lessons 1, 2, and 3. Other students draw the scene, and the pair describing the scene picks the the most accurate drawing.

Make Cultural Connections

Have students describe any festivals from their home country that celebrate the sun and/or moon.

Name: ______________________________

Up in the Sky

Use Newcomer Card, page 9

Draw what you can see in the sky. Label the objects. Write a sentence describing the scene.

____

My Body

Newcomer Card, p. 10

LESSONS	MATERIALS	LANGUAGE OBJECTIVES	LANGUAGE STRUCTURES/ GRAMMAR	VOCABULARY
Lesson 1: Parts of My Body, p. 60–61	Newcomer Card p. 10 Phonics Card 16 Song/Chant p. T3	Name different parts of the body and describe what people look like	What do/does you/she/he look like? I/She/He have/has ___ ___. **Helping verbs:** do/does **Wh- questions:** What **Pronouns:** he, she, you, I	Parts of the body and adjectives **High-Frequency Words:** *what, he, she, look, like*
Lesson 2: Healthy Routines, p. 62–63	Newcomer Card p. 10 Phonics Card 21 Song/Chant p. T3	Describe the different ways we take care of our bodies	How do/does you/she/he stay healthy? I/She/He ____. ***How* questions** **Pronouns:** I, he, she, my, her, his	Healthy activities **High-Frequency Words:** *take, wash, after, before, go*
Lesson 3: Five Senses, p. 64–65	Newcomer Card p. 10 Phonics Cards 18 and 24 Song/Chant p. T3	Ask and answer questions about the five senses	We ____ with our ____. What do you ___? I ___ a ___. **Wh- questions:** What **Articles:** a, an, the	Senses **High-Frequency Words:** *what, with, do, our*

Clothing

Newcomer Card, p. 11

LESSONS	MATERIALS	LANGUAGE OBJECTIVES	LANGUAGE STRUCTURES/ GRAMMAR	VOCABULARY
Lesson 1: What I Wear, p. 66–67	Newcomer Card p. 11 Phonics Card 18 Song/Chant p. T3	Name and describe clothing	That is a ___ ___ and ___ ___. This is a ___ ___. Those are ___ ___ and ___ ___. **Nouns and adjectives** **Conjunction:** and	Items of clothing **High-Frequency Words:** *that, this, what, like*
Lesson 2: Clothing and Seasons, p. 68–69	Newcomer Card p. 11 Phonics Card 23 and 30 Song/Chant p. T3	Name clothing needed for different seasons	What do you wear in the ____? I wear ____. **Helping verb:** to do **Pronouns:** you, I	Clothing and seasons **High-Frequency Words:** *what, do, you, in, the*
Lesson 3: Activities and Clothing, p. 70–71	Newcomer Card p. 11 Phonics Card 7 Song/Chant p. T3 Language Transfers Handbook	Name items of clothing needed for different activities	When do you need (a) ____? I need (a) ____ when I go ____. **Verbs:** to need **Wh- questions:** When **Pronouns:** you, I	Clothing and activities **High-Frequency Words:** *when, do, you, go, I*

Feelings

Newcomer Card, p. 12

LESSONS	MATERIALS	LANGUAGE OBJECTIVES	LANGUAGE STRUCTURES/ GRAMMAR	VOCABULARY
Lesson 1: How I Feel, p. 72–73	Newcomer Card p. 12 Phonics Card 2 and 21 Song/Chant p. T3	Describe different feelings	How do/does you/she/he feel? I/She/He am/is ____. When are you ____? I'm happy when ____. **Verb:** to be **Wh- questions:** When	Feelings **High-Frequency Words:** *how, when, you, he, she*
Lesson 2: Friendship, p. 74–75	Newcomer Card p. 12 Phonics Card 27 and 42 Song/Chant p. T3	Ask and answer questions about friends	What do we like to do with friends? We like to ____ with our friends. **Verb:** to like **Pronouns:** their, his, our	Activities with friends **High-Frequency Words:** *what, like, with, to, do*
Lesson 3: Helping Others, p. 76–77	Newcomer Card p. 12 Phonics Cards 9 Song/Chant p. T3	Ask and answer questions about helping friends and others	How do/does you/she/he help a/ her/his friend? I/She/He ____ my/ her/his friend. **Helping verbs:** do/does **Pronouns:** my, her	Ways of helping friends **High-Frequency Words:** *how, with, to, for, help*

My Family

Newcomer Card, p. 13

LESSONS	MATERIALS	LANGUAGE OBJECTIVES	LANGUAGE STRUCTURES/ GRAMMAR	VOCABULARY
Lesson 1: Family Members, p. 78–79	Newcomer Card p. 13 Phonics Card 18 Song/Chant p. T4	Name the people in a family	Do you have any _____? No, I don't have any ____. I/She/He have/has ____ ____. **Verbs:** to have **Questions with** *do*	Family members **High-Frequency Words:** *who, this, that, how, many*
Lesson 2: Physical Characteristics, p. 80–81	Newcomer Card p. 13 Phonics Card 18 Song/Chant p. T4	Describe and compare family members	What does the _____ look like? She/He has _____ _____. **Verb:** to have **Wh- questions:** What **Comparatives and Superlatives**	Descriptions of family members **High-Frequency Words:** *has, does, look, like, than*
Lesson 3: Family Activities, p. 82–83	Newcomer Card p. 13 Phonics Card 28 Song/Chant p. T4	Describe family activities	What does their/his/her/your family do together? They/We _____ together. **Helping verb:** to do **Pronoun:** they	*Family activities* **High-Frequency Words:** *what, do, they, and, together*

My Home

Newcomer Card, p. 14

LESSONS	MATERIALS	LANGUAGE OBJECTIVES	LANGUAGE STRUCTURES/ GRAMMAR	VOCABULARY
Lesson 1: Where We Live, p. 84–85	Newcomer Card p. 14 Phonics Card 37 Song/Chant p. T4	Name different kinds of homes	What kind of home do you live in? I live in a/an _____. **Verb:** to live **Wh- questions:** What	*Types of homes* **High-Frequency Words:** *what, kind, of, in, live*
Lesson 2: Rooms in Our Home, p. 86–87	Newcomer Card p. 14 Phonics Card 36 Song/Chant p. T4	Describe the location of objects in a home	Where is/are the _____? The _____ is/are in the _____. **Regular plurals** **Prepositions of place** **Wh- questions:** Where	*Home rooms and objects* **High-Frequency Words:** *where, in, on, is, are*
Lesson 3: Helping Around the House, p. 88–89	Newcomer Card p. 14 Phonics Card 37 Song/Chant p. T4	Name things people do around the house	What is ____ doing? She/He is _____ in the _____. **Present continuous verbs** **Pronouns:** she, he **Wh- questions:** What	Activities at home **High-Frequency Words:** *what, the, is, she, he*

Progress Monitoring

Use the **Oral Language Proficiency Benchmark Assessment** on pages T40–T41 to monitor students' oral language proficiency growth.

Use the **Student Profile** on pages T43–T44 to record observations throughout the units.

My Body

Language Objective:
Name different parts of the body and describe what people look like

Content Objective:
Identify the different parts of the body and physical characteristics

Sentence Frames:
What do you look like?
What does she/he look like?
I/You have ____ ____.
She/He has ____ ____.
She/He has ____ ____ ____ and ____ ____.

VOCABULARY
head, hair, ears, face, eyes, nose, mouth, teeth, neck, arm, hand, fingers, leg, foot, long, short
False Cognate: fase

>> Go Digital

Language Transfers Handbook
See pages 16-19 for grammatical structures that do not transfer. Some Cantonese, Korean, Vietnamese, Spanish, Arabic, or Hmong speakers may struggle with the word order of adjectives and nouns.

Grades 2-3 Foundational Skills Kit
Use Phonics Card 16 to teach final *e* (*face, nose*); Structural Analysis Card 1 to teach plural noun *-s* (*ears, eyes*); Routine Card 5 with the high-frequency words *what, he, she, look, like.*

eBook Use digital material for vocabulary practice.

LESSON 1: Parts of My Body

Set Purpose

- Tell students that today they will discuss parts of the body. Show page 10 of the Newcomer Cards.

Teach/Model Vocabulary

- Lead students through the song/chant on page T3.
- Display the Newcomer Card and ask: *What do you see?* Point to and name each body part. Have students repeat. Help with pronunciation. Then point to a body part and have the class tell you the name. Model putting adjectives and nouns together by pointing to your eyes and saying, for example: *I have brown eyes.*
- Say these sentence frames as you point to a part of the body: **What does he look like? He has brown eyes.** Then say the sentences again as you write them on the board. Have students repeat after you. Then point to the boy's hair and ask: **What does he look like?** Have students answer chorally: **He has short hair**. Repeat for other parts of the body on the card and on the vocabulary list.
- **Talk About It** Introduce the sentence frames: **What do you look like? I have brown hair**. Then have students describe themselves to a partner.
- Extend by introducing sentence frames that contain more detail: **What does she/he look like? She/He has long black hair and green eyes.**

Practice/Apply

- **Talk About It** Have partners use the card and the sentence frames they learned to ask and answer questions about different parts of the body.
- Have partners stand back to back. One student in the pair describes an imaginary person, and the other student draws it. Then have partners switch roles.
- Guide students to complete the activity on page 61.

Make Connections

Have students work in pairs. One student describes a person in school, and the other student guesses the identity based on the description. Encourage students to use adjectives they've learned.

Name: ____________________

Parts of My Body

Use Newcomer Card, page 10

Draw a picture of a friend and label it using words from the box. Talk to a partner about it.

hair	ears	face	eyes	nose	mouth
arm	hand	fingers	leg	foot	

My Body

Language Objective:
Describe the different ways we take care of our bodies

Content Objective:
Understand the different ways we take care of our bodies

Sentence Frames:
How does she/he stay healthy?
She/He ____ .
How do you stay healthy?
I ____ and ____ .
I ____ before/after I ____ .

VOCABULARY
brush teeth, brush hair, take a bath, take a shower, wash hands, healthy, stay, before, after

>> Go Digital

Language Transfers Handbook
See pages 16-19 for grammatical structures that do not transfer. Some Cantonese, Korean, Arabic, or Hmong speakers may struggle with transitive and intransitive verbs.

Grades 2-3 Foundational Skills Kit
Use Phonics Card 21 to teach long *a* sounds (*stay*); Phonological Awareness Card 19 to teach syllable addition (*healthy*); Routine Card 5 with the high-frequency words *take, wash, after, before, go.*

eBook Use digital material for vocabulary practice.

LESSON 2: Healthy Routines

Set Purpose

- Tell students that today they will discuss how we take care of our bodies. Show page 10 of the Newcomer Cards.

Teach/Model Vocabulary

- Elicit vocabulary from Lesson 1.
- Lead students through the song/chant on page T3.
- Display the Newcomer Card and ask: *What are the kids doing?* Then point to, name, and pantomime each action. Have students repeat. Help with pronunciation.
- Say these sentence frames as you point to the first picture: **How does she stay healthy? She brushes her teeth.** Then say the sentences again as you write them on the board, completing the second sentence with the action. Point to the second picture and ask: **How does he stay healthy?** Have students answer chorally: **He washes his hands,** filling in the action. Repeat for brushing hair and for the other ways included in the vocabulary list.
- **Talk About It** Have partners talk about the different ways people take care of their bodies.
- Expand by introducing the sentence frames: **How do you stay healthy? I wash my hands and take a shower.** Then extend by reusing the frames with the words *before* and *after* and previously learned vocabulary.

Practice/Apply COLLABORATIVE

- **Talk About It** Have partners use the Newcomer Card and the sentence frames they learned to ask and answer questions about why it's important to wash our hands and brush our teeth.
- Have partners work together. One student acts out two of the actions discussed. The other student fills in the sentence frame with action verbs: **I ____ and ____**. Then have partners switch roles.
- Guide students to complete the activity on page 63.

Make Connections

Ask students: *What are some other things you do to stay healthy?* Have students act out and talk about things they do to stay healthy *(eat good food, sleep, take a walk).* Provide vocabulary as needed.

Name: ______________________________

Use Newcomer Card, page 10

Look at the pictures. Then complete each sentence using words from the box.

brush teeth	brush hair
take a bath	wash hands

1.  She ______________________________ .

2.  She ______________________________ .

3.  He ______________________________ .

4.  He ______________________________ .

My Body

Language Objective:
Ask and answer questions about the five senses

Content Objective:
Demonstrate understanding of the five senses

Sentence Frames:
We ____ with our ____.
What do you ____?
I ____ a/an/the ____.
What do you ____ with your ____?
I ____ ____ with my ____.

VOCABULARY
see, hear, taste, smell, feel, tongue, skin

>> Go Digital

Language Transfers Handbook
See pages 16-19 for grammatical structures that do not transfer. Some Cantonese or Hmong speakers may omit prepositions.

Grades 2-3 Foundational Skills Kit
Use Phonics Card 18 to teach *s*-blends (*skin, smell*); Phonics Card 24 to teach long *e* sounds (*see, feel*); Routine Card 5 with the high-frequency words *what, with, do, our.*

eBook and Games Provide audio support, interaction, and practice with the vocabulary.

LESSON 3: Five Senses

Set Purpose

- Tell students that today they will discuss the five senses. Show page 10 of the Newcomer Cards.

Teach/Model Vocabulary

- Elicit vocabulary you discussed in Lessons 1 and 2.
- Lead students through the song/chant on page T3.
- Display the Newcomer Card and ask: *What do these parts of the body help us to do?* Then point to and read the sentences about the senses. Use gestures to indicate each sense. Have students repeat. Help with pronunciation.
- Say these sentence frames as you point to a sense: **We hear with our ears. What do you hear?** Clap your hands and say: **I hear a clap.** Say the sentences again as you write them on the board. Have students repeat after you. Then, point to the eyes and say: **We see with our eyes. What do you see?** Point to a book and have students answer chorally: **I see a book.** Repeat for the other senses on the card.
- **Talk About It** Have partners talk about what they can see, feel, taste, hear, and smell using their five senses.
- Expand by introducing the sentence frames: **What do you see with your eyes? I see stars with my eyes.**

Practice/Apply INTERPRETIVE

- **Talk About It** Have partners use the card and the sentence frames they learned to talk about what the boy might use his five senses to see, hear, feel, smell, and taste while skateboarding at the park.
- Have partners work together to locate items in the classroom that they can see, hear, smell, taste, and feel. After items are gathered, have partners use the sentence frames to present each object to the class.
- Guide students to complete the activity on page 65.

Make Cultural Connections

Have students respond to the following prompt: *Tell me about your favorite things to hear, see, taste, smell, and feel from your home country.*

Name: ______________________

Five Senses

Use Newcomer Card, page 10

A. Match the sense to the correct part of the body.

1. hear — a.

2. taste — b.  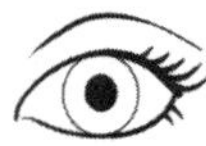

3. feel — c. 

4. smell — d. 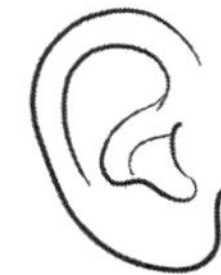 

5. see — e. 

B. Write a sentence about a sound you like to hear.

____

Clothing

Language Objective:
Name and describe clothing

Content Objective:
Demonstrate knowledge of clothing

Sentence Frames:
This is a ____ ____.
That is a ____ ____ *and a* ____ ____.
Those are ____ ____ *and* ____ ____.
What do you like to wear?
I like to wear ____ ____.
I don't like to wear ____ ____.

VOCABULARY
shirt, dress, pants, jeans, shorts, shoes, socks, boots, sneakers, jacket, wear
Cognates: pantalones, botas

>> Go Digital

Language Transfers Handbook See pages 16-19 for grammatical structures that do not transfer. Cantonese or Hmong speakers may confuse *one* with *a/an*.

Grades 2-3 Foundational Skills Kit Use Phonics Card 18 to teach the consonant digraph *sh* (*shirt, shorts*); Structural Analysis Card 1 to teach plural nouns with the ending *-s* (*socks*); Routine Card 5 with the high-frequency words *that, this, what, like.*

eBook Use digital material for vocabulary practice.

LESSON 1: What I Wear

Set Purpose

- Tell students that today they will discuss what we wear. Show page 11 of the Newcomer Cards.

Teach/Model Vocabulary

- Lead students through the song/chant on page T3.
- Display the Newcomer Card and ask: *What do you see?* Then point to and name items of clothing on the card and others that you and the students are wearing. Have students repeat. Help with pronunciation.
- Say these sentence frames as you point to items of clothing: **This is a white shirt. That is a red shirt and green shorts. Those are pink sneakers and pink shorts.** Then say the sentences again as you write them on the board. Have students repeat after you. Then point to the boy in the fall scene and say: **Those are . . .** Students chorally fill in: **brown pants and a green jacket.** Repeat for other clothing on the card and in the vocabulary list.
- **Talk About It** Have partners describe clothing they're wearing.
- Extend by introducing the sentence frames: **What do you like to wear? I like to wear blue jeans. I don't like to wear dresses.** Use these sentence frames to review likes and dislikes.

Practice/Apply PRODUCTIVE

- **Talk About It** Have partners use the sentence frames they learned to name and describe clothing that other people in the class are wearing.
- Guide students to complete the activity on page 67.
- Provide magazines or catalogs with pictures of clothing. Have partners cut out pictures to make a poster, then take turns describing the clothing to the class.

Make Connections

- Have partners fill in a Venn diagram to compare and contrast their clothing. Have them write or draw the things that are the same in the middle and the things that are different on the sides. Then have them describe the similarities and differences to another pair.

Name: ______________________________

Use Newcomer Card, page 11

A. Use words from the box to complete each sentence.

shirt	shoes	socks	boots

1. 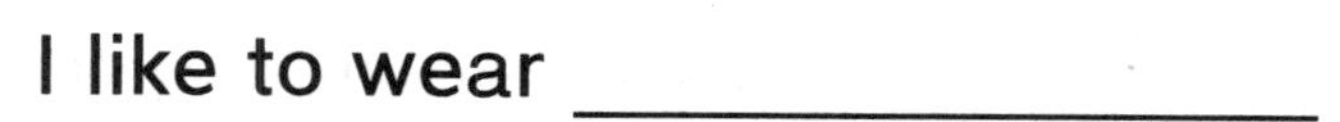 I like to wear ______________ .

2. I like to wear a ______________ .

3.  I like to wear ______________ .

4.  I like to wear ______________ .

B. Complete each sentence with what you like and don't like to wear.

1. I don't like to wear ________________________ .

2. I like to wear ____________________________ .

Clothing

Language Objective:
Name clothing needed for different seasons

Content Objective:
Determine what clothing is needed for each season

Sentence Frames:
What do you wear in the ____?
I wear ____.
I wear a ____.
I wear a ____ and ____.

VOCABULARY
coat, hat, mittens, raincoat, boots, bathing suit, t-shirt, shorts, scarf, gloves, spring, summer, winter, fall
Cognates: mitones, botas

>> Go Digital

Language Transfers Handbook
See pages 16-19 to identify grammatical structures that do not transfer. Some Cantonese, Hmong, Korean, Vietnamese, Arabic, Spanish, or Tagalog speakers may omit or overuse articles.

Grades 2-3 Foundational Skills Kit
Use Phonics Card 23 to teach long *o* sounds (*coat*); Phonics Card 30 to teach the *r*-controlled vowel *ear* (*wear*); Routine Card 5 with the high-frequency words *what, do, you, in, the.*

eBook Use digital material for vocabulary practice.

LESSON 2: Clothing and Seasons

Set Purpose

- Tell students that today they will discuss clothing for different seasons. Show page 11 of the Newcomer Cards.

Teach/Model Vocabulary

- To review, elicit vocabulary from Lesson 1.
- Lead students through the song/chant on page T3.
- Display the Newcomer Card and ask: *What seasons do you see?* Then point to and name the clothing worn in different seasons. Have students repeat. Help with pronunciation.
- Say these sentence frames as you point to a season: **What do you wear in the summer? I wear a bathing suit.** Then say the sentences again as you write them on the board, completing the sentences with the season and item of clothing. Have students repeat after you. Then point to spring and say: **What do you wear in the spring?** Have students answer chorally: **I wear shorts**. Repeat for other seasons and clothing on the card and vocabulary list.
- **Talk About It** Have partners talk about the current season, what they are wearing, and why.
- Extend by reusing the sentence frames with the conjunction *and* to name multiple items.

Practice/Apply

- **Talk About It** Have partners use the Newcomer Card and the sentence frames they learned to talk about clothing they might need during a spring rain shower.
- Guide students to complete the activity on page 69.
- Divide the class into four groups. Whisper to each group which season they will represent. Then ask each group one at a time to make exaggerated gestures to show the season. The other three groups guess the season and describe the clothes needed for that season.

Make Connections

Have students name their favorite season and describe what they wear during that season and why. Encourage them to use descriptive words.

Name: ______________________________

Use Newcomer Card, page 11

Write the name of a season. Then write clothes in the circles that you wear during that season.

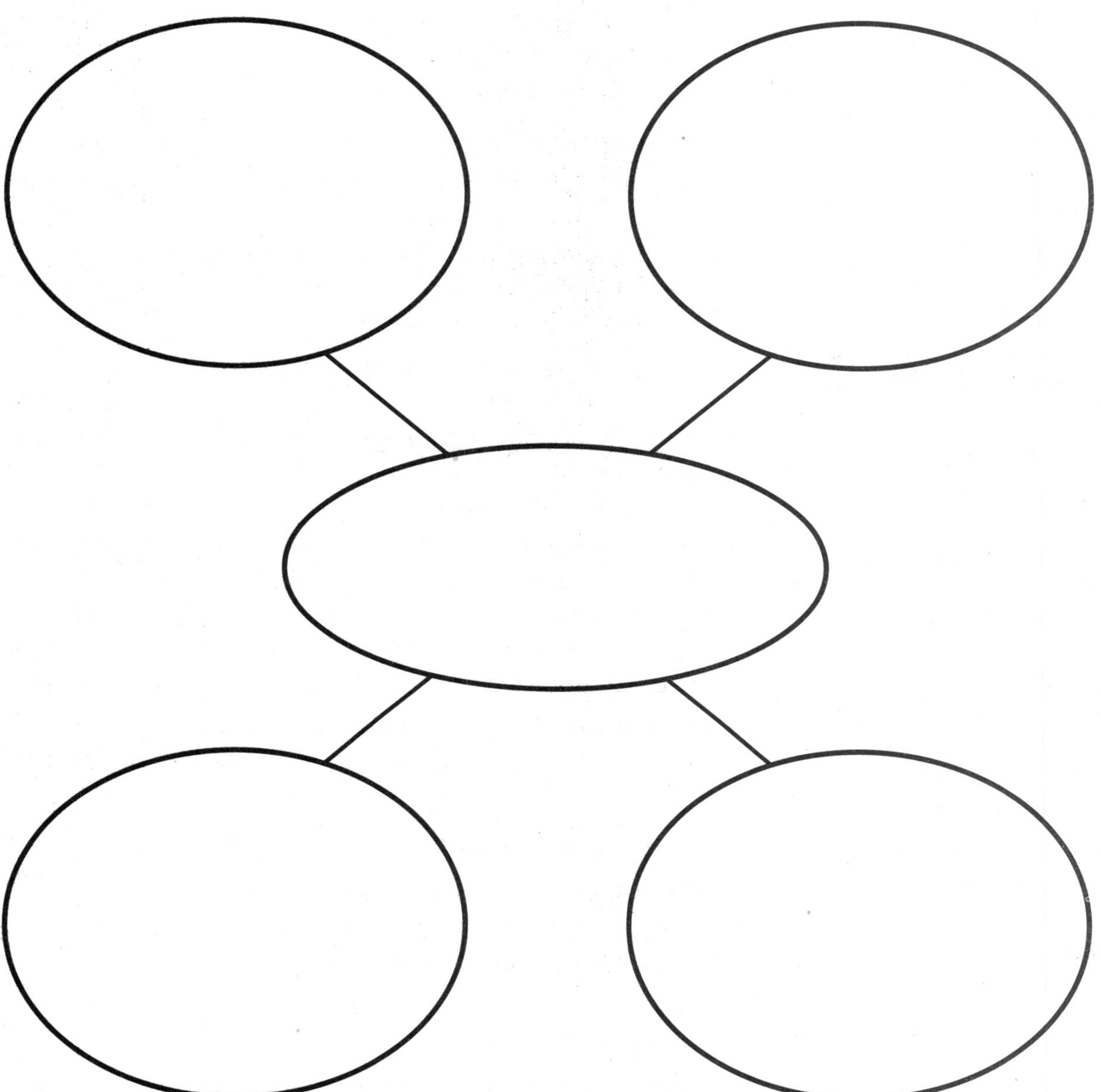

B. Complete this sentence about what you like to wear during the summer.

I like to wear ______________________________.

Clothing

Language Objective:
Name items of clothing needed for different activities

Content Objective:
Determine items of clothing needed for different activities

Sentence Frames:
When do you need a ____?
I need a ____ when I go ____.
When do you need ____?
I need ____ when I go ____.

VOCABULARY

running, swimming, hiking, biking, camping

>> Go Digital

Language Transfers Handbook
See pages 16-19 for grammatical structures that do not transfer. Cantonese, Hmong, Korean, Vietnamese, Arabic, or Spanish speakers may forget to use the plural marker *-s* on nouns.

Grades 2-3 Foundational Skills Kit
Use Phonics Card 7 to teach consonant digraph *-ng;* Structural Analysis Card 10 to teach inflectional ending *-ing* with a doubled final consonant (*running*); Routine Card 5 with the high-frequency words *when, do, go, you, I.*

eBook and Games Provide audio support, interaction, and practice with the vocabulary.

LESSON 3: Activities and Clothing

Set Purpose

- Tell students that today they will discuss clothing needed for different activities. Show page 11 of the Newcomer Cards.

Teach/Model Vocabulary

- To review, elicit vocabulary from Lessons 1 and 2.
- Lead students through the song/chant on page T3.
- Display the card and ask: *What are they doing?* Students can name activities they know. Then point to and name each activity and the clothing needed. Have students repeat. Help with pronunciation. Have students turn to a partner and talk about other activities they like.
- Say these sentence frames as you point to an activity: **When do you need a <u>bathing suit</u>? I need a <u>bathing suit</u> when I go <u>swimming</u>.** Then say the sentences again as you write them on the board, completing the sentences with the name of each item of clothing and activity. Have students repeat after you. Then point to the boy hiking and ask: **When do you need <u>boots</u>?** Have students answer chorally: **I need <u>boots</u> when I go <u>hiking</u>.** Repeat for other activities on the card, in the vocabulary list, and ones students have talked about.
- **Talk About It** Have partners act out each activity. Then have them talk about the clothing needed for each one.

Practice/Apply

COLLABORATIVE

- **Talk About It** Have partners use the sentence frames they learned to discuss clothing they've worn for different activities.
- Guide students to complete the activity on page 71.
- In pairs, have one student tell about a trip including the season and activities, while his/her partner draws the clothing that should be packed. Partners can talk about the drawings. Then they switch roles.

Make Cultural Connections

Have students respond to the following prompt: *Tell us about clothing you wore for different seasons in your home country.* Have students present to the class as they compare clothing they wore with clothing they see on the card and in school.

Name: ______________________________

A. Circle the correct clothing for each activity.

1. biking 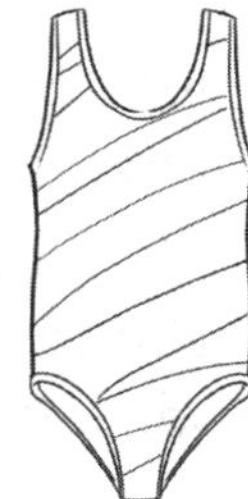 

2. camping  

3. hiking  

4. swimming 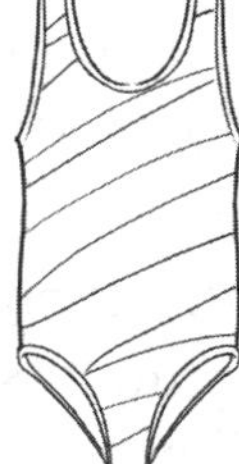 

B. Write about the clothing you need for your favorite activity.

____.

Feelings

Language Objective:
Describe different feelings

Content Objective:
Identify different feelings

Sentence Frames:
How does she/he feel?
She/He is ____.
How do you feel?
I am _____.
When are you ____?
I'm ____ when/because ____.

VOCABULARY
afraid, angry, confused, happy, sad

>> Go Digital

Language Transfers Handbook
See pages 16–19 for grammatical structures that do not transfer. Cantonese, Hmong, or Vietnamese speakers may omit linking verbs.

Grades 2–3 Foundational Skills Kit
Use Phonics Card 2 to teach short *a* (*sad, happy*); Phonics Card 21 to teach long *a* (as in the second *a* in *afraid*); Routine Card 5 to teach high-frequency words *how, when, you, he, she*.

eBook Use digital material for vocabulary practice.

LESSON 1: How I Feel

Set Purpose

- Tell students that today they will discuss feelings. Show page 12 of the Newcomer Cards.

Teach/Model Vocabulary

- Lead students through the song/chant on page T3.
- Display the Newcomer Card and ask: *What do you see?* Then point to and name each feeling as you copy the expression. Students repeat. Help with pronunciation.
- Say these sentence frames as you point to a feeling: **How does she feel? She is <u>confused</u>.** Then say the sentences again as you write them on the board, completing the second sentence with the name of the feeling. Have students repeat after you. Then point to the happy boy and ask: **How does he feel?** Have students answer chorally: **He is <u>happy</u>.** Repeat for the other feelings shown on the Newcomer Card.
- Introduce the sentence frames: **How do you feel? I am <u>sad</u>.** Have partners use the Conversation Starters on page T29 to talk about how they are feeling.
- Extend by introducing the sentence frames: **When are you <u>happy</u>? I'm <u>happy</u> when/because <u>it is warm outside.</u>/<u>I'm in the gym.</u>/<u>I'm with my friends</u>.** Use these for discussing *when* and *why* students have different feelings.

Practice/Apply PRODUCTIVE

- **Talk About It** Have partners use the card and the sentence frames they learned. Have them discuss why they think the kids on the card feel the way they do.
- As a class, have students make up sounds that go with feelings, such as laughing, growling, or sighing. Then have students play a guessing game. One student uses facial expressions and sounds to indicate a feeling. The other students guess by saying: **She/He is ____.** Play until each student has had a turn acting out a feeling.
- Guide students to complete the activity on page 73.

Make Connections

Ask partners to discuss what they do when they feel happy. Have students share their responses with you.

Name: ______________________________

A. Complete each sentence with the correct feeling.

angry	confused	happy	sad

1.  I am ______________________________.

2.  I am ______________________________.

3.  I am ______________________________.

4.  I am ______________________________.

B. Describe how you feel when you watch a funny video.

____

Feelings

Language Objective:
Ask and answer questions about friends

Content Objective:
Understand what friends do together

Sentence Frames:
What does he/she like to do with his/her friend(s)?
What do you/they like to do with your/their friend(s)?
They/We like to ____ with their/ our friend(s).
She/He likes to ____ with her/his friend(s).
I like to ____ with my friend(s).

VOCABULARY
play, laugh, work, eat, friend

>> Go Digital

Language Transfers Handbook
See pages 16–19 for grammatical structures that do not transfer. Korean, Vietnamese, or Spanish speakers may omit subject pronouns.

Grades 2–3 Foundational Skills Kit
Use Phonics Card 27 to teach *r*-controlled vowel /ûr/ (*work*); Phonics Card 42 to teach consonant digraph *gh* (*laugh*); Routine Card 5 to teach high-frequency words *what, like, with, to,* and *do.*

eBook Use digital material for vocabulary practice.

LESSON 2: Friendship

Set Purpose

- Tell students that today they will discuss friendship and show page 12 of the Newcomer Cards.

Teach/Model Vocabulary

- Use the card to elicit the feelings learned in Lesson 1.
- Lead students through the song/chant on page T3.
- Display the Newcomer Card and ask: *What are the kids doing in the picture? What do you do with your friends?* Point to, name, and pantomime the actions. Have students repeat. Help with pronunciation.
- Say these sentence frames as you point to the kids laughing: **What do they like to do with their friends? They like to laugh with their friends.** Then say the sentences again as you write them on the board, completing the second sentence with the action. Have students repeat after you. Pantomime the words in the vocabulary list and ask what people like to do with friends. Have students chorally answer: **They like to eat with their friends.**
- **Talk About It** Have partners talk about the things their friends like to do.
- Extend by introducing the other sentence frames in the sidebar. Have students talk about what others like to do.

Practice/Apply COLLABORATIVE

- **Talk About It** Have partners talk about the fun activities they do with their friends. Have them explain why they think these activities are fun.
- Guide students to complete the activity on page 75.
- Have partners make a tally chart with three different activities at the top. Have the partners survey classmates and ask if his/her classmates like to do these activities with friends. Have partners tally how many students like each activity and report their findings to the class.

Make Connections

Have each partner draw and describe a picture showing a time when they laughed with their friends. Then partners describe their partner's picture to the class. After each telling, have a student ask a follow-up question.

Name: ______________________________

Friendship

Use Newcomer Card, page 12

Complete each sentence with a word that tells what the person is doing.

1.

They like to ________ with their friends.

2.

She likes to ________ with her friend.

3.

She likes to ________ with her friend.

4.

He likes to ________ with his friend.

Feelings

Language Objective:
Ask and answer questions about helping friends and others

Content Objective:
Understand how we help friends and others

Sentence Frames:
How does he/she help his/her friend?
She/He ____ her/his friend ____.
How do you help your friend(s)?
I ____ my friend ____.

VOCABULARY
help, friend(s), talk to, listen to, care for, call, eat with, share with
False Cognates: col

>> Go Digital

Language Transfers Handbook
See pages 16–19 for grammatical structures that do not transfer. Cantonese or Hmong speakers may omit prepositions.

Grades 2–3 Foundational Skills Kit
Use Phonics Card 9 to teach *r* blends (*friend*); Structural Analysis Card 2 to teach inflectional ending *-s* (*talks, cares*); Routine Card 5 to teach high-frequency words *how, with, to, for,* and *help.*

eBook and Games Provide audio support, interaction, and practice with the vocabulary.

LESSON 3: Helping Others

Set Purpose

- Tell students that today they will discuss helping others and show page 12 of the Newcomer Cards.

Teach/Model Vocabulary

- Elicit the names of feelings and activities done with friends from Lessons 1 and 2.
- Lead students through the song/chant on page T3.
- Display the Newcomer Card and ask: *What do you see here? What are the two boys doing?*
- Say these sentence frames as you point to the boy helping his friend walk: **How does he help his friend? He <u>helps</u> his friend <u>walk</u>.** Then say the sentences again as you write them on the board, completing the second sentence. Have students repeat after you. Then pantomime and say the other actions in the vocabulary list, and ask: **How do you help your friend?** Have students chorally answer with the corresponding vocabulary word.
- **Talk About It** Have partners talk about different ways they help their friends. Expand the conversation by encouraging children to fill in the second half of the sentence frames with different vocabulary they know: **I <u>help</u> my friend <u>read/when she needs me/use a computer/in the morning/brush her hair/etc.</u>**

Practice/Apply PRODUCTIVE

- **Talk About It** Have partners ask each other how they help their friends and have them explain why.
- Guide students to complete the activity on page 77.
- Have partners talk about and write two different ways they help friends on two separate slips of paper. Have students put the slips in one pile. Have students take turns choosing a slip and acting out what is written. Have others guess what way to help a friend is written.

Make Cultural Connections

Have students respond to this prompt: *What activities did you do with your friends in your home country? How did you help your friends?* Partners can share their responses with each other and then with the class. Other students ask follow-up questions.

Name: ______________________

Write four ways to help a friend. Then draw a picture for each sentence.

How do you help a friend?	
1. ______________________	2. ______________________
3. ______________________	4. ______________________

My Family

Language Objective:
Name the people in a family

Content Objective:
Name the people in a family

Sentence Frames:
Do you have any ____?
No, I don't have any ____.
I/She/He have/has ____ ____.
How many ____ do(es) she/he/you have?

VOCABULARY
father, mother, daughter, son, grandfather, grandmother, sister, brother, or
False Cognates: son

>> Go Digital

Language Transfers Handbook
See pages 16-19 for grammatical structures that do not transfer. Cantonese, Hmong, Korean, Spanish, Tagalog, or Vietnamese speakers may struggle with gender-specific pronouns.

Grades 2-3 Foundational Skills Kit
Use Phonics Card 18 to teach the consonant digraph *th* (*mother*); Structural Analysis Card 14 to teach compound words (*grandmother*); Routine Card 5 to teach high-frequency words *who, this, that, how, many.*

eBook Use digital material for vocabulary practice.

LESSON 1: Family Members

Set Purpose

- Tell students that today they will discuss family members. Show page 13 of the Newcomer Cards.

Teach/Model Vocabulary

- Lead students through the song/chant on page T4.
- Display the Newcomer Card and ask: *Who do you see?* Then point to and name each family member. Have students repeat. Help with pronunciation.
- Draw your family tree. Say the sentence frames as you point to the people in your family tree: **I have a/an/ one/two/etc. (member(s)).** Then say the sentences again as you write them on the board, complete with the number and the family member name. Cover other members on the vocabulary list with: **I don't have any (members).** Have students repeat after you. Ask students: **Do you have any brothers or sisters?** Have them turn to a partner and talk about it.
- **Talk About It** Have students talk about the number of different family members they have. Expand their conversations by teaching extended family members: aunt, uncle, cousin, etc.
- Use the card to extend the lesson with the other sentence frames in the sidebar: **How many brothers does she have? She has one brother.** Have partners use these sentence frames to talk about the relationships on the card.

Practice/Apply

- **Talk About It** Have partners use the sentence frames they learned to ask and answer questions about the family members of someone they both know.
- Guide students to complete the activity on page 79.
- In pairs, have students ask and answer questions about each other's family tree, such as: *Who is she/he? What does she/he look like?* Encourage students to use previously learned vocabulary.

Make Connections

Have students compare and contrast their family trees. Have partner present their findings to the class, and have the rest of the class ask follow-up questions.

Name: ______________________________

Family Members

Use Newcomer Card, page 13

Draw your family tree. Then write a sentence about your family.

____

My Family

Language Objective:
Describe and compare family members

Content Objective:
Understand differences between family members

Sentence Frames:
What does his/her/your ____ look like?
She/he has ____ ____.
She/he is ____.
She/He is ____ than his/her ____.
____ is the ____.

VOCABULARY
tall, long, short, dark, light, taller than, tallest, shorter than, shortest, eyes, hair, brown, black, blonde, blue, curly, straight

>> Go Digital

Language Transfers Handbook
See pages 16-19 for grammatical structures that do not transfer. Hmong, Korean, Spanish, or Tagalog speakers may struggle with comparative and superlative endings.

Grades 2-3 Foundational Skills Kit
Use Phonics Card 18 to teach consonant digraph *sh* (*short*); Structural Analysis Card 25 to teach comparative inflectional endings *-er* and *-est* (*taller, tallest*); Routine Card 5 to teach high-frequency words *has, does, look, like, than.*

eBook Use digital material for vocabulary practice.

LESSON 2: Physical Characteristics

Set Purpose

- Tell students they will discuss physical characteristics of family members. Show page 13 of the Newcomer Cards.

Teach/Model Vocabulary

- To review, elicit names of family members from Lesson 1.
- Lead students through the song/chant on page T4.
- Display the card and ask: *What do these people look like?* Then point to and describe their physical characteristics, using gestures when possible. Be sure to cover all vocabulary listed. Have students repeat. Help with pronunciation.
- Say these sentence frames as you point to the brother: **What does his sister look like? She has straight hair.** Then say the sentences again as you write them on the board. Have students repeat after you. Then say these sentence frames as you point to the father: **What does his father look like?** Have students answer chorally: **He is tall.** Repeat for other people and physical characteristics on the card and vocabulary list.
- **Talk About It** Have partners talk about the physical characteristics of the family members on the card and in their own families.
- Extend the partners' conversations by introducing these comparative and superlative sentence frames: **She is shorter than her brother. She is the shortest.**

Practice/Apply

- **Talk About It** Have partners use the sentence frames they learned to ask and answer questions about the physical characteristics of their favorite teachers.
- Have students draw two members of their family and then describe them to a partner. Encourage them to use comparative and/or superlative adjectives to compare.
- Guide students to complete the activity on page 81.

Make Connections

Partners cut out pictures from magazines of people with different physical characteristics creating "families" with the pictures and describing the family, in detail, to another pair.

Name: ______________________________

Write the name of a family member. Then write words in the circles to describe that person.

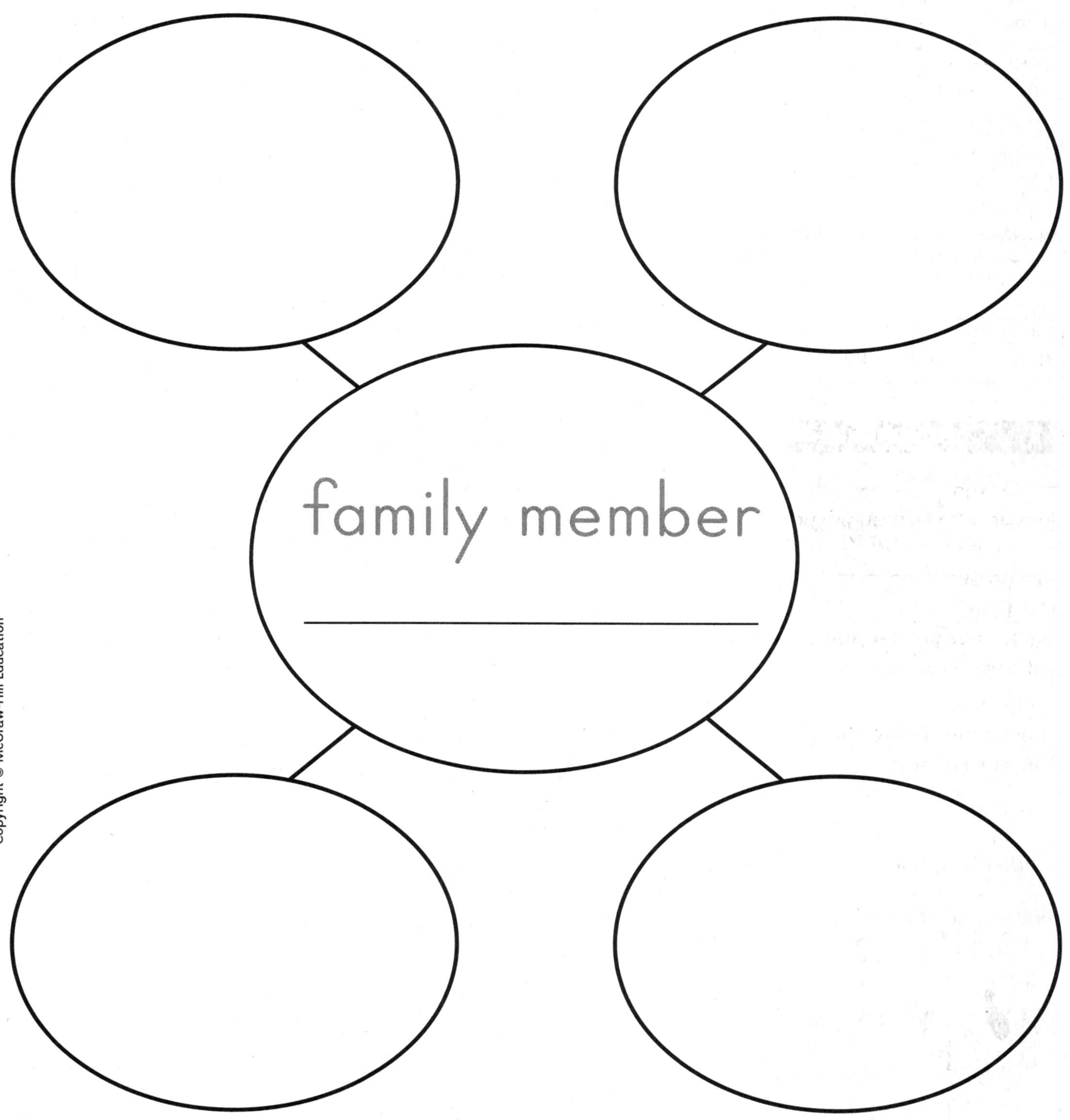

My Family

Language Objective:
Describe family activities

Content Objective:
Identify family activities

Sentence Frames:
What does their/his/her/your family do together?
They/We ____ together.
They/We ____ and ____ together.

VOCABULARY
visit relatives, meet relatives, go to the park, go shopping, eat, play, fly a kit, play in the park
Cognates: visitar, parque

>> Go Digital

Language Transfers Handbook See pages 16-19 to identify grammatical structures that do not transfer. Korean, Spanish, or Vietnamese speakers may omit subject pronouns.

Grades 2-3 Foundational Skills Kit Use Phonics Card 28 to teach *r*-controlled vowel /är/ (*park*); Structural Analysis Card 18 to teach inflectional endings and plurals (*families*); Routine Card 5 to teach high-frequency words *what, do, they, and, together.*

eBook and Games Provide audio support, interaction, and practice with the vocabulary.

LESSON 3: Family Activities

Set Purpose

- Tell students that today they will discuss family activities. Show page 13 of the Newcomer Cards.

Teach/Model Vocabulary

- Elicit family member names and physical characteristics from Lessons 1 and 2.
- Lead students through the song/chant on page T4.
- Display the Newcomer Card. Ask students: *What are the families doing?* Then point to and name each activity, using gestures when possible. Have students repeat. Help with pronunciation.
- Say these sentence frames as you point to each family: **What does their family do together? They <u>fly a kite</u> together.** Then say the sentences again as you write them on the board, completing the second sentence with the name of the activity. Have students repeat after you. Then point to the other family and ask: **What does their family do together?** Have students answer chorally: **They <u>visit relatives</u> together.** Repeat for other activities on the card, on the vocabulary list, and ones that students do with their own families.
- **Talk About It** Have partners talk about the different things their families do together.
- Extend the conversations by introducing the sentence frame naming multiple activities: **We <u>go shopping</u> and <u>eat</u> together.**

Practice/Apply COLLABORATIVE

- **Talk About It** Have partners use the Newcomer Card and the sentence frames to ask and answer questions about the activities families are doing together.
- Have pairs sit back to back. Students take turns describing the physical characteristics and activities of a family, and the partner draws what he/she hears. Have partners talk about their drawings with the class.
- Guide students to complete the activity on page 83.

Make Cultural Connections

Have partners talk about activities they did with their family in their home country. Have them present to the class.

Name: ______________________

A. Match the sentence to the correct image.

1. They visit relatives together.

a. 

2. They play in the park together.

b. 

3. They go shopping together.

c. 

B. Write what you like to do with your family.

____

My Home

Language Objective:
Name different kinds of homes

Content Objective:
Identify different kinds of homes

Sentence Frames:
What kind of home do you live in?
I live in a/an ____.

VOCABULARY
house, apartment building, mobile home
Cognates: apartamento, móvil

>> Go Digital

Language Transfers Handbook
See pages 16-19 for grammatical structures that do not transfer. Korean, Spanish, or Arabic speakers may confuse related phrasal verbs (*live in/on*).

Grades 2-3 Foundational Skills Kit
Use Phonics Card 37 to teach the variant vowel /ů/ in *house*; Structural Analysis Card 26 to teach the three or more syllable word (*apartment*); Routine Card 5 to teach high-frequency words *what, kind, of, in, live.*

eBook Use digital material for vocabulary practice.

LESSON 1: Where We Live

Set Purpose

- Tell students that today they will discuss different kinds of homes. Show page 14 of the Newcomer Cards.

Teach/Model Vocabulary

- Lead students through the song/chant on page T4.
- Display the Newcomer Card and ask: *What do you see?* Students can name things they know and describe them to a partner. Then point to and name each kind of home. Have students repeat. Help with pronunciation.
- Say these sentence frames as you point to the apartment building: **What kind of home do you live in? I live in an apartment building.** Then say the sentences again as you write them on the board. Have students repeat after you. Then point to the house and ask: **What kind of home do you live in?** Have students answer chorally: **I live in a house.** Repeat for other kinds of homes on the card.
- **Talk About It** Have partners talk about different kinds of homes they see in their neighborhood.
- Have students expand the conversation with descriptive adjectives to review colors and shapes.

Practice/Apply COLLABORATIVE

- **Talk About It** Have partners use the Newcomer Card and the sentence frames they learned to ask and answer questions about different kinds of homes.
- Guide students to complete the activity on page 85.
- In pairs, have students write three sentences describing a home on the Newcomer Card using previously learned vocabulary. Pairs share with their classmates. Then they name the home being described. Model for students, for example: *It's the tallest. It has square windows. It has brown paint.* (*It's the apartment building.*)

Make Connections

Have partners cut out shapes from colored paper. They then use the shapes to create a two-dimensional home. Then they share with classmates by naming the kind of home and describing the shapes and colors they used to build it.

Use Newcomer Card, page 14

Name: ______________________________

A. Look at the picture. Then complete each sentence.

1. I live in a  .

a. 

2. I live in an ____________________ .

b. 

3. I live in a ____________________ .

c. 

B. Choose a home on your street. Write about the kind of home using the words *They* or *We*.

____

My Home

Language Objective:
Describe the location of objects in a home

Content Objective:
Identify objects and rooms in a home

Sentence Frames:
Where is/are the ____?
The ____ is /are in the ____.
The ____ is/are on the ____ in the ____.

VOCABULARY
bedroom, bathroom, kitchen, living room, pillow, bed, dresser, mirror, shower, toilet, bathtub, table, cabinet, sink, coffee table, couch, window, refrigerator, television
Cognates: refrigerador, televisión **False Cognate:** mirar

>> Go Digital

Language Transfers Handbook
See pages 16-19 for grammatical structures that do not transfer. Hmong or Cantonese speakers may omit prepositions.

Grades 2-3 Foundational Skills Kit
Use Phonics Card 36 to teach the diphthong *oi* (*toilet*); Structural Analysis Card 14 to teach compound words (*bedroom, bathtub*); Routine Card 5 to teach high-frequency words *where, in, on, is, are.*

eBook Use digital material for vocabulary practice.

LESSON 2: Rooms in Our Home

Set Purpose

- Tell students that today they will discuss objects and rooms in a home. Show page 14 of the Newcomer Cards.

Teach/Model Vocabulary

- Elicit names of different kinds of homes from Lesson 1.
- Lead students through the song/chant on page T4.
- Display the Newcomer Card and say: *Look at the rooms in the home. What do you see?* Partners can name and discuss things they know. Then point to and name the objects and rooms. Have students repeat. Help with pronunciation.
- Say these sentence frames as you point to the bedroom: **Where is the bed? The bed is in the bedroom.** Then say the sentences again as you write them on the board. Then point to the couch and ask: **Where is the couch?** Have students answer chorally: **The couch is in the living room**. Repeat for other objects and rooms on the card. Repeat for other objects in the vocabulary list drawn by you or using images you gathered beforehand.
- **Talk About It** Have students talk with a partner about different objects and rooms in their home.
- Expand by using the sentence frame with *are* and plural nouns. Expand further by using the preposition *on* to talk about the location of more things found in a home.

Practice/Apply

- **Talk About It** Have partners use the Newcomer Card and the sentence frames they learned to ask and answer questions about objects they see in the kitchen.
- Have partners sit back to back. One student describes the location of objects in a room in his or her home using the prepositions *next to, between, in,* and *on.* The other student draws what she/he hears. Then have them switch roles. Afterwards, have partners share and talk about their pictures.
- Guide students to complete the activity on page 87.

Make Connections

Ask students to name their favorite room in their home and tell why it's their favorite. Have students discuss with a partner and then present to their classmates.

Name: ____________________

Draw a bathroom in a home and label it using words from the box. Talk to a partner about it.

shower	toilet	sink	towel	bathtub

My Home

Language Objective:
Name things people do around the house

Content Objective:
Identify things people do around the house

Sentence Frames:
What is the ____ doing?
She/He ____ in the ____ .

VOCABULARY
recycle, mop, dust, cook, sweep, making the bed, empty the trash can
Cognates: reciclar

>> Go Digital

Language Transfers Handbook See pages 16-19 for grammatical structures that do not transfer. Korean, Spanish, or Vietnamese speakers may omit subject pronouns.

Grades 2-3 Foundational Skills Kit Use Phonics Card 37 to teach variant vowel /ů/ (*cooking*); Structural Analysis Card 9 to teach inflectional endings that drop the final *e* (*recycling*); Routine Card 5 to teach high-frequency words *what, is, the, she, the.*

eBook and Games Provide audio support, interaction, and practice with the vocabulary.

LESSON 3: Helping Around the House

Set Purpose

- Tell students that today they will discuss what people do around the house. Show page 14 of the Newcomer Cards.

Teach/Model Vocabulary

- To review, elicit vocabulary from Lessons 1 and 2.
- Lead students through the song/chant on page T4.
- Display the Newcomer Card and ask: *What are the people doing?* Partners can share their ideas about activities people do around the house. Then point to, pantomime, and name each household activity. Have students repeat. Help with pronunciation.
- Say these sentence frames as you point to the kitchen: **What is the father doing? He cooks in the kitchen.** Then say the sentences again as you write them on the board. Have students repeat after you. Then point to the bathroom and ask: **What is the mother doing?** Have students chorally answer: **She empties the trash can in the bathroom**. Repeat for other activities on the card and in vocabulary list.
- **Talk About It** Have partners talk about different things they like to do around the house.
- Expand by using the sentence frames with other activities students know.

Practice/Apply

- **Talk About It** Have partners use the Newcomer Card and the sentence frames they learned to describe different things people do to keep a bedroom clean.
- Have small groups play charades. One student acts out helping around the house and other students try to guess the action and the room where that action takes place. Continue until every student has had a turn to act.
- Guide students to complete the activity on page 89.

Make Cultural Connections

Have partners describe different household activities they participated in while they lived in their home country. Students can tell about these activities, as well as the rooms where they ate their meals, played games, and spent time with friends.

Name: ______________________________

Complete each sentence with a word that tells what the person in the picture is doing.

1. 

She is ________________
in the living room.

2. 

They are ________________
in the kitchen.

3. 

He is ________________
in the kitchen.

4. 

He is ________________
in the bedroom.

UNIT 3: Community OVERVIEW

My Community

Newcomer Card, p. 15

LESSONS	MATERIALS	LANGUAGE OBJECTIVES	LANGUAGE STRUCTURES/ GRAMMAR	VOCABULARY
Lesson 1: Community Places, p. 92–93	Newcomer Card p. 15 Phonics Card 28 Song/Chant p. T4	Describe the location of places in the community	Where is the ______? It is next to/across from the ______. **Prepositions of place** **Wh- questions:** Where	Community places **High-Frequency Words:** *is, it, from, to*
Lesson 2: Community Workers, p. 94–95	Newcomer Card p. 15 Phonics Card 27 Song/Chant p. T4	Name the different workers in a community and the places where they work	Who works in/on a ______? Where does a/an ______ work? A/an ______ works in/on a ______. **Verb:** to work **Articles:** a, an	Community workers **High-Frequency Words:** *who, where, in, on*
Lesson 3: Helping in My Community, p. 96–97	Newcomer Card p. 15 Phonics Card 18 Song/Chant p. T4	Describe ways people can help in their community	What is she/he doing? She's/He's ______. I can help by ______. **Modal verb:** can **Contractions:** she's, he's	Ways to help **High-Frequency Words:** *I, you, he, she, they*

Technology

Newcomer Card, p. 16

LESSONS	MATERIALS	LANGUAGE OBJECTIVES	LANGUAGE STRUCTURES/ GRAMMAR	VOCABULARY
Lesson 1: Equipment, p. 98–99	Newcomer Card p. 16 Phonics Card 19 Song/Chant p. T5	Name equipment we use to communicate and get information	What are those? Those are ______. What is that? That is a ______. **Wh- questions:** What **Pronouns:** that, those	Technology equipment **High-Frequency Words:** *what, is, are, that, those*
Lesson 2: Using Technology, p. 100–101	Newcomer Card p. 16 Phonics Card 19 Song/Chant p. T5	Describe the different things we can do with technology	What can you do with a ______? I can ______ with a ______. **Modal verb:** can **Wh- questions:** What	Technology and its uses **High-Frequency Words:** *what, can, you, and, with*
Lesson 3: How Technology Helps Us, p. 102–103	Newcomer Card p. 16 Phonics Card 27 Song/Chant p. T5	Describe how technology helps us	I need ______. I can ______. **Verb:** to need **Modal verb:** can **Pronouns:** I, her, my, him	Needs and technology **High-Frequency Words:** *I, can, him, her, my*

Transportation

Newcomer Card, p. 17

LESSONS	MATERIALS	LANGUAGE OBJECTIVES	LANGUAGE STRUCTURES/ GRAMMAR	VOCABULARY
Lesson 1: Signs, p. 104–105	Newcomer Card p. 17 Phonics Card 33 Song/Chant p. T5	Name different signs we see in the community	What's this/are those signs? This is a/those are ______. **Wh- questions:** What **Pronouns:** this, that, those	Signs **High-Frequency Words:** *what, this, that, those*
Lesson 2: Getting Around Town, p. 106–107	Newcomer Card p. 17 Phonics Card 44 Song/Chant p. T5	Describe the different ways to get around	How do/does you/they/she/he get to the ______? I/They/She/He ______. **Pronouns:** I, you, he, she, they **Conjunction:** or	Modes of transportation **High-Frequency Words:** *how, do, you, get, to, or*
Lesson 3: Directions, p. 108–109	Newcomer Card p. 17 Phonics Card 34 Song/Chant p. T5	Use sequence and direction words to provide directions	How do I get to the ______ from the ______? First /Then/ Next ______. Finally look for the ______. **Helping verb:** to do **Sequence words**	Direction words **High-Frequency Words:** *do, get, from, make, go*

Food and Meals

Newcomer Card, p. 18

LESSONS	MATERIALS	LANGUAGE OBJECTIVES	LANGUAGE STRUCTURES/ GRAMMAR	VOCABULARY
Lesson 1: At a Restaurant, p. 110–111	Newcomer Card p. 18 Phonics Card 24 Song/Chant p. T5	Use language to ask for and order things in a restaurant	May I take your order? Can I have a/the ____, please? **Modal verb**: can, may **Articles:** a, the	Restaurant dialogue **High-Frequency Words:** *may, see, have, please, thank*
Lesson 2: Healthy Eating, p. 112–113	Newcomer Card p. 18 Phonics Card 46 Song/Chant p. T5	Name healthy foods	What are you ____? I'm ____ ____. Do you like ____? Yes, I like ____. No, I don't like ____. **Questions with** *do* **Contractions:** I'm, don't	Healthy food **High-Frequency Words:** *do, don't, you, I, like*
Lesson 3: Lunchtime at School, p. 114–115	Newcomer Card p. 18 Phonics Card 17 Song/Chant p. T5	Name things we eat during lunch at school	What is he/she having for lunch? He's/She's having a ____. **Present continuous verbs** **Pronouns:** I, you, he, she, they **Contractions:** he's, she's, they're, I'm	Lunch food **High-Frequency Words:** *what, is, are, for, some*

Shopping

Newcomer Card, p. 19

LESSONS	MATERIALS	LANGUAGE OBJECTIVES	LANGUAGE STRUCTURES/ GRAMMAR	VOCABULARY
Lesson 1: Grocery Store, p. 116–117	Newcomer Card p. 19 Phonics Card 17 Song/Chant p. T6	Name the different items in a grocery store	What do you need to buy? I need ____. **Verbs:** to need **Contractions:** it's, they're **Wh- questions:** where	Food and departments at the grocery store **High-Frequency Words:** *what, do, the, buy, where*
Lesson 2: Using Money, p. 118–119	Newcomer Card p. 19 Phonics Card 40 Song/Chant p. T6	Ask and answer questions about buying items in a grocery store	What is this? This is a ____. How much are the ____? They cost ____ each. **Pronouns:** this, these, those ***How* questions**	Money **High-Frequency Words:** *more, much, another, yes, no*
Lesson 3: Grocery Shopping, p. 120–121	Newcomer Card p. 19 Phonics Card 11 Song/Chant p. T6	Ask and answer questions about what we do in the grocery store	Does she/he ____? Yes/No, ____. Who in your family ____? My/I ____ ____. **Questions with** *do* **Wh- questions:** Who	Activities in a grocery store **High-Frequency Words:** *do, does, don't, he, she*

Progress Monitoring

Use the **Oral Language Proficiency Benchmark Assessment** on pages T40–T41 to monitor students' oral language proficiency growth.

Use the **Student Profile** on pages T43–T44 to record observations throughout the units.

My Community

Language Objective:
Describe the location of places in the community

Content Objective:
Identify names and locations of places in the community

Sentence Frames:
Where's the ____?
It's next to/across from the ____.
Is the ____ ____ the ____?
No/Yes, it's ____ to the ____.

VOCABULARY
school, fire station, supermarket, park, hospital, post office, bank, gas station, community center, police station
Cognates: supermercado, banco, estación, centro, comunidad, parque

>> Go Digital

Language Transfers Handbook
See pages 16–19 for grammatical structures that do not transfer. Korean or Vietnamese speakers may avoid pronouns and repeat nouns.

Grade 2–3 Foundational Skills Kit
Use Phonics Card 28 to teach *r*-controlled vowel /är/ *(park)*; Routine Card 5 to teach high-frequency words *is, it, to, from.*

eBook Use digital material for vocabulary practice.

LESSON 1: Community Places

Set Purpose

- Tell students that today they will discuss places in the community. Show page 15 of the Newcomer Cards.

Teach/Model Vocabulary

- Lead students through the song/chant on page T4.
- Display the Newcomer Card and ask: *What places do you see in the community?* Point to and name each place. Have students repeat. Help with pronunciation.
- Say these sentence frames as you point to each community place: **Where's the <u>fire station</u>? It's next to the <u>school</u>. It's across from the <u>park</u>.** Then say the sentences again as you write them on the board. Have students repeat after you. Then point to the school and ask: **Where is the <u>school</u>?** Students answer chorally: **It's across from the <u>park</u>. It's next to the <u>post office</u>.** Repeat for other places on the card and places listed in the vocabulary box that are in your community.
- **Talk About It** Students can compare places on the card to places in their own community. Then partners can ask and answer questions about the location of their school to other places in the community.
- Extend by introducing the sentence frames: **Is the <u>post office</u> <u>across from</u> the <u>school</u>? No, it's <u>next to</u> the <u>school</u>.** Expand by having students talk about places that are *between* other place.

Practice/Apply COLLABORATIVE

- **Talk About It** Have partners use the Newcomer Card and the sentence frames they've learned to ask and answer questions about places in the community.
- Guide students to complete the activity on page 93.
- Have pairs create three sentences to describe a place on the Newcomer Card using previously-learned vocabulary, and let others guess the place. Model for students: *It's next to the post office. It has a red door. It's a rectangle.*

Make Connections

Have students draw a map of their community. Have them ask a partner: **Where's the ____?** Their partner will answer with the sentence frame: **It's next to/across from ____.**

Name: ______________________________

Draw a picture of places in your community. Then write a sentence about the location of one of the places.

____

My Community

Language Objective:
Name the different workers in a community and the places where they work

Content Objective:
Determine where different people work in a community

Sentence Frames:
Who works in/on a ____?
Where does a/an ____ work?
A/An ____ works in/on a ____.

VOCABULARY
teacher, fire fighter, nurse, doctor, mail carrier, bus driver, artist, writer, police officer, works
Cognates: doctor, artista, policía

>> Go Digital

Language Transfers Handbook
See pages 16–19 for grammatical structures that do not transfer. Cantonese or Hmong speakers may omit prepositions from sentences.

Grades 2–3 Foundational Skills Kit
Use Phonics Card 27 to teach *r*-controlled vowel /ûr/ (*works, nurse, writer*); Routine Card 5 to teach high-frequency words *who, where, in, on.*

eBook Use digital material for vocabulary practice.

LESSON 2: Community Workers

Set Purpose

- Tell students that today they will discuss community workers. Show page 15 of the Newcomer Cards.

Teach/Model Vocabulary

- To review, elicit names of places in the community.
- Lead students through the song/chant on page T4.
- Display the Newcomer Card and ask: *Who do you see?* Point to and name each community worker. Have students repeat. Help with pronunciation.
- Say these sentence frames as you point to each community worker: **Who works in a fire station? A fire fighter works in a fire station.** Then say the sentences again as you write them on the board, completing the sentence frames with the names of places and workers. Have students repeat after you. Then, point to yourself and ask: **Who works in a school?** Have students respond chorally: **A teacher works in a school**. Repeat for the other workers on the card and vocabulary list.
- **Talk About It** Have partners talk about workers on the card and in their own community.
- Extend by introducing the sentence frames: **Where does a/an ____ work?** Have partners explain to each other when to use *a* and when to use *an*.

Practice/Apply

INTERPRETIVE

- **Talk About It** Have partners use the sentence frames they learned to ask and answer questions about different community workers they know.
- Guide students to complete the activity on page 95.
- Have partners use the Speech Balloons on T26 to create a dialogue between two community workers. Have them present to the class and other students can guess the community workers in the conversation.

Make Connections

Provide a variety of magazines and newspapers. Have partners cut and paste pictures to create a collage of community workers. Have partners present to the class by pointing to and talking about the pictures of community workers they found. Have the class ask follow-up questions.

Name: ______________________________

A. Match each sentence to the correct picture.

1. A doctor works in a hospital.

a. 

2. A teacher works in a school.

b. 

3. A fire fighter works in a fire station.

c.  

4. A police officer works in a police station.

d. 

5. A bus driver works on a bus.

e. 

B. Write a sentence telling where a mail carrier works.

____

My Community

Language Objective:
Describe ways people can help in their community

Content Objective:
Identify and describe ways to help in the community

Sentence Frames:
What is/are she/he/they doing?
She's/He's/They are ____.
What can you do to help your community?
I can help by ____.

VOCABULARY
picking up garbage, helping neighbor, planting flowers, recycling plastic/bottles, paper, community
Cognates: reciclar, plástico, papel, botellas, communidad

>> Go Digital

Language Transfers Handbook
See pages 16–19 for grammatical structures that do not transfer. Cantonese, Hmong, Korean, Spanish, Tagalog, or Vietnamese speakers may struggle with gender-specific pronouns.

Grades 2–3 Foundational Skills Kit
Use Phonics Card 18 to teach consonant digraph *ng* (*picking*); Structural Analysis Card 7 to teach inflectional ending *-ing*; Routine Card 5 to teach high-frequency words *you, I, he, she, they*.

eBook and Games Provide audio support, interaction, and practice with the vocabulary.

LESSON 3: Helping in My Community

Set Purpose

- Tell students that today they will discuss ways to help in the community. Show page 15 of the Newcomer Cards.

Teach/Model Vocabulary

- Elicit vocabulary from Lessons 1 and 2.
- Lead students through the song/chant on page T4.
- Display the Newcomer Card and say: *Look at the people in the community. What are they doing?* Then point to and name ways people are helping in the community. Have students repeat. Help with pronunciation.
- Say these sentence frames as you point to people in the community: **What is she doing? She's recycling bottles.** Then say the sentences again as you write them on the board. Have students repeat after you. Then point to the boy throwing away garbage and ask: **What is he doing?** Have students answer chorally: **He's picking up garbage**. Repeat for the other ways to help shown on the card and in vocabulary list.
- **Talk About It** Have partners talk about the different ways people help in their community.
- Extend by introducing the sentence frames: **What are they doing? They are ____. What can you do to help in your community? I can help by ____.**

Practice/Apply PRODUCTIVE

- **Talk About It** Have partners use the Newcomer Card and the sentence frames they learned to ask and answer questions about the ways they can help in their own community.
- Guide students to complete the activity on page 97.
- Have students survey their classmates to learn how they help in their community. Help students make their survey.

Make Cultural Connections

Have students tell about the ways they helped in their home-country's community. After each telling, have another student ask a follow-up question. Model correct form.

Name: ____________________________

Use the words in the box to complete each sentence. Write the words on the line.

recycling paper	planting flowers	recycling bottles
picking up garbage	helping her neighbor	

1.  She is ____________________________.

2.  He is ____________________________.

3.  She is ____________________________.

4.  He is ____________________________.

5.  They are ____________________________.

Technology

Language Objective:
Name equipment we use to communicate and get information

Content Objective:
Identify technology equipment

Sentence Frames:
What is that?
That is a ____.
What are those?
Those are ____.

VOCABULARY
smartphone, tablet, camera, wifi, computer, printer
Cognates: computadora, cámara

>> Go Digital

Language Transfers Handbook
See pages 16-19 for grammatical structures that do not transfer. Cantonese, Hmong, or Vietnamese speakers may omit the linking verb.

Grades 2-3 Foundational Skills Kit
Use Phonics Card 19 to teach consonant digraph *ph* (*phone*); Routine Card 5 to teach high-frequency words *what, is, are, that, those.*

eBook Use digital material for vocabulary practice.

LESSON 1: Equipment

Set Purpose

- Tell students that today they will discuss equipment we use to communicate and get information. Show page 16 of the Newcomer Cards.

Teach/Model Vocabulary

- Lead students through the song/chant on page T5.
- Display the Newcomer Card and ask: *What do you see?* Point to and name each piece of equipment. Have students repeat. Help with pronunciation. Have students talk about other equipment they know of.
- Say these sentence frames as you point to the equipment: **What is that? That is a <u>smartphone</u>.** Then say the sentences again as you write them on the board, completing the second sentence with the name of the equipment. Have students repeat. Then, point to the printer and ask: **What is that?** Have students answer chorally: **That is a <u>printer</u>.** Repeat for the other equipment on the Newcomer Card, in the classroom, and in the vocabulary list.
- **Talk About It** Have partners talk about different technology equipment they have or use and why they use them. Model complete sentences, as needed.
- Extend by introducing the sentence frames for multilple items: **What are those? Those are ____.**

Practice/Apply INTERPRETIVE

- **Talk About It** Have partners use the Newcomer Card and the sentence frames they've learned to ask and answer questions about technology equipment in their home, school, and library.
- Guide students to complete the activity on page 99.
- In pairs, one student describes the things in his/her graphic organizer (color, what it does, how it works) while the other student guesses the items. Then they switch roles. Model the activity before students begin.

Make Connections

Have students name their favorite piece of technology to use and explain why it's their favorite. Have students share their response with a partner and then share with you.

Name: ______________________________

Equipment

Use Newcomer Card, page 16

Write the names of technology you use.

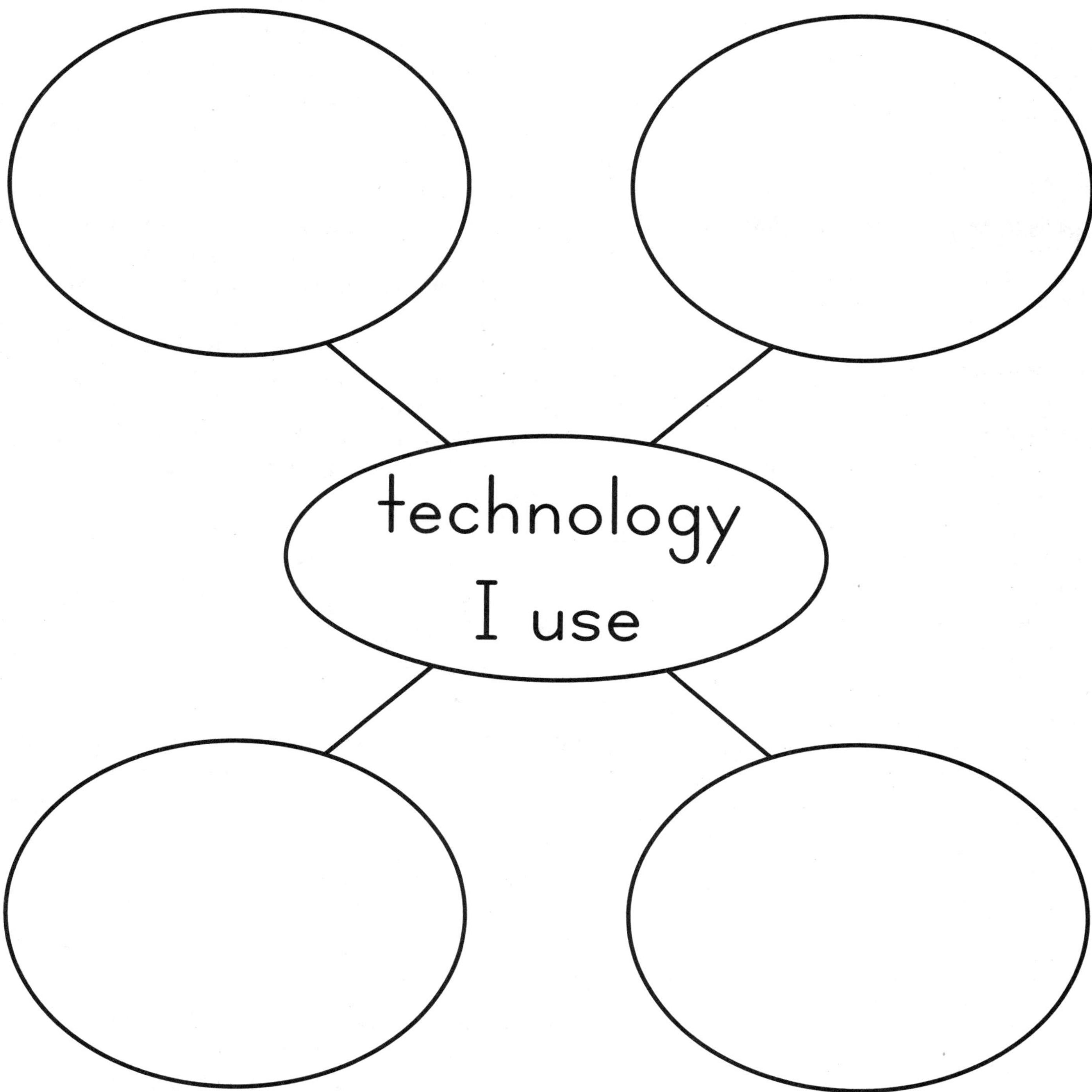

Technology

Language Objective:
Describe the different things we can do with technology

Content Objective:
Identify the different things we can do with technology

Sentence Frames:
What can you do with a ____?
I can ____ with a ____.
I can ____ and ____ with a ____.

VOCABULARY
text, call, chat, video chat, email, watch movies, watch videos, take pictures, print
Cognates: video

>> Go Digital

Language Transfers Handbook
See pages 16-19 for grammatical structures that do not transfer. Cantonese, Hmong, Korean, Vietnamese, Arabic, or Spanish speakers may forget to use the plural marker *-s*.

Grades 2-3 Foundational Skills Kit
Use Phonics Card 19 to teach consonant digraphs *ch* and *tch* *(chat, watch)*; Fluency Card 13 to teach phrasing with conjunctions and prepositions; Routine Card 5 to teach high-frequency words *what, can, you, and, with.*

eBook Use digital material for vocabulary practice.

LESSON 2: Using Technology

Set Purpose

- Tell students that today they will discuss what we do with technology. Show page 16 of the Newcomer Cards.

Teach/Model Vocabulary

- To review, elicit names of technology equipment.
- Lead students through the song/chant on page T5.
- Display the Newcomer Card and ask: *What are they doing?* Point to, name, and pantomime each action. Have students repeat your words and actions. Help with pronunciation. Have students talk about the videos and movies they like to watch.
- Say these sentence frames as you point to equipment: **What can you do with a smartphone? I can text with a smartphone.** Then say the sentences again as you write them on the board, completing the sentence frames with the technology and actions. Have students repeat after you. Then, point to the printer and ask: **What can you do with a printer?** Students answer chorally: **I can print with a printer.** Repeat for other things we do with technology on the card and listed in the vocabulary list.
- **Talk About It** Have partners talk about the different technology they use, the things they do, and why.
- Extend with the sentence frame: **I can text and video chat with a smartphone.**

Practice/Apply COLLABORATIVE

- **Talk About It** Have partners use the Newcomer Card and the sentence frames they learned to ask and answer questions about things we can do with technology.
- Guide students to complete the activity on page 101.
- Have partners survey their classmates to find what they do with technology. Encourage them to use vocabulary from previous lessons. Help students make the survey.

Make Connections

Have students use vocabulary from Lessons 1 and 2 to talk about how they use different technology. Then have students play charades. A student acts out using technology and the others guess the technology being used and the action.

Name: ______________________________

A. Match each sentence with a picture.

1. I can email on a computer.

2. I can text with a smartphone.

3. I can video chat on a tablet.

4. I can print with a printer.

a. 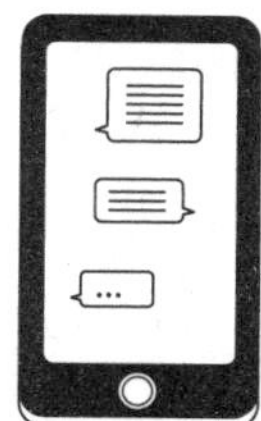

b. 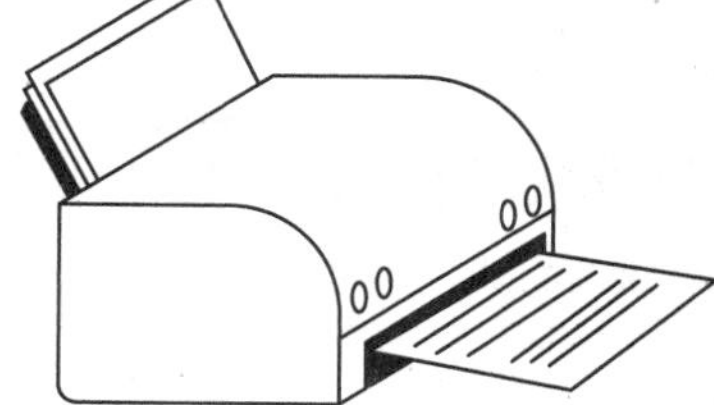

c. 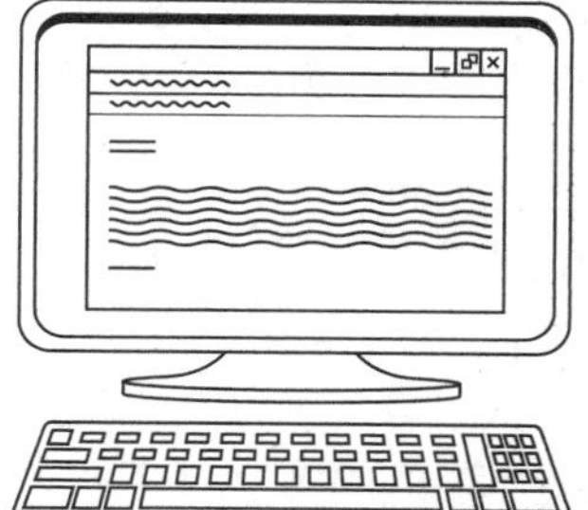

d. 

B. Write a sentence about what you like to do with a smartphone or tablet.

____

Technology

Language Objective:
Describe how technology helps us

Content Objective:
Understand how technology helps in different situations

Sentence Frames:
I need/want ________.
I can ________.

VOCABULARY
text, call, 9-1-1, information, Internet, police officer, mother, father
Cognates: información, policía

>> Go Digital

Language Transfers Handbook
See pages 16–19 for grammatical structures that do not transfer. Korean, Spanish, or Vietnamese speakers may omit subject pronouns.

Grades 2–3 Foundational Skills Kit
Use Phonics Card 27 to teach *r*-controlled vowel /ûr/ *(mother)*; Routine Card 2 to teach multisyllabic words *(information, Internet)*; Routine Card 5 to teach high-frequency words *I, can, him, her, my*.

eBook and Games Provide audio support, interaction, and practice with the vocabulary.

LESSON 3: How Technology Helps Us

Set Purpose

- Tell students that today they will discuss how technology helps us. Show page 16 of the Newcomer Cards.

Teach/Model Vocabulary

- Elicit the equipment and uses covered in Lessons 1 and 2.
- Lead students through the song/chant on page T5.
- Display the Newcomer Card and ask: *What are the people doing? Why do you think they're using technology?* Then point to each person and describe how technology helps them. Have students repeat. Help with pronunciation.
- Say these sentence frames as you point to a person: **I need <u>my father</u>. I can <u>text him</u>.** Then say the sentences again as you write them on the board, completing the sentence frames. Have students repeat after you. Then point to the boy looking at a tablet and say: **I want <u>to watch a video</u>. What can I do?** Have students chorally respond: **I can <u>watch a video on my tablet</u>.** Repeat, covering the other ways technology helps us listed in the vocabulary box.
- **Talk About It** Have partners talk about how technology has helped them in the past. Expand by having students tell partners a sequential story.

Practice/Apply

- **Talk About It** Have partners talk about their needs and wants. Have them ask and answer questions and explain how technology helps or could help their partner.
- Guide students to complete the activity on page 103.
- Have students discuss what they think are the most important uses of technology. In pairs, one student gives his or her opinion about which technology is the most helpful and useful. Have the other students agree or disagree and explain why. Model the activity before students begin.

Make Cultural Connections

Have students tell about the ways technology was used in their community in their home country. Have other students ask detailed follow-up questions. Model correct form, as needed.

Name: ______________________________

Write things that you need or want and how technology helps. Then discuss with a partner.

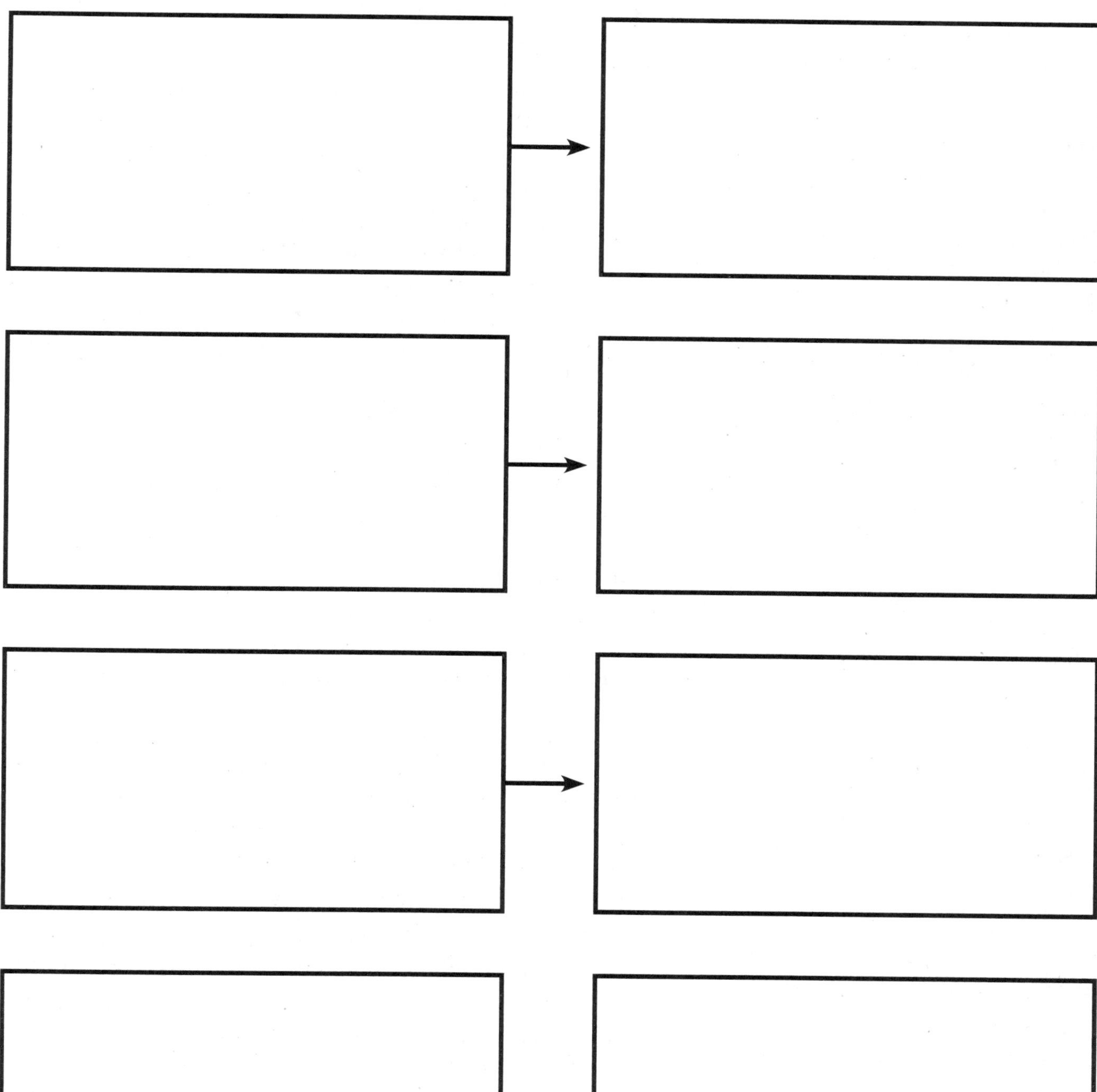

Transportation

Language Objective:
Name different signs we see in the community

Content Objective:
Distinguish between different signs in a community

Sentence Frames:
What's this/What are those sign(s)?
This is a/Those are ____ sign(s).
Is that a ____ sign?
Yes/No, that's a ____ sign.

VOCABULARY
bus stop sign, hospital sign, crosswalk sign, walk sign, don't walk sign, stop sign, street sign, exit sign
Cognates: signo de hospital **False Cognates:** éxito

>> Go Digital

Language Transfers Handbook See pages 16–19 for grammatical structures that do not transfer. Cantonese, Hmong, Korean, Arabic, or Tagalog speakers may struggle with the irregular subject-verb agreement of *to be*.

Grades 2–3 Foundational Skills Kit Use Phonics Card 33 to teach silent letters *gn* in *sign*; Routine Card 5 to teach high-frequency words *what, this, that, those*.

eBook For further practice with the lesson.

LESSON 1: Signs

Set Purpose

- Tell students that today they will discuss signs we see in the community. Show page 17 of the Newcomer Cards.

Teach/Model Vocabulary

- Lead students through the song/chant on page T5.
- Display the Newcomer Card and ask: *What signs do you see?* Point to and name the signs on the card. Have students repeat. Help with pronunciation. Have students talk about signs they know of in the community.
- Say these sentence frames as you point to each sign on the card: **What is this sign? This is a stop sign.** Then say the sentences again as you write them on the board, completing the second sentence. Have students repeat after you. Then point to the walk sign and ask: **What is this sign?** Have students answer chorally: **This is a walk sign.** Repeat for other signs on card, in the vocabulary list, and signs offered up by students.
- **Talk About It** Have partners talk about the colors and sizes of different signs on the card and in the community. Have partners talk about why they think different signs are different colors and shapes.
- Extend by introducing the sentence frames: **What are those signs? Those are street signs. Is that a hospital sign? Yes/No, that is a hospital/bus stop sign.**

Practice/Apply INTERPRETIVE

- **Talk About It** Have partners use the card and the sentence frames they learned to ask and answer questions about signs in their own community.
- Guide students to complete the activity on page 105.
- Have pairs write three sentences, using previously-learned vocabulary, describing a sign that's on the card, in the school, or in the community. Others guess which sign is being described. Model for the students. For example: *This sign is a triangle. It's red and white. It's near the bank. (Yield sign)*

Make Connections

Have students list three signs in their school, then discuss with a partner why these signs are important. Then have students create signs to put up in the classroom.

Name: ______________________________

Use Newcomer Card, page 17

Complete each sentence. Use words from the box.

bus stop sign	street sign	walk sign	stop sign

1. 

This is a ____________________.

2. 
This is a ____________________.

3. 

This is a ____________________.

4. 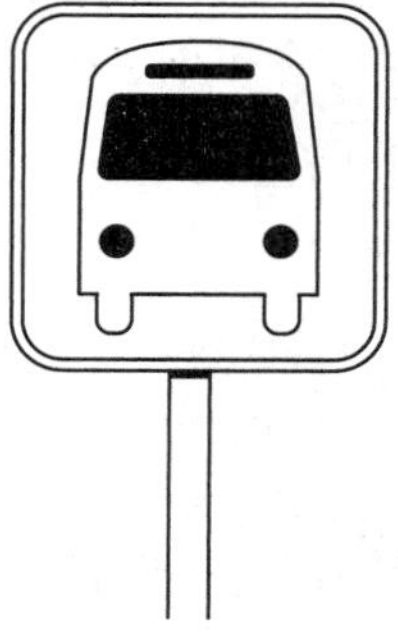
This is a ____________________.

Transportation

Language Objective:
Describe the different ways to get around

Content Objective:
Identify the different ways people get around

Sentence Frames:
How does she/he get to the ____?
She/He ____ a ____.
He/She/They/We ____.
How do you/they get to the ____?
I/They ____ a ____.
I ____ or I ____.

VOCABULARY
car, truck, airplane, bus, train, taxi, bike, walk, drive, take, ride
Cognates: *carro, tren, bus, taxi* **False Cognate:** *caro*

>> Go Digital

Language Transfers Handbook
See pages 16–19 for grammatical forms that do not transfer. Cantonese or Hmong speakers may omit prepositions from sentences.

Grades 2–3 Foundational Skills Kit
Use Phonics Card 44 to teach CVCe syllables *(bike)*; Fluency Card 13A to teach how to phrase sentences with conjunctions; Routine Card 5 to teach high-frequency words *how, do, you, get, to, or.*

eBook Use digital material for vocabulary practice.

LESSON 2: Getting Around Town

Set Purpose

- Tell students that today they will discuss ways to get around town. Show page 17 of the Newcomer Cards.

Teach/Model Vocabulary

- Elicit names of street signs covered in Lesson 1.
- Lead students through the song/chant on page T5.
- Display the Newcomer Card and ask: *What are the people doing? How are they getting around?* Point to and name each mode of transportation. Have students repeat. Help with pronunciation.
- Say these sentence frames as you point to a person: **How does she get to the post office?** Point to the taxi and say: **She takes a taxi.** Then say the sentences again as you write them on the board. Have students repeat after you. Then point to the grocery store and ask: **How do they get to the grocery store?** Point to the people walking near the grocery and have students answer chorally: **They walk**. Repeat for other places and ways to get around on the card and listed in the vocabulary.
- **Talk About It** Partners can talk about their favorite ways to get around and explain why it's their favorite way.
- Extend with the sentence frames: **How do you get to the park? I walk.** Then teach the conjunction *or* with the sentence frame: **I walk or bike.**

Practice/Apply

COLLABORATIVE

- **Talk About It** Have partners use the card and sentence frames to discuss the ways people get around town. Elicit action and descriptive words.
- Guide students to complete the activity on page 107.
- Have partners work together to create a survey about different modes of transportation students have taken. Have the partners survey the class and present their results.

Make Connections

Have partners ask each other how they get to the park and write the answers on a sticky note. Students place the sticky notes in a bar graph on the board to display the results. Then they ask and answer questions about the graph.

Use Newcomer Card, page 17

Name: ______________________________

Circle the caption that tells about the picture. Then write a sentence in your notebook about how you get to school.

1.

Claudia walks to school.

Claudia bikes to school.

2.

Jonathan takes a taxi to the mall.

Jonathan takes a train to the mall.

3.

Alex takes a bus to the bank.

Alex drives a car to the bank.

4.

Martin takes an airplane to the store.

Martin drives a truck to the store.

Transportation

Language Objective:
Use sequence and direction words to provide directions

Content Objective:
Understand and give directions

Sentence Frames:
How do I get to the ____ from ____?
First/Then/Next ________.
Finally look for the ____.

VOCABULARY
school, Park Street, Main Street, make a right/left, go straight, look for the, one, two, three, four, five, blocks, corner, cross, crosswalk, thanks
Cognate: cruzar

>> Go Digital

Language Transfers Handbook
See pages 16–19 for grammatical structures that do not transfer. Hmong, Spanish, Arabic, Tagalog, Cantonese, or Korean speakers may omit articles (*the*).

Grades 2–3 Foundational Skills Kit
Use Phonics Card 34 to teach silent letters *gh* in *straight* and *right*; Fluency Card 13B to teach phrasing with prepositions; Routine Card 5 to teach high-frequency words *do, get, from, make, go*.

eBook and Games Provide audio support, interaction, and practice with the vocabulary.

LESSON 3: Directions

Set Purpose

- Tell students that today they will discuss directions. Show page 17 of the Newcomer Cards.

Teach/Model Vocabulary

- To review, elicit names of signs and ways to get around.
- Lead students through the song/chant on page T5.
- Display the Newcomer Card and point to the woman outside of the bank. Say: *Imagine this woman needs help getting to the grocery store. How can we give her directions?* Provide directions, pantomiming the direction words. Have students repeat. Help with pronunciation.
- Say these sentence frames as you point to the grocery store and then yourself: **How do I get to the bank from the grocery store? First cross Park Street. Then make a left. Next cross Main Street. Finally, look for the bank.** Then say the sentences again as you write them on the board. Have students repeat after you. Then point to the post office and ask: **How do I get to the post office from the stop sign?** Have students chorally answer, filling in the sentence frames. Repeat for other places on the card.
- Extend by adding more phrases from the vocabulary list to the sentence frames: *make a right, make a left, go one/two block(s), cross at the crosswalk, thanks,* etc.

Practice/Apply PRODUCTIVE

- **Talk About It** Have partners use the sentence frames they learned to use sequence and direction words to provide directions to each other from place to place on the card.
- Guide students to complete the activity on the page 109.
- Have partners share their maps from the activity on page 109. Have them take turns asking for directions from one place to another while the other student uses sequence and direction words to provide directions.

Make Cultural Connections

Have partners talk about how people travel in their home countries. Have the partners share some of the interesting conversation points with the class.

Name: ______________________________

Directions

Use Newcomer Card, page 17

Think about a place near your home. How do you get there from your home? Draw a map. Then write the directions.

First ______________________________.

Then ______________________________.

Next ______________________________.

Finally look for the ______________________________.

Food and Meals

Language Objective:
Use language to ask for and order things in a restaurant

Content Objective:
Demonstrate understanding of language used in a restaurant

Sentence Frames:
May I take your order?
Can I have a/the _____, please?
The _____ is more/less expensive than the _____.

VOCABULARY
meal, menu, order, bill, burger, soup, may I, please, thank you, more/less expensive than
Cognates: menú, sopa, hamburguesa

>> Go Digital

Language Transfers Handbook
See pages 16–19 for grammatical structures that do not transfer. Hmong, Vietnamese, Korean, Arabic, Tagalog, or Cantonese speakers may omit articles.

Grades 2-3 Foundational Skills Kit
Use Phonics Card 24 to teach the long *e* sound in *meal* and *please*; Routine Card 5 to teach high-frequency words *may, see, have, please, thank*.

eBook Use digital material for vocabulary practice.

LESSON 1: At a Restaurant

Set Purpose

- Tell students that today they will discuss language used a restaurant. Show page 18 of the Newcomer Cards.

Teach/Model Vocabulary

- Lead students through the song/chant on page T5.
- Display the Newcomer Card and ask: *What do you see?*
- Say and write the sentence frames: **May I take your order? Can I have a _____, please?** Explain that this exchange takes place at a restaurant. Fill in the sentence with what you would order at a restaurant. Then have students take turns saying their own order.
- Read aloud the speech balloons: **May I take your order? Can I have a <u>cheese sandwich</u>, please?** Point to the choice of sandwiches in the menu. Repeat the instruction for other items on the menu. Tell students that when we get the food we say "Thank you."
- **Talk About It** Have partners discuss their favorite food to order in a restaurant and explain why it's their favorite.
- Extend with the sentence frame: **May I have the <u>bill</u>, please?** to request the menu or bill, and use the following to compare prices: **The <u>burger</u> is <u>more expensive than</u> the <u>vegetables</u>.**

Practice/Apply COLLABORATIVE

- **Talk About It** Have partners use the sentence frames they learned to role-play ordering in a restaurant, requesting the bill, and saying "Thank you."
- Guide students to complete the activity on page 111.
- Using pictures of restaurant items, have students play Flashcard Relay. Model the game first. For example, hold up several pictures, including a picture of a sandwich, and ask: *May I have the <u>sandwich</u>, please?* A student selects the correct picture and hands it to you, and you say: *Thank you*. Then have students play with partners.

Make Connections

Have partners create a menu for a restaurant by drawing or cutting out pictures of food and drink items and labeling them. Students practice ordering from different menus.

Name: ____________________

Use Newcomer Card, page 18

A. Write the correct item on the line.

menu soup bill sandwich burger restaurant

B. Write what you say when you order in a restaurant.

____.

Food and Meals

Language Objective:
Name healthy foods

Content Objective:
Identify healthy foods

Sentence Frames:
What are you ____?
I'm ____ ____.
Do you like ____/____ food?
Yes, it's my favorite.
Yes/No, I like ____/____ food.
No, I don't like ____.

VOCABULARY

noodles, cereal, eggs, cheese, soup, fish, vegetables, carrots, potatoes, rice, bread, milk, tea, water, orange juice, fruit, yogurt, burger, sandwich, favorite, meals, sides, drinks, spicy, sweet

>> Go Digital

Language Transfers Handbook
See pages 16–19 for grammatical structures that do not transfer. Spanish or Tagalog speakers may struggle with countable and uncountable nouns.

Grades 2–3 Foundational Skills Kit
Use Phonics Card 46 to teach consonant *+le (noodle)*; Structural Analysis Card 1 to teach plural nouns with *-s*; Routine Card 5 to teach high-frequency words *do, don't, you, I, like.*

eBook Use digital material for vocabulary practice.

LESSON 2: Healthy Eating

Set Purpose

- Tell students that today they will discuss healthy eating. Show page 18 of the Newcomer Cards.

Teach/Model Vocabulary

- To review, elicit names of items in a restaurant.
- Lead students through the song/chant on page T5.
- Display the Newcomer Card and ask: *What do you see on the menu?* Point to and name the food and drinks on the card. Have students repeat. Help with pronunciation.
- Say these sentence frames as you point to the burger on the menu: **What are you ordering? I'm ordering a burger**. Then say the sentences again as you write them on the board. Have students repeat after you. Then point to the milk and ask: **What are you ordering?** Have students respond chorally: **I'm ordering milk**. Repeat for other items on the card and vocabulary list.
- **Talk About It** Have partners pretend they are in a restaurant and use the Conversation Starters on page T30 to talk about what they are eating.
- Extend the conversation with the sentence frames: **Do you like soup? Yes, it's my favorite. Yes, I like soup. No, I don't like soup. I like tuna sandwiches.** Then incorporate the sentence frames: **Do you like sweet/spicy food? Yes/No, I like/don't like spicy food.**

Practice/Apply

- **Talk About It** Have partners use the Newcomer Card and the sentence frames they've learned to ask and answer questions about different foods in a restaurant.
- Guide students to complete the activity on page 113.
- Have students use their graphic organizers to ask their partner which foods they like and dislike.

Make Connections

Have partners describe and discuss their favorite healthy foods, such as fruits or vegetables. Remind students to use descriptive words, such as colors and shapes, and tell why they like these foods. Encourage students to talk about foods from their home countries.

Name: ______________________________

Use Newcomer Card, page 18

List healthy foods you like and don't like.

Like	Don't Like

Food and Meals

Language Objective:
Name things we eat during lunch at school

Content Objective:
Identify items we eat for lunch at school

Sentence Frames:
What are you having for lunch?
I'm having ____.
What is she/he having for lunch?
She's/He's having (a)____.
What are they having for lunch?
They're having/sharing ____.

VOCABULARY
lunch, sandwich, burger, soup, noodles, yogurt, fruit, apple, orange, orange juice, milk, water
Cognates: sándwich, sopa, fruta

>> Go Digital

Language Transfers Handbook
See pages 16–19 for grammatical structures that do not transfer. Cantonese, Hmong, Korean, Spanish, Tagalog, or Vietnamese speakers may struggle with gender-specific pronouns.

Grades 2-3 Foundational Skills Kit
Use Phonics Card 17 to teach soft *g* (*orange*); Structural Analysis Card 15 to teach contractions with *'s* and *'re*; Routine Card 5 to teach high-frequency words *what, is, are, for, some.*

eBook and Games Provide audio support, interaction, and practice with the vocabulary.

LESSON 3: Lunchtime at School

Set Purpose

- Tell students that today they will discuss lunchtime at school. Show page 18 of the Newcomer Cards.

Teach/Model Vocabulary

- Elicit vocabulary from Lessons 1 and 2.
- Lead students through the song/chant on page T5.
- Display the Newcomer Card, point to the menu, and ask: *What are some things you can order for lunch at school?* Then point to and name each item on the menu. Do the same for your school's lunch menu. Have students repeat. Help with pronunciation.
- Say these sentence frames as you point to the boy: **What is he having for lunch? He's having a <u>cheese sandwich</u>.** Then say the sentences again as you write them on the board, completing the second sentence with the item he ordered. Have students repeat after you. Then point to the woman in the background and ask: **What is she having for lunch?** Have students chorally answer: **She's having <u>orange juice</u> and a <u>burger</u>.** Repeat for other items on the card and vocabulary list.
- **Talk About It** Have partners talk about their favorite foods and drinks to have for lunch.
- Extend the conversation with the sentence frames using subject pronouns *you, I,* and *they,* and with *sharing.*

Practice/Apply COLLABORATIVE

- **Talk About It** Have partners use the Newcomer Card and the sentence frames they learned to discuss what different people in the restaurant may have for lunch.
- Guide students to complete the activity on the page 115.
- Have students role-play eating in a restaurant, using the sentence frames, the Speech Balloons on T26, and vocabulary they learned. Have partners take turns playing the waiter and the customer.

Make Cultural Connections

Have partners discuss restaurants they enjoyed going to in their home country and the food they ordered. Then partners share with the group. Other students ask follow-up questions.

Name: ______________________________

Lunchtime at School

Use Newcomer Card, page 18

Write the names of foods and drinks you are having for lunch today.

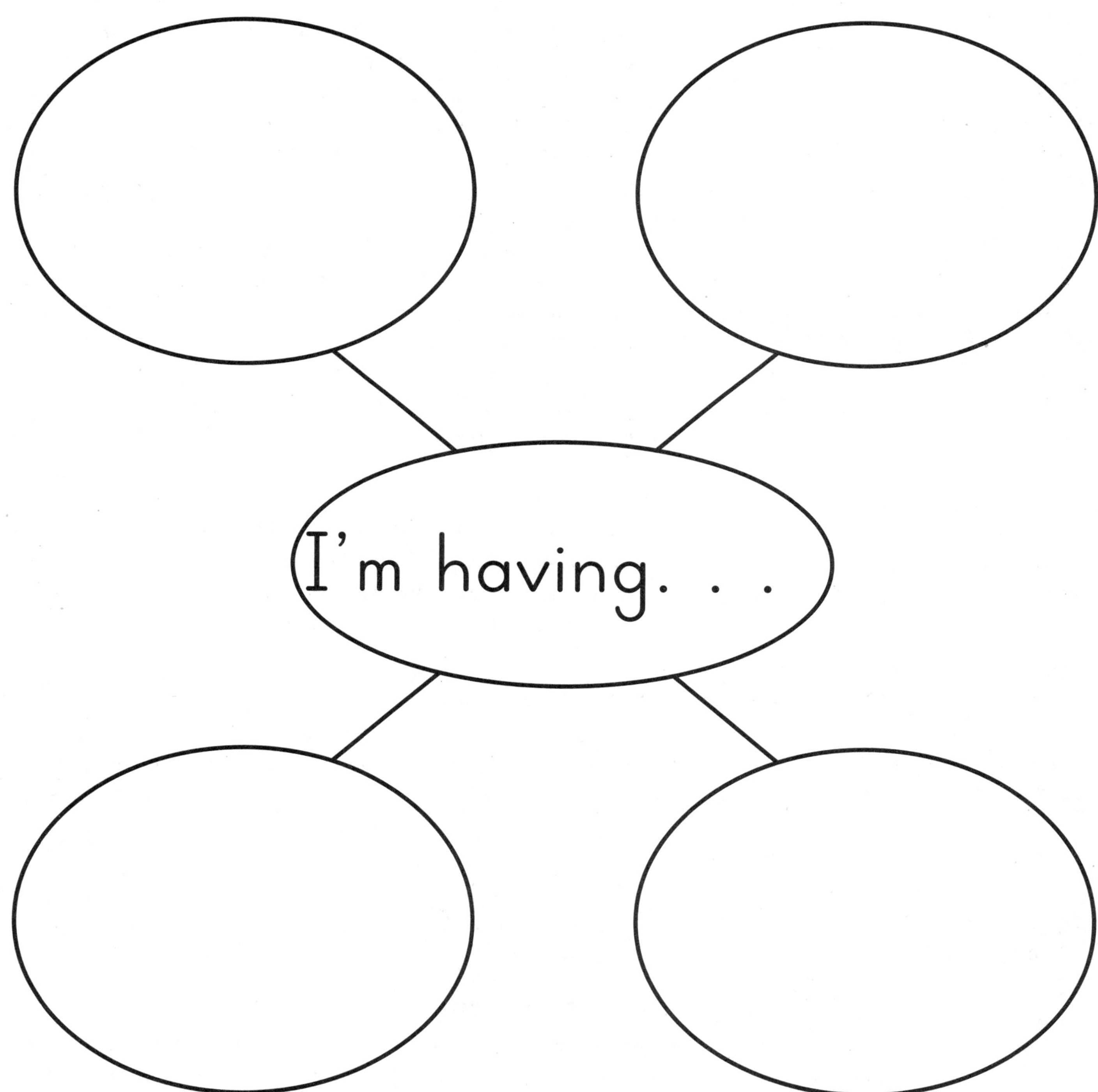

Shopping

Language Objective:
Name the different items in a grocery store

Content Objective:
Demonstrate understanding of items and departments in a grocery store

Sentence Frames:
What do you need to buy?
I need ____.
She/He needs ____.
Where is/are the ____?
It's/They're in the ____.

VOCABULARY
grocery store, cash register, bakery, meat department, cart, basket, produce department, buy, bread, apples, oranges, onions, cashier
Cognates: *registradora, departamento*
False Cognates: *produce*

>> Go Digital

Language Transfers Handbook
See pages 16–19 for grammatical structures that do not transfer. Cantonese, Korean, or Arabic speakers may use the wrong pronouns.

Grades 2–3 Foundational Skills Kit
Use Phonics Card 17 to teach the soft *c* sound in *grocery* and *produce*; Routine Card 5 to teach high-frequency words *what, do, the, buy, where.*

eBook Use digital material for vocabulary practice.

LESSON 1: Grocery Store

Set Purpose

- Tell students that today they will discuss items in a grocery store. Show page 19 of the Newcomer Cards.

Teach/Model Vocabulary

- Lead students through the song/chant on page T6.
- Display the Newcomer Card and ask: *What do you see?* Point to and name the departments, the foods shown, and words in the vocabulary list. Have students repeat. Help with pronunciation. Have students tell a partner the foods that are missing from the scene.
- Say these sentence frames as you point to the bakery: **Where is the <u>bread</u>? It's in the <u>bakery</u>.** Then say the sentences again as you write them on the board, completing the sentences with the name of the food and department. Have students repeat after you. Then point to the produce department and ask: **Where are the <u>apples</u>?** Have students answer chorally: **They're in the <u>produce department</u>.** Repeat for other departments, foods shown on the card, and food items volunteers provide.
- **Talk About It** Have partners talk about items and departments in their neighborhood grocery store.
- Extend by having students pretend to be grocery shopping and use the Conversation Starters on page T30 to have a conversation.

Practice/Apply

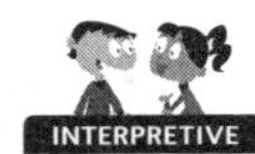

- **Talk About It** Have partners talk about their favorite food items and departments in a grocery store. Have students tell why they like the foods and the department.
- Guide students to complete the activity on the page 117.
- Have pairs write two sentences about an item in a grocery store using previously learned vocabulary. Others guess what is being described. Model for students. For example: *It's in the produce department. It's purple.*

Make Connections

Have partners cut pictures of food from magazines to create a collage of grocery store departments. Have them label the pictures, then share with classmates.

Name: ______________________________

Grocery Store

Use Newcomer Card, page 19

Write the names of items you can find in each department.

Bakery Department	Produce Department

Shopping

Language Objective:
Ask and answer questions about buying items in a grocery store

Content Objective:
Identify costs of items

Sentence Frames:
What is this?
This is a ____.
How much are the ____?
How much are these/those?
They cost ____ each.

VOCABULARY
coin, cent, penny, nickel, dime, quarter, dollar, apples, oranges, cost, money, enough, another, each, bag
Cognates: cuesta, dólar, centavo **False Cognates:** dime

>> Go Digital

Language Transfers Handbook
See pages 16–19 for grammatical structures that do not transfer. Spanish or Tagalog speakers may struggle with countable and uncountable nouns.

Grades 2–3 Foundational Skills Kit
Use Phonics Card 40 to teach variant vowel *ough* in *enough*; Structural Analysis Card 15 to teach contractions with *not* (*don't*); Routine Card 5 to teach high-frequency words *more, much, another, yes, no.*

eBook Use digital material for vocabulary practice.

LESSON 2: Using Money

Set Purpose

- Tell students that today they will discuss costs of items in a grocery store. Show page 19 of the Newcomer Cards.

Teach/Model Vocabulary

- Elicit grocery store items and departments from Lesson 1.
- Lead students through the song/chant on page T6.
- Display the Newcomer Card and ask: *What do you see at the top of the card?* Point to and name the types of money using the sentence frames: **What is this? This is a dollar.** Have students repeat. Help with pronunciation. Then explain and write on the board *a penny=1 cent,* etc.
- Show a local grocery store advertisement with foods and prices. Have students talk about the items, their prices, and the different denominations of money they would need to buy certain items.
- Point to the price tags on different items on the card. Use the sentence frames: **How much are the apples? They cost 25 cents each.** Etc.
- **Talk About It** Have students use the sentence frames to ask each other the prices of items on the card and in the grocery store advertisement.
- Expand the conversation by giving students a budget and having "shoppers" see if they have enough money with the following sentence frames: **How much are these/those? They cost $3.00 each. Do I have enough money? Yes, you do./No, you don't. You need $1.00.**

Practice/Apply

- **Talk About It** Have partners use the sentence frames they learned to ask and answer questions about the cost of items in a grocery store.
- Guide students to complete the activity on page 119.
- Have partners make a shopping list for a party with a budget of $5.00. Partners list the items and costs of things they want to buy, up to $5.00. Encourage students to use previously learned vocabulary, such as food items.

Make Connections

Have students use grocery store ads to take turns pointing to items, asking, and answering questions about their costs.

Name: ______________________

A. Circle the caption that tells about the picture.

1.

The apples cost 75 cents each.

The oranges cost one dollar each.

2.

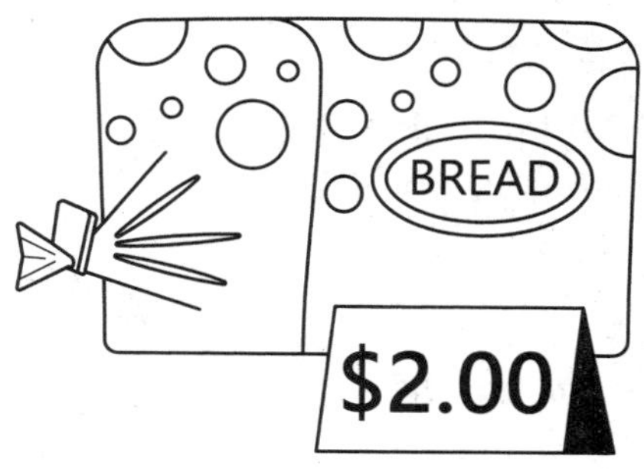

The bread costs two dollars.

The bread costs one dollar.

3.

The vegetables cost $3.00.

The fish costs $3.00.

4.

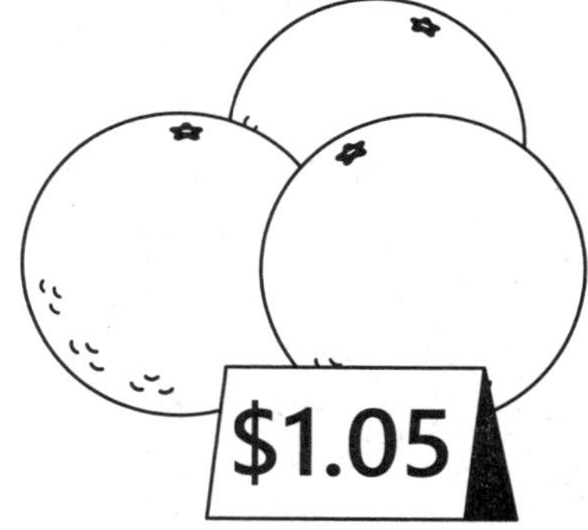

The oranges cost one dollar and five cents.

The oranges cost one dollar.

B. What do you like to buy at the grocery store?

____

Shopping

Language Objective:
Ask and answer questions about what we do in the grocery store

Content Objective:
Identify what people do in a grocery store

Sentence Frames:
Who in your family ____?
Do you/Does she/he ____?
Do you ____ or do you ____?
My ____/I ____.

VOCABULARY
make a shopping list, compare prices, look for something, ask for help, push a cart, carry a basket
Cognates: comparar, precio

>> Go Digital

Language Transfers Handbook
See pages 16–19 for grammatical structures that do not transfer. Korean, Spanish, or Arabic speakers may struggle with the phrasal verbs *look for* and *ask for*.

Grades 2–3 Foundational Skills Kit
Use Phonics Card 11 to teach end blends (*list*); Structural Analysis Card 15 to teach contractions with *not* (*doesn't, don't*); Routine Card 5 to teach high-frequency words *do, does, don't, he, she*.

eBook and Games Provide audio support, interaction, and practice with the vocabulary.

LESSON 3: Grocery Shopping

Set Purpose

- Tell students that today they will discuss what we do in the grocery store. Show page 19 of the Newcomer Cards.

Teach/Model Vocabulary

- Elicit vocabulary from Lessons 1 and 2.
- Lead students through the song/chant on page T6.
- Display the card and ask: *What are the people doing?* Point to, name, and pantomime each action, covering all actions on the card and in the vocabulary list. Have students repeat. Help with pronunciation.
- Say these sentence frames as you point the woman holding a basket: **Does she carry a basket? Yes, she does.** Then say the sentences again as you write them on the board, completing the first sentence with the action. Have students repeat after you. Then, point to the woman talking to the store clerk and ask: **Does she ask for help?** Have students answer chorally: **Yes, she does.** Repeat for other actions on the card.
- Extend by introducing the sentence frames: **Who in your family makes a shopping list? Do you push a cart or do you carry a basket? My mother pushes a cart. I carry a basket.**
- **Talk About It** Have partners talk about which action they like to do in the grocery store.

Practice/Apply

PRODUCTIVE

- **Talk About It** Have partners use the sentence frames they learned to ask and answer questions about what their partner's family members do in the grocery store.
- Guide students to complete the activity on the page 121.
- Have students stand in a circle. Have one student say what they do in a grocery store while pantomiming the action. The whole class repeats the action. Continue around the circle with each student telling what she/he does and what the previous students do in a grocery store, until all students have had a turn.

Make Cultural Connections

Have students respond to this prompt: *Tell your partner and then the class about grocery shopping in your home country.*

Use Newcomer Card, page 19

Name: ______________________________

Write what you and your family members do in the grocery store.

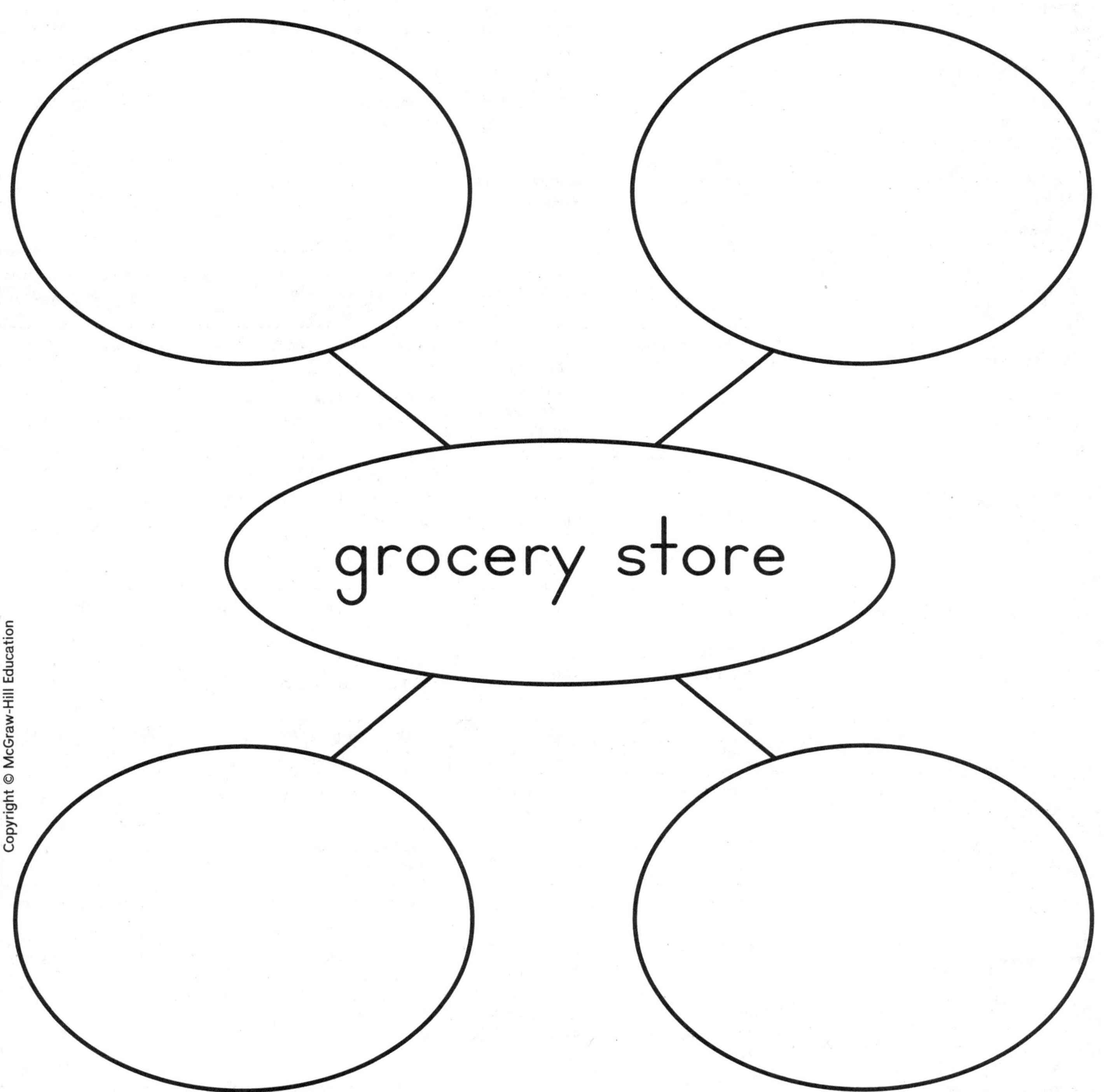

Measurement	LESSONS	MATERIALS	LANGUAGE OBJECTIVES	LANGUAGE STRUCTURES/ GRAMMAR	VOCABULARY
Newcomer Card, p. 20	**Lesson 1:** Comparing Objects, p. 124–125	Newcomer Card p. 20 Phonics Card 34 Song/Chant p. T6	Use language to compare objects by length, height, and weight	What is the ____ of the ____? I measure with a ____. The ____ is/are ____. **Verb:** to be **Comparatives** **Articles:** a, the	Units of measurement **High-Frequency Words:** *what, do, you, need*
	Lesson 2: Same and Different, p. 136–127	Newcomer Card p. 20 Phonics Card 11 Song/Chant p. T6	Use language to compare and contrast different objects	Observe the ____ and ____. How are they ____? They both need ____. **Imperative** **Conjunction:** and	Comparison Words **High-Frequency Words:** *same, different, both, than, they*
	Lesson 3: Measuring in the Classroom, p. 128–129	Newcomer Card p. 20 Phonics Card 8 Song/Chant p. T6	Build on understanding of measurement	How ____ is the ____? It is ____. The ____ is ____ the ____. ***How* questions** **Pronoun:** it	Measurements **High-Frequency Words:** *long, your, my, his, her*

Animals	LESSONS	MATERIALS	LANGUAGE OBJECTIVES	LANGUAGE STRUCTURES/ GRAMMAR	VOCABULARY
Newcomer Card, p. 21	**Lesson 1:** Wild Animals and Insects, p. 130–131	Newcomer Card p. 21 Phonics Card 22 Song/Chant p. T6	Describe the actions of different wild animals and insects	What is the ____ doing? The ____ is ____. **Present continuous verbs** **Wh- questions:** What	Wild animals and insects **High-Frequency Words:** *what, is, the, no*
	Lesson 2: Pets, p. 132–133	Newcomer Card p. 21 Phonics Card 44 Song/Chant p. T6	Describe what people do with their pets	Do you have pets? Yes, I have a ____ and a ____. No, I don't have a pet. **Questions with *do*** **Negatives**	Pets **High-Frequency Words:** *have, like, to, do, my*
	Lesson 3: Farm Animals, p. 134–135	Newcomer Card p. 21 Structural Analysis Cards 19 and 25 Song/Chant p. T6	Ask and answer questions about the sizes of farm animals	Which animal is the ____? The ____ is the ____. **Wh- questions:** Which **Comparatives and Superlatives**	Farm animals **High-Frequency Words:** *which, big, small, than, is, or*

Growth and Change	LESSONS	MATERIALS	LANGUAGE OBJECTIVES	LANGUAGE STRUCTURES/ GRAMMAR	VOCABULARY
Newcomer Card, p. 22	**Lesson 1:** Animal Growth Cycle, p. 136–137	Newcomer Card p. 22 Phonics Card 26 Song/Chant p. T7	Recount the stages in a buttlerfly's growth cycle	First/then/Next/finally, it is a/an ____. **Sequence words** **Articles:** a, an	Animal growth cycle **High-Frequency Words:** *first, then, it, is*
	Lesson 2: Plant Growth Cycle, p. 138–139	Newcomer Card p. 22 Phonics Card 24 Song/Chant p. T7	Ask and answer questions about the growth cycle of plants	How does the ____ change? The ____ changes into a ____. **Verb:** to change ***How* questions**	Parts of plant life cycle **High-Frequency Words:** *how, does, the, a, into*
	Lesson 3: Human Growth, p. 140–141	Newcomer Card p. 22 Structural Analysis Cards 18 and 20 Song/Chant p. T7	Ask and answer questions about human growth	The ____ is ____ the ____. Is the ____ ____ the ____? Yes/No, the ____ is/is not ____ the ____. **Regular and irregular plurals** **Comparatives and Superlatives**	Stages in human growth **High-Frequency Words:** *yes, no, the, is, than*

United States	LESSONS	MATERIALS	LANGUAGE OBJECTIVES	LANGUAGE STRUCTURES/ GRAMMAR	VOCABULARY
Newcomer Card, p. 23	**Lesson 1:** States and Regions, p. 142–143	Newcomer Card p. 23 Phonics Card 35 Song/Chant p. T7	Ask and answer questions about where you and others live.	Where do you live? I live in the ____. **Verb:** to live **Wh- questions:** Where	States and regions **High-Frequency Words:** *where, do, live, to, in*
	Lesson 2: National Landmarks, p. 144–145	Newcomer Card p. 23 Phonics Card 17 Song/Chant p. T7	Ask and answer questions about visiting United States landmarks	Do you want to go to the ____ or the ___? I want to go to the ____. I don't want to go to the ____. **Verbs:** to want, to go **Conjunction:** or	United States Landmarks **High-Frequency Words:** *do, you, want, but, not*
	Lesson 3: Natural Features, p. 146–147	Newcomer Card p. 23 Phonics Cards 12 and 28 Song/Chant p. T7	Ask and answer questions about living near natural features	Do you want to live near a/an ____ ? Yes/No, I want to live near a/an ____. **Verbs:** to want, to live **Pronouns:** you, I	Natural features **High-Frequency Words:** *live, want, no, do, yes*

My World	LESSONS	MATERIALS	LANGUAGE OBJECTIVES	LANGUAGE STRUCTURES/ GRAMMAR	VOCABULARY
Newcomer Card, p. 24	**Lesson 1:** Where I'm From, p. 148–149	Newcomer Card p. 24 Phonics Cards 9 and 29 Song/Chant p. T7	Ask and answer questions about where you are from	What ____ are you from? I'm from ____. **Wh- questions:** What **Contractions:** I'm	Countries **High-Frequency Words:** *you, I, are, am, from*
	Lesson 2: Land and Water Animals, p. 150–151	Newcomer Card p. 24 Phonics Card 7 Song/Chant p. T7	Ask and answer questions about animals in your home country	What land/water animals live in your home country? ____ live on land/in the water in ____. **Verb:** to live **Wh- questions:** What	Animals **High-Frequency Words:** *live, water, what, on, in*
	Lesson 3: In My New Country, p. 152–153	Newcomer Card p. 24 Phonics Card 39 Song/Chant p. T7	Ask and answer questions about two different places	I am from ____. At ____, we ____. I ____ in my home country. Here I ____. **Present and past tense verbs** **Pronouns:** I, we	Activities and currency **High-Frequency Words:** *school, money, ate, used, saw*

Progress Monitoring

Use the **Oral Language Proficiency Benchmark Assessment** on pages T40–T41 to monitor students' oral language proficiency growth.

Use the **Student Profile** on pages T43–T44 to record observations throughout the units.

Measurement

Language Objective:
Use language to compare objects by length, height, and weight

Content Objective:
Compare the length, height, and weight of objects

Sentence Frames:
What is the ____ of the ____?
She/He measures ___ with a ___.
The ____ is/are ____.
The ____ is ____ the ____.

VOCABULARY
taller than, longer than, shorter than, heavier than, lighter than, foot, yard, inch, ruler, tape measure, yard stick, scale, measure, weigh, pounds, strawberries, tomato plant, sunflower, leaf, height, length, weight
Cognates: *tomate, planta*

>> Go Digital

Language Transfers Handbook
See pages 16–19 for grammatical structures that do not transfer. Cantonese, Hmong, or Vietnamese speakers may omit the linking verbs *is* or *are*.

Grades 2-3 Foundational Skills Kit
Use Phonics Card 34 to teach silent letters *gh (weight)*; Routine Card 5 with high-frequency words *what, do, need, you*; Fluency Card 13B to teach chunking text with prepositions.

eBook Use digital material for vocabulary practice.

LESSON 1: Comparing Objects

Set Purpose

- Tell students that today they will discuss comparing objects. Show page 20 of the Newcomer Cards.

Teach/Model Vocabulary

- Lead students through the song/chant on page T6.
- Display the Newcomer Card and ask: *What do you see?* Students name things they know. Then point to and name the objects on the card. Have students repeat.
- Say these sentence frames as you point to the boy measuring the plant with a ruler: **What is the height of the plant?** Read aloud the speech balloon: **The plant is 5 inches tall.** Ask: *What does he use to measure the plant?* Point to the ruler and have students chorally answer: **He measures height with a ruler.** Then point to the strawberries and ask: **What is the weight of the strawberries?** Point to the scale and ask: *What does she use to measure the strawberries' weight?* Have students answer chorally: **She measures weight with a scale.** Repeat for other objects on the card and in the vocabulary list.
- **Talk About It** Have partners talk about what they might use a ruler and scale to measure in the classroom.
- Extend by reviewing *taller/shorter than* and introducing *longer than* and *heavier than* with the sentence frames in the sidebar. Have partners work together to compare the height and length of plants and their leaves and vegetables shown on the card.

Practice/Apply

- **Talk About It** Have partners discuss things they or their family have measured and why.
- Guide students to complete the activity on page 125.
- Provide students with pictures of objects. Have partners talk about what they would measure (height, weight, etc.) and compare objects.

Make Connections

Partners use rulers to measure the length of objects in the classroom. Partners present their findings to the class. Elicit descriptive, comparative, and superlative words.

Name: ______________________________

Comparing Objects

Use Newcomer Card, page 20

A. Read the name of the measuring tool.
Write if you need it to measure weight or length.

1. 

ruler

____

2. 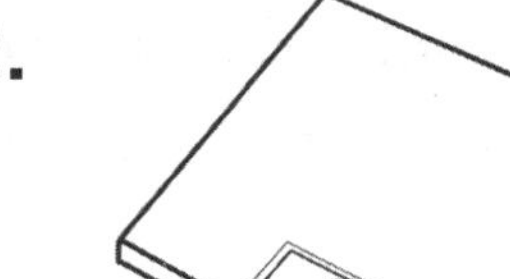
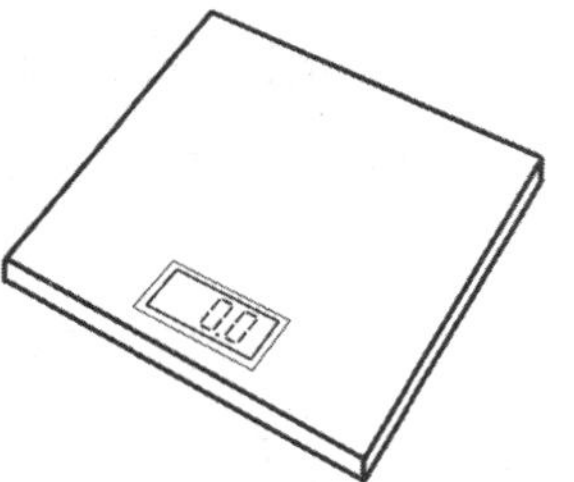

scale

____

3.

tape measure

____

B. Circle what you measure in each sentence. Then write if you measure weight or length.

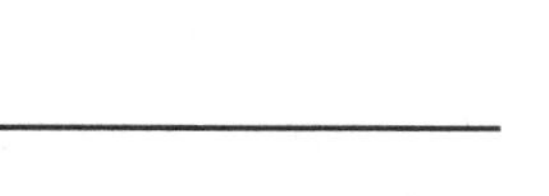

1. I measure my hand. __________

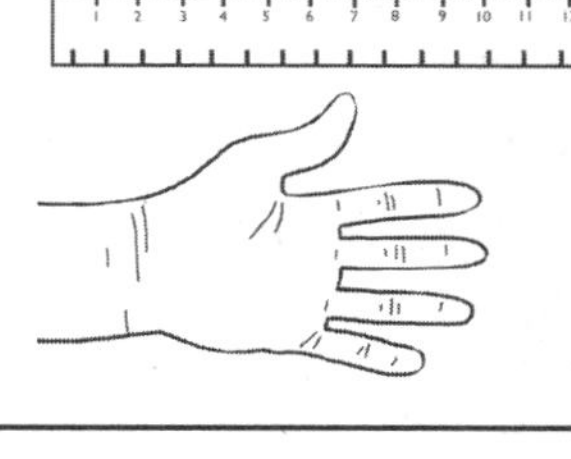

2. I measure the bicycle. __________

3. I measure the apples. __________

Measurement

Language Objective:
Use language to compare and contrast different objects

Content Objective:
Identify similarities and differences

Sentence Frames:
Observe the ____ and ____.
How are they ____?
They/They're both ____.
How are the ____ and the ____ different?
The ____ ____ and the ____ ____.
The ____ is ____ the ____.

VOCABULARY
same, different, both, similar, alike
Cognates: *diferente, similar*

>> Go Digital

Language Transfers Handbook
See pages 16–19 for grammatical structures that do not transfer. Cantonese, Hmong, Korean, Vietnamese, Arabic, or Tagalog speakers may consistently omit articles.

Grades 2-3 Foundational Skills Kit
Use Phonics Card 11 to teach end blends *(different)*; Routine Card 5 to teach high-frequency words *same, different, both, than,* and *they*; Structural Analysis Card 26 to teach three or more syllable words *(different, similar)*.

eBook Use digital material for vocabulary practice.

LESSON 2: Same and Different

Set Purpose

- Tell students that today they will discuss objects that are the same and different. Show page 20 of the Newcomer Cards.

Teach/Model Vocabulary

- Elicit the vocabulary from Lesson 1.
- Lead students through the song/chant on page T6.
- Display the Newcomer Card and ask: *What do you see*? Point to the objects and ask students to name them.
- Say these sentence frames as you point to two different objects: **Observe the sunflower and the tomato plant. How are they alike? They're both green.** Then say the sentences again as you write them on the board. Have students repeat after you. Then point to the strawberries and tomatoes and say: **Observe the strawberries and tomatoes. How are they similar?** Have partners discuss how they are alike and have them say: **They're both red**. Elicit other adjectives. Repeat for other objects.
- **Talk About It** Have partners discuss other ways that plants, fruits, and vegetables are alike. Extend the conversation with comparative adjectives and the sentence frame: **The sunflower is taller than the tomato plant.**
- Repeat instruction for differences by using the sentence frames: **How are the sunflower and the tomato plant different? The sunflower has a yellow flower and the tomato plant has a red fruit.**

Practice/Apply

- **Talk About It** Have partners use the card and the sentence frames to discuss plants that people have and talk about how they are the same or different.
- Guide students to complete the activity on the page 127.
- Have partners discuss how the plants or flowers they drew on page 127 are the same and different.

Make Connections

Have partners compare and contrast the trees, plants, fruits, or vegetables in their home, garden, park, or school playground.

Name: ______________________________

Draw two plants or flowers. Then write a sentence that tells how they are the same or different.

____

____

Measurement

Language Objective:
Build on understanding of measurement

Content Objective:
Understand measurement

Sentence Frames:
How ____ is the ____?
The ____/It is ____.
The ____ is ____ the ____.

VOCABULARY
inches, yards, foot, feet, heavier than, lighter than, taller than, shorter than, longer than, long
Cognates: *planta*

>> Go Digital

Language Transfers Handbook
See pages 16–19 for grammatical structures that do not transfer. Hmong, Korean, Spanish, or Tagalog speakers may avoid -*er* endings (*taller, longer*).

Grades 2-3 Foundational Skills Kit
Use Phonics Card 8 to teach *r*-controlled vowel /ôr/ *(shorter)*; Structural Analysis Card 20 to teach irregular plurals *(foot/feet)*; Routine Card 5 to teach high-frequency words *long, your, my, his,* and *her.*

eBook and Games Provide audio support, interaction, and practice with the vocabulary.

LESSON 3: Measuring in the Classroom

Set Purpose

- Tell students that today they will discuss measuring in the classroom. Show page 20 of the Newcomer Cards.

Teach/Model Vocabulary

- Elicit vocabulary from Lessons 1 and 2.
- Lead students through the song/chant on page T6.
- Say these sentence frames as you measure objects in your classroom: **How tall is the door? It is 7 feet tall. The door is six inches taller than the cabinet.** Say the sentences again as you write them on the board. Have students repeat after you. Then point to a student's desk and ask: **How long is the desk?** Have pairs measure the desk and your desk. Help them report their results with the sentence frames: **The student desk is 2 feet long. The teacher's desk is 3 feet long. The student desk is shorter than the teacher's desk**.
- **Talk About It** Have partners measure, compare, and contrast the length and height of different objects in the classroom.
- Extend with the sentence frames: **How heavy is the book? The book is heavier than the pencil.**

Practice/Apply PRODUCTIVE

- **Talk About It** Have partners compare what has been measured in the classroom with what's being measured on the Newcomer Card. Ask: *Is the door taller than the sunflower? How do you know?*
- Guide students to complete the activity on page 129.
- Have students line up against the wall from shortest to tallest. Measure each student's height and record on the board. Then have students discuss the different heights using the sentence frames they learned.

Make Cultural Connections

Have partners discuss the different units of measurement from their home country. Have partners talk about the similarities and differences in those units of measurement compared to what we use in theUnited States.

Name: ___________________________

Measuring in the Classroom

Use Newcomer Card, page 20

Measure different classroom objects. Write the name of the object, the measurement, and how it compares to another object.

Classroom Object	Measurement	How It Compares

Animals

Language Objective:
Describe the actions of different wild animals and insects

Content Objective:
Distinguish the different actions of wild animals and insects

Sentence Frames:
What is the ____ doing?
The ____ is ____.
Is the ____ ____?
Yes, the ____ is ____.
No, the ____ is ____.

VOCABULARY
deer, snake, bear, raccoon, zebra, antelope, giraffe, squirrel, coyote, bee, ant, fly, mosquito, buzzing, swimming, running, jumping, eating, flying, walking, drinking
Cognates: *coyote, mosquito*

>> Go Digital

Language Transfers Handbook See pages 16–19 for grammatical structures that do not transfer. Cantonese, Hmong, or Vietnamese speakers may omit the linking verb *is*.

Grades 2-3 Foundational Skills Kit Use Phonics Card 22 to teach the long /i/ sound in *fly* and *coyote*; Routine Card 5 to teach high-frequency words *what, is, the,* and *no*; Structural Analysis Card 10 to teach the inflectional ending *-ing* with double final consonant *(swimming, running)*.

eBook Use digital material for vocabulary practice.

LESSON 1: Wild Animals and Insects

Set Purpose

- Tell students that today they will discuss wild animals and insects. Show page 21 of the Newcomer Cards.

Teach/Model Vocabulary

- Lead students through the song/chant on page T6.
- Display the Newcomer Card and ask students what they see. Point to and name the wild animals and insects. Have students repeat. Help with pronunciation.
- Say these sentence frames as you point to the wild animals and insects and pantomime the actions: **What is the zebra doing? The zebra is drinking.** Then say the sentences again as you write them on the board. Have students repeat after you. Then gesture flying, point to the bee, and ask: **What is the bee doing?** Have students respond chorally: **The bee is flying**. Repeat the instruction with other wild animals and insects on the card and in the vocabulary list.
- **Talk About It** Have partners talk about different wild animals and insects on the card and their actions.
- Extend by introducing the sentence frames: **Is the zebra eating? No, the zebra is drinking.**

Practice/Apply COLLABORATIVE

- **Talk About It** Have partners use the Newcomer Card and the sentence frames they learned to ask and answers questions about what wild animals and insects do.
- Guide students to complete the activity on page 131.
- Have students play 20 questions. Have students take turns drawing a picture of a wild animal or insect in action. They don't show it to anyone. Then the rest of the class takes turns asking *yes* or *no* questions to figure out which animal or insect the student drew and what it is doing. For example: *Is it bigger than a zebra? Is it brown? Is it drinking?*

Make Connections

Partners compare and contrast one of the wild animals or insects on the card to one of their favorite animals or insects. Have partners present one student's animal/insect comparison to the class.

Name: ______________________

Write the names of wild animals and insects. Then talk to your partner about what the animals do or how they move.

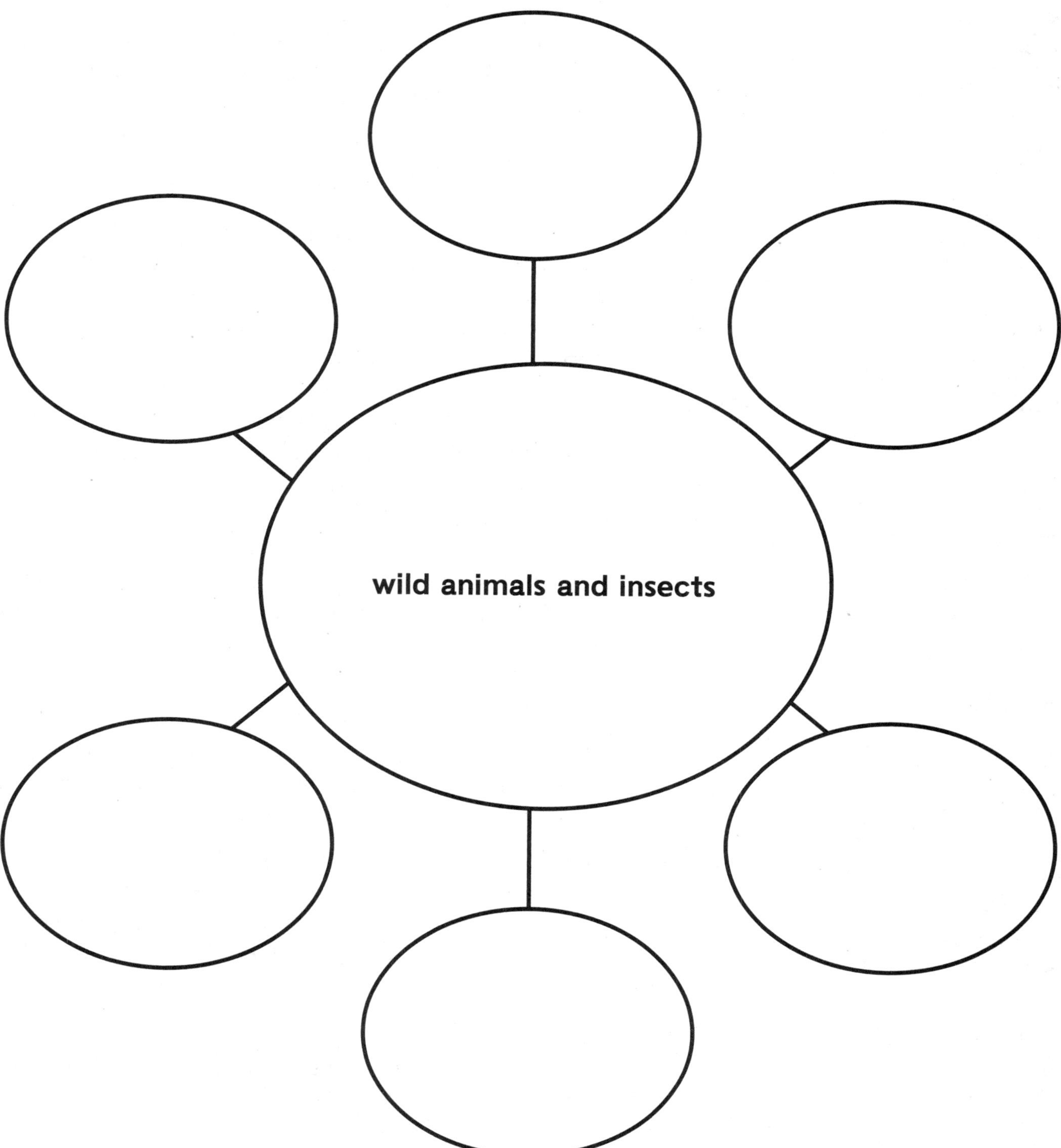

Animals

Language Objective:
Describe what people do with their pets

Content Objective:
Identify animals that people have as pets

Sentence Frames:
Do you have pets?
Yes, I have (a) ____ and (a) ____.
No, I don't have a pet.
My friend has a ____.
Do you like to ____ your (friend's) ____?
Yes/No, I like to ____ my (friend's) ____.

VOCABULARY
cat, dog, bird, turtle, fish, rabbit, hamster, snake, feed, give water to, play with, brush, take care of, walk the dog

>> Go Digital

Language Transfers Handbook See pages 16–19 for grammatical structures that do not transfer. Cantonese, Hmong, Korean, Arabic, or Tagalog speakers may have problems with irregular subject-verb agreement.

Grades 2-3 Foundational Skills Kit Use Phonics Card 44 to teach CVCe syllables *(take, snake)*; Routine Card 5 to teach high-frequency words *have, like, to, do,* and *my;* Fluency Card 13 to teach phrasing of sentences with conjunctions and prepositions.

eBook Use digital material for vocabulary practice.

LESSON 2: Pets

Set Purpose

- Tell students that today they will discuss pets. Show page 21 of the Newcomer Cards.

Teach/Model Vocabulary

- To review, elicit vocabulary from Lesson 1.
- Lead students through the song/chant on page T6.
- Display the Newcomer Card and ask: *What pets do you see?* Then point to and name the pets. Have students repeat. Help with pronunciation. Have partners talk about other pets they know of.
- Say these sentence frames as you point to the pets: **Do you have pets? Yes, I have a cat and fish.** Then say the sentences again as you write them on the board, completing the sentences with the names of pets. Have students repeat after you. Then point to the dog and cat and ask: **Do you have pets?** Have students respond chorally: **Yes, I have a dog and a cat.** Repeat for other pets on the vocabulary list and ones that students know.
- **Talk About It** Have partners name and describe the animals they, their friends, or their family has as pets.
- Extend by naming and pantomiming the different actions to take care of pets. Have students repeat after you. Then review likes with the sentence frames: **Do you like to feed your (friend's) dog?** and **Yes/No, I like to feed my (friend's) dog.**

Practice/Apply COLLABORATIVE

- **Talk About It** Have partners use the card and sentence frames to discuss animals people have as pets and what they do with them. Elicit action and descriptive words.
- Guide students to complete the activity on page 133.
- Have pairs write three sentences to describe a pet in the picture using previously learned vocabulary. Have others guess which pet is being described. Model for students. For example: *It's orange. It has short hair. It says* meow.

Make Connections

Have partners describe a pet they have cared for. Then have the partners explain why they like or don't like taking care of this pet.

Name: ________________________

Pets

Use Newcomer Card, page 21

Write the name of each pet. Use words from the box. Then complete the sentence.

fish	bird	dog	rabbit	hamster	cat

My favorite pet is a ________________________.

Animals

Language Objective:
Ask and answer questions about the sizes of farm animals

Content Objective:
Understand the different sizes of farm animals

Sentence Frames:
Which animal is ____/the ____?
The ____ is ____ /the____.
The ____ is ____ the ____.

VOCABULARY
chicken, cow, goat, horse, sheep, pig, turkey, small, smaller than, smallest, big, bigger than, biggest

>> Go Digital

Language Transfers Handbook See pages 16–19 for grammatical structures that do not transfer. Hmong, Korean, Spanish, or Tagalog speakers may struggle with the comparative and superlative endings *-er* and *-est*.

Grades 2-3 Foundational Skills Kit Use Structural Analysis Card 19 to teach comparative inflectional endings with no spelling change *(smaller, smallest)*; Structural Analysis Card 25 to teach comparative inflectional endings with a spelling change *(bigger, biggest)*; Routine Card 5 to teach high-frequency words *which, big, small, than, is,* and *or.*

eBook and Games Provide audio support, interaction, and practice with the vocabulary.

LESSON 3: Farm Animals

Set Purpose

- Tell students that today they will discuss farm animals. Show page 21 of the Newcomer Cards.

Teach/Model Vocabulary

- To review, elicit vocabulary from Lessons 1 and 2.
- Lead students through the song/chant on page T6.
- Display the Newcomer Card and say: *Describe the farm animals.* Then point to, name, and describe each farm animal. Have students repeat. Help with pronunciation.
- Say these sentence frames as you point to the farm animals: **Which animal is small? The chicken is small. The chicken is smaller than the cow.** Then say the sentences again as you write them on the board, completing the sentences with the names of animals and the comparative adjectives. Have students repeat after you. Then point to the card again and say: **The sheep is big. Which animal is bigger?** Have students respond chorally: **The cow is bigger than the sheep.** Repeat for other animals on the card and in the vocabulary list.
- **Talk About It** Have partners compare the sizes of other animals they know.
- Expand by introducing the sentence frames: **Which animal is the biggest/smallest? The ____ is the biggest/smallest.**

Practice/Apply

- **Talk About It** Have partners use the Newcomer Card to explain to each other the differences between wild animals, insects, pets, and farm animals.
- Guide students to complete the activity on page 135.
- Have each student cut out a picture of an animal from a magazine. Have them tell a partner about the animal. Then have all students interact with each other, comparing and contrasting their chosen animals.

Make Cultural Connections

Have partners describe, compare, and contrast different animals in their home countries. Then each student presents to the class and the other students ask follow-up questions.

Name: ______________________________

Use Newcomer Card, page 21

Complete the sentences with words from the box.

big	small

The horse is ______________________ .

The pig is __________________________ .

bigger	biggest	smaller	smallest

The chicken is the ______________________ .

The pig is ________________ than the sheep.

The sheep is ________________ than the pig.

The horse is the ____________________ .

Growth and Change

Language Objective:
Recount the stages in a butterfly's growth cycle

Content Objective:
Identify stages of the butterfly growth cycle

Sentence Frames:
First, it is a/an ____, and then, it is a ____.
Next, it is a ____, and finally, it is a ____.

VOCABULARY
egg, caterpillar, pupa, butterfly, first, then, next, finally

>> Go Digital

Language Transfers Handbook
See pages 16–19 for grammatical structures that do not transfer. Spanish or Arabic speakers may confuse the verbs *have* and *be*.

Grades 2-3 Foundational Skills Kit
Use Phonics Card 26 to teach long *u* (*pupa*); Structural Analysis Card 26 to teach multi-syllable words (*caterpillar, butterfly*); Routine Card 5 to teach high-frequency words *first, then, it,* and *is*.

eBook Use digital material for vocabulary practice.

LESSON 1: Animal Growth Cycle

Set Purpose

- Tell students that today they will discuss the animal growth cycle. Show page 22 of the Newcomer Cards.

Teach/Model Vocabulary

- Lead students through the song/chant on page T7.
- Display the Newcomer Card, point to the Animal Growth box, and ask: *What do you see?* Point to and name each stage of the butterfly's growth cycle. Have students repeat. Help with pronunciation.
- Say these sentence frames as you point to the stages of the growth cycle: **First, it is an egg, and then, it is a caterpillar.** Then say the sentences again as you write them on the board, completing the sentences with the sequence word and the stage of the growth cycle. Have students repeat after you. Then point to the pupa and butterfly and have students fill in the sentences frames for: **Next, it is a ____, and finally, it is a ____.** Repeat for other animal growth cycles the students know.
- **Talk About It** Have partners talk about how their favorite animal changes as it grows.
- Extend by using adjectives with the sentences: **First, it is a small egg, and then, it is a black and yellow caterpillar. Next, it is a green pupa, and finally, it is a big butterfly**. Expand by showing the growth of a frog.

Practice/Apply

- **Talk About It** Have partners use the Newcomer Card and the sentence frames they learned to ask and answer questions about the butterfly's growth cycle.
- Guide students to complete the activity on the page 137.
- Have partners work together to draw a picture of each stage of the butterfly's growth cycle on index cards. Then have students take turns putting the stages in order and narrating each stage as they hold up the card.

Make Connections

Have students draw butterflies they have seen. Then have partners take turns describing their pictures, describing colors, shapes, and sizes. Have partners compare their drawings for the class.

Name: ______________________

Use Newcomer Card, page 22

Write the stages of a butterfly's growth cycle in order. Describe it to a partner.

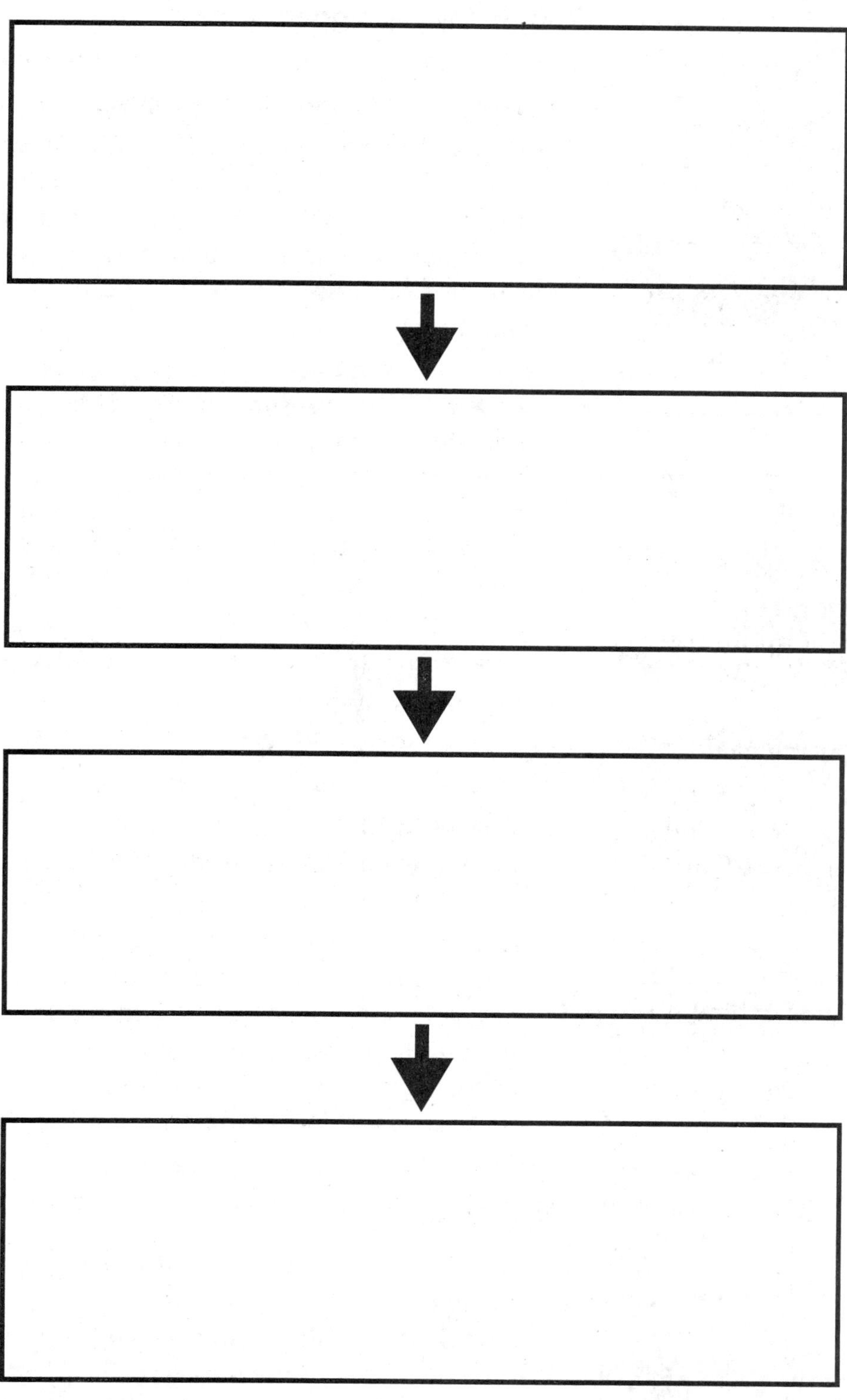

Growth and Change

Language Objective:
Ask and answer questions about the growth cycle of plants

Content Objective:
Identify the stages of the plant growth cycle

Sentence Frames:
How does the ____ change?
The ____ changes into a ____.

VOCABULARY
seed, seedling, budding plant, flower
Cognate: *planta*

>> Go Digital

Language Transfers Handbook
See pages 16–19 for grammatical structures that do not transfer. Cantonese, Korean, or Spanish speakers may struggle with inflectional ending *-s* in *changes.*

Grades 2-3 Foundational Skills Kit
Use Phonics Card 24 to teach the long *e* sound in *seed;* Routine Card 5 to teach high-frequency words *how, does, the, a,* and *into;* Structural Analysis Card 2 to teach the inflectional ending *-s* in *changes.*

eBook Use digital material for vocabulary practice.

LESSON 2: Plant Growth Cycle

Set Purpose

- Tell students that today they will discuss the plant growth cycle. Show page 22 of the Newcomer Cards.

Teach/Model Vocabulary

- Elicit stages of the butterfly's growth cycle from Lesson 1.
- Lead students through the song/chant on page T7.
- Display the card, point to the Plant Growth box, and ask what students see. Then point to and name the stages of the plant's growth cycle. Have students repeat. Help with pronunciation. Have students turn to a partner and use the previous lesson's sentence frames to describe the plant growth cycle.
- Say these sentence frames as you point to the seeds: **How does the seed change? The seed changes into a seedling.** Then say the sentences again as you write them on the board. Have students repeat after you. Then point to the seedling and ask: **How does the seedling change?** Have students answer chorally: **The seedling changes into a budding plant.** Repeat for the last stage of the plant growth cycle.
- **Talk About It** Have partners describe what happens during the different stages.

Practice/Apply

- **Talk About It** Have partners use the Newcomer Card and the sentence frames they learned to ask and answer questions about the plant growth cycle.
- Have students create a plant growth cycle story chain. Have students in small groups take turns telling one stage of the "story" about how a seed changes into a seedling, the seedling changes into a budding plant, and so on. Encourage students to use as much detail as possible, such as describing size, color, and shape at each stage.
- Guide students to complete the activity on the page 139.

Make Connections

In pairs, have one student use previously learned vocabulary to describe a plant in a particular stage of growth while the other student draws it. Then they switch roles. Afterwards, have them compare drawings.

Name: ________________________________

Observe the plant's growth cycle. Write about the changes using *first, then, next,* and *finally*.

Growth and Change

Language Objective:
Ask and answer questions about human growth

Content Objective:
Understand the different stages of human growth

Sentence Frames:
The ____ is ____ the ____.
Is the ____ ____the ____?
Yes/No, the ____ is/is not ____ the ____.
____ are ____ ____.

VOCABULARY
baby, child, children, teenager, adult, younger than, older than, youngest, oldest
Cognates: *bebé, adulto*

>> Go Digital

Language Transfers Handbook
See pages 16–19 for grammatical structures that do not transfer. Hmong, Korean, Spanish, or Tagalog speakers may avoid using the comparative ending *-er.*

Grades 2-3 Foundational Skills Kit
Use Structural Analysis Card 18 to teach plural that change the *y* to *i* (*babies*); Structural Analysis Cards 20 to teach irregular plurals (*children*); Routine Card 5 to teach high-frequency words *yes, no, the, is,* and *than.*

eBook and Games Provide audio support, interaction, and practice with the vocabulary.

LESSON 3: Human Growth

Set Purpose

- Tell students that today they will discuss the stages in human growth. Show page 22 of the Newcomer Cards.

Teach/Model Vocabulary

- Elicit vocabulary from Lessons 1 and 2.
- Lead students through the song/chant on page T7.
- Display the Newcomer Card, point to the last box, and ask: *What do you see?* Point to and name the different stages. Have students repeat. Help with pronunciation.
- Say these sentence frames as you point to people: **The baby is younger than the child. The adult is older than the teenager.** Then say the sentences again as you write them on the board. Have students repeat after you. Then point to the teenager and ask: *Who is younger than the teenager?* Have students answer chorally: **The child is younger than the teenager.**
- Introduce the sentence frame: **The baby is the youngest.** Have students discuss the youngest and oldest people on the card and their families.
- **Talk About It** Have partners talk about and compare the people on the card and the people they both know.
- Extend by introducing the sentence frames: **Is the child older than the baby? Yes/No, the child is/is not older than the baby. Babies are younger than children.**

Practice/Apply COLLABORATIVE

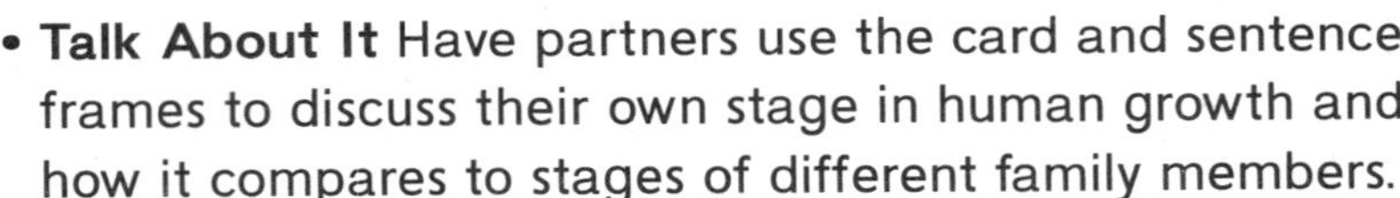

- **Talk About It** Have partners use the card and sentence frames to discuss their own stage in human growth and how it compares to stages of different family members.
- Guide students to complete the activity on the page 141.
- Have partners use the vocabulary in Lessons 1, 2, and 3 to play charades. One student acts out a stage of a growth cycle while the other student guesses the stage. Then partners can discuss the previous and next stage.

Make Cultural Connections

Have students share what is different about being a child in the United States compared with being a child in their home country. Have other students ask follow-up questions.

Name: ______________________________

Human Growth

Use Newcomer Card, page 22

A. Draw pictures of your family members. Label the stage of growth for each person.

B. Write a sentence about your stage of growth.

____

United States

Language Objective:
Ask and answer questions about where you and others live

Content Objective:
Understand that the United States has different states and regions

Sentence Frames:
Where do you live?
I live in (the) ____.
Do you live ____ (the) ____?
Yes/No, I live ____(the) ____.

VOCABULARY

Northeast, Midwest, West, Southeast, Southwest, Great Plains, Rocky Mountains, Mississippi River, Appalachian Mountains, near, closer to, region, state

>> Go Digital

Language Transfers Handbook
See pages 16–19 for grammatical structures that do not transfer. Cantonese or Hmong speakers may omit prepositions.

Grades 2-3 Foundational Skills Kit
Use Phonics Card 35 to teach the diphthong *ou* in *Southwest* and *mountains*; Routine Card 5 to teach high-frequency words *where, do, live, to,* and *in*; Fluency Card 7 to teach the intonation of reading different sentence types.

eBook Use digital material for vocabulary practice.

LESSON 1: States and Regions

Set Purpose

- Tell students that today they will discuss the United States. Show page 23 of the Newcomer Cards.

Teach/Model Vocabulary

- Lead students through the song/chant on page T7.
- Display the Newcomer Card and ask: *What do you see?* Students can name the places they know. Then point to and name the states and regions. Have students repeat. Help with pronunciation.
- Say these sentence frames as you point to your state: **Where do you live? I live in (your state).** Then say the sentences again as you write them on the board. Have students repeat after you. Then point to your region and ask: **Where do you live?** Have students chorally answer: **I live in the (your region).**
- **Talk About It** Have partners talk about the states and regions shown on the card and where they live.
- Extend by introducing the following sentence frames students can use to discuss their proximity to states or areas such as Montana, the Rocky Mountains, or the Great Plains: **Do you live near the Great Plains? Yes/ No, I live near/closer to the Rocky Mountains.**

Practice/Apply

- **Talk About It** Have partners use the card to describe the different features in and around their state.
- Guide students to complete the activity on the page 143.
- Have each student write a state name on a piece of paper. Then shuffle and distribute the papers. Have students pretend they live in the state written on the paper they receive. Then students ask each other questions about what they live near to find out which state the other lives in. For example: *Do you live in the Southwest? Do you live near Texas?*

Make Connections

Have partners discuss the states they have lived in or visited. Then have them describe some of the places they've visited.

Name: ______________________________

States and Regions

Use Newcomer Card, page 23

Draw a picture of the state you live in. Then write a sentence telling where you live.

United States

Language Objective:
Ask and answer questions about visiting United States landmarks

Content Objective:
Identify and locate United States landmarks

Sentence Frames:
Do you want to go to the ____?
I want to go to the ____.
I don't want to go to the ____, but I want to go to the ____.
Do you want to go to the ____ or the ____?
I want to go to the ____.

VOCABULARY

Yosemite Park, Grand Canyon, Statue of Liberty, Mount Rushmore, Golden Gate Bridge, Gateway Arch, Everglades, White House

>> Go Digital

Language Transfers Handbook See pages 16–19 for grammatical structures that do not transfer. Cantonese, Hmong, Korean, Spanish, Tagalog, or Vietnamese speakers may omit verbs from negative sentences.

Grades 2-3 Foundational Skills Kit Use Phonics Card 17 to teach the soft /dge/ in *Bridge*; Routine Card 5 to teach high-frequency words *do, you, want, but,* and *not*.

eBook Use digital material for vocabulary practice.

LESSON 2: National Landmarks

Set Purpose

- Tell students that today they will discuss landmarks in the United States. Show page 23 of the Newcomer Cards.

Teach/Model Vocabulary

- To review, elicit vocabulary from Lesson 1.
- Lead students through the song/chant on page T7.
- Display the Newcomer Card and ask: *What do you see in the pictures?* Then point to and name the landmarks. Have students repeat. Help with pronunciation.
- Say these sentence frames as you point to a landmark: **Do you want to go to the White House? I want to go to the White House.** Then say the sentences again as you write them on the board, completing the sentences with the name of the place. Have students repeat after you. Then point to the Grand Canyon and ask: **Do you want to go to the Grand Canyon?** Have students answer chorally: **I want to go to the Grand Canyon.** Repeat for other landmarks on the card and in or near your state.
- **Talk About It** Have partners talk about the landmarks they know of or have visited. Afterwards, have them ask each other if they want to visit these landmarks.
- Extend by introducing the sentence frames: **I don't want to go to the Golden Gate Bridge, but I want to go to the Statue of Liberty. Do you want to go to the Grand Canyon or the Gateway Arch? I want to go to the Gateway Arch.**

Practice/Apply

- **Talk About It** Have partners use the Newcomer Card and the sentence frames they learned to have a conversation about different landmarks they would like to visit.
- Guide students to complete the activity on page 145.
- Have students write the vocabulary from Lesson 1 and 2 on index cards. Then have students take turns choosing slips and asking and answering questions about wanting to visit landmarks, states, and regions.

Make Connections

Have partners discuss *why* they would like to visit different landmarks and/or states. Then have students share with you.

Name: ______________________________

Use Newcomer Card, page 23

Write the names of the landmarks you want to visit.

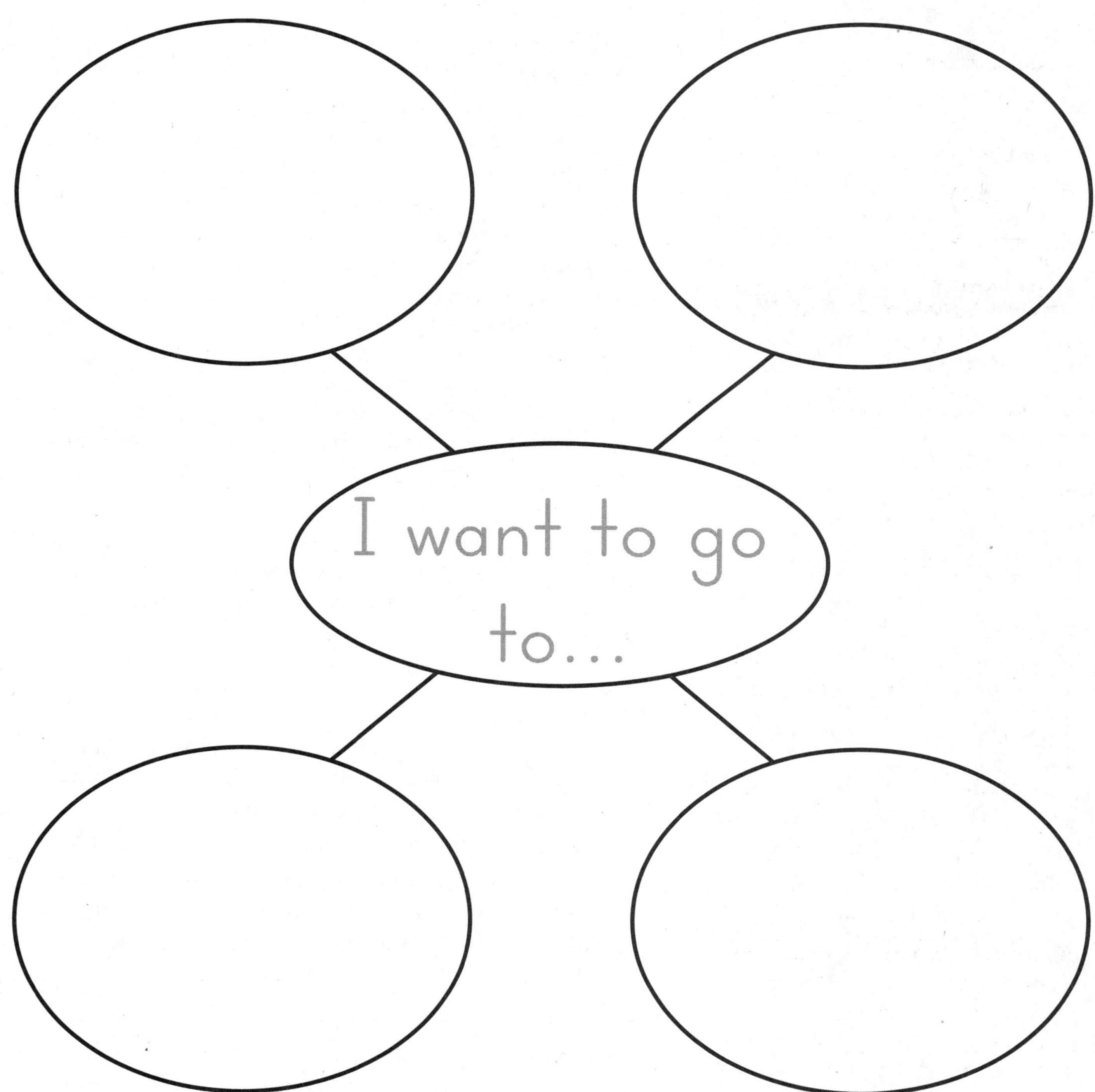

United States

Language Objective:
Ask and answer questions about living near natural features

Content Objective:
Identify natural features

Sentence Frames:
Do you want to live near a/an ____?
Yes/No, I want to live near a/an ____.
Do you want to live near a(n) ____ or a(n) ____?

VOCABULARY
mountain, river, pond, lake, farm, ocean, tree, plain, prairie, valley, live, near
Cognates: *montaña, lago, océano, valle*

>> Go Digital

Language Transfers Handbook
See pages 16–19 for grammatical structures that do not transfer. Some Cantonese or Hmong speakers may omit prepositions.

Grades 2-3 Foundational Skills Kit
Use Phonics Card 12 to teach the long *a* sound in *lake*; Phonics Card 28 to teach the *r*-controlled vowel in *farm*; Routine Card 5 to teach the high-frequency words *live, want, yes, no,* and *do*.

eBook and Games Provide audio support, interaction, and practice with the vocabulary.

LESSON 3: Natural Features

Set Purpose

- Tell students that today they will discuss natural features in the United States. Show page 23 of the Newcomer Cards.

Teach/Model Vocabulary

- Elicit vocabulary from Lessons 1 and 2.
- Lead students through the song/chant on page T7.
- Display the Newcomer Card and ask: *What things do you see?* Then point to and name the natural features. Have students repeat. Help with pronunciation.
- Say these sentence frames as you point to a feature: **Do you want to live near a river? Yes, I want to live near a river.** Then say the sentences again as you write them on the board, completing the sentences with the name of the natural feature. Have students repeat after you. Then point to the ocean and ask: **Do you want to live near an ocean?** Have students answer chorally: **Yes, I want to live near an ocean.** Repeat for the other natural features on the card and in the vocabulary box.
- **Talk About It** Have partners talk about natural features in and around their own state.
- Expand by introducing the sentence frames: **No, I want to live near a/an ____.** Review negative statements and the use of *a(n)*. Introduce: **Do you want to live near a/an ____ or a/an ____?**

Practice/Apply

COLLABORATIVE

- **Talk About It** Have partners use the Newcomer Card and the sentence frames they learned to ask and answer questions about where they want to live.
- Guide students to complete the activity on page 147.
- Have pairs work together. One student says what natural feature he/she wants to live near and explains why using previously-learned vocabulary. The listener agrees or disagrees and explains why. Then they switch roles.

Make Cultural Connections

Have partners talk about the natural features in their home country. Then students present to the class and other students ask follow-up questions.

Natural Features

Use Newcomer Card, page 23

Name: ____________________

Write the names of water or land features in the correct column.

water	land

My World

Language Objective:
Ask and answer questions about where you are from

Content Objective:
Identify the country you are from and activities done there

Sentence Frames:
What country are you from?
I'm from ____.
Are you from a ____ ____ or a ____ ____?
I lived in a ____ ____.
What do people do in your home country?
In ____, people like to ________.
Did you live in/near a/the ____?
I lived in/near a/the ____.

VOCABULARY
celebrate, play, sports, eat, country, city, town, big, small

>> Go Digital

Language Transfers Handbook
See pages 16–19 for grammatical structures that do not transfer. Cantonese, Hmong, Korean, Arabic, or Tagalog speakers may struggle with irregular subject-verb agreement *(I am, you are).*

Grades 2-3 Foundational Skills Kit
Use Phonics Card 9 to teach *r*-blends *(Africa, country)*; Phonics Card 29 to teach the soft *c* sound in *celebrate* and *city*; Routine Card 5 to teach high-frequency words *you, I, are, am,* and *from.*

eBook Use digital material for vocabulary practice.

LESSON 1: Where I'm From

Set Purpose

- Tell students that today they will discuss where they are from. Show page 24 of the Newcomer Cards.

Teach/Model Vocabulary

- Lead students through the song/chant on page T7.
- Display the Newcomer Card and ask: *What do you see?*
- Review sentence frames for meeting a new friend: **Hello. I'm ____.** Introduce the sentence frame: **What country are you from? I'm from ____.** Then read the text in the speech balloon: **Hola. I'm Miguel. I'm from Mexico.**
- **Talk About It** Have partners or small groups greet each other with their name and the country they're from.
- Point to the pictures and have volunteers read the labels. Say these sentence frames as you point to the soccer player: **What do people like to do in your home country? In Mexico, people like to play soccer.** Students say the sentences as you write them.
- **Talk About It** Partners can discuss what sports or hobbies people like to do in their home country.
- Repeat the instructional routine covering the sentence frames in the sidebar. When discussing the city and town pictures, note that the city is Mexico City and the town is San Sebastian.

Practice/Apply INTERPRETIVE

- **Talk About It** Have partners ask and answer questions about their favorite activities in their home country and explain why they like these activities.
- Ask students *yes* or *no* questions about their home countries. Have students that answer "yes" move to one side of the room and "no" to the other. For example, ask: *Are you from a big city?* Then have volunteers take turns asking questions.
- Guide students to complete the activity on page 149.

Make Connections

Have partners respond to this prompt: *Tell me more about your home country and community*. Students can share details about sports, food, celebrations, and the kind of town or city they lived in.

Name: ____________________

Where I'm From

Use Newcomer Card, page 24

Draw a picture of yourself doing something in your home country. Write sentences about it.

My World

Language Objective:
Ask and answer questions about animals in your home country

Content Objective:
Identify which animals live on land and in the water

Sentence Frames:
What land animals live in your home country?
____ live on land in ____.
What animals live in the water in your home country?
____ live in the water in ____.

VOCABULARY
camel, panda, kangaroo, alligator, giraffe, dolphin, whale, octopus, crab, starfish, monkey, parrot
Cognates: camello, panda, canguro, jirafa, delfín

>> Go Digital

Language Transfers Handbook
See pages 16–19 for grammatical structures that do not transfer. Cantonese or Hmong speakers may omit prepositions.

Grades 2-3 Foundational Skills Kit
Use Phonics Card 7 to teach short *a, e, i, o, u* sounds *(alligator, octopus)*; Routine Card 5 to teach high-frequency words *live, water, what, on, in.*

eBook Use digital material for vocabulary practice.

LESSON 2: Land and Water Animals

Set Purpose

- Tell students that today they will discuss animals in their home country. Show page 24 of the Newcomer Cards.

Teach/Model Vocabulary

- Elicit vocabulary from Lesson 1.
- Lead students through the song/chant on page T7.
- Display the Newcomer Card and ask: *What animals do you see?* Then point to and name the animals. Have students repeat. Help with pronunciation.
- Say these sentence frames as you point to the animals: **What land animals live in your home country? Monkeys live on land in Mexico. What animals live in the water in your home country? Dolphins live in the water in Mexico**. Then say the sentences again as you write them on the board. Have students repeat after you. Repeat for the other animals from the vocabulary list and those that students provide.
- **Talk About It** Have partners talk about the animals they have seen in their home country and whether they live on land or in the water.
- Expand with the sentence frames: **What other animals are in your home country? There are ____ and ____ in ____.**

Practice/Apply

PRODUCTIVE

- **Talk About It** Have partners use the Newcomer Card and the sentence frames they learned to ask and answer questions about the land and water animals they know. Elicit descriptive words.
- Guide students to complete the activity on page 151.
- Have partners work together to create a survey to ask about animals in their home countries. Have them ask their classmates if they have ever seen the animals. Afterwards have students share the results of their survey with the class.

Make Connections

Have partners discuss animals from their home countries as they fill in a Venn diagram comparing and contrasting them. Partners share their finished diagram with the class.

Use Newcomer Card, page 24

Name: ______________________

Write the name of your home country. Then write the names of animals living there. Tell a partner if each one lives on land or in the water.

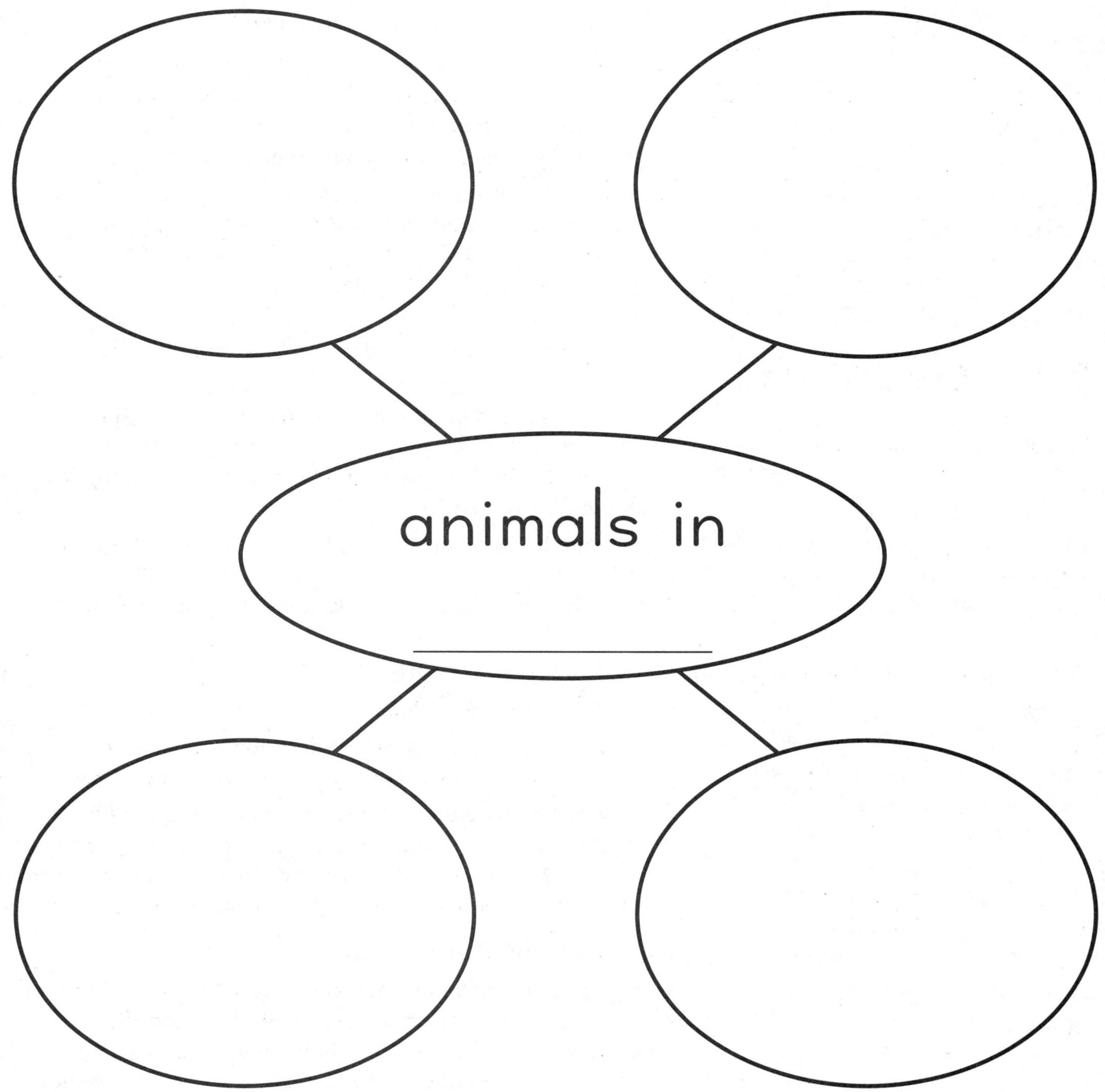

My World

Language Objective:
Ask and answer questions about two different places

Content Objective:
Identify special things about two different places

Sentence Frames:
I am from ____.
We spoke ____ there.
At school, we played ____.
We ate ____ in my home country.
We used ____ for money.
In the United States, we play____.
We eat ____. We speak ____.
We use ____ for money.

VOCABULARY
school, played, ate, eat, play, speak, spoke, dollars

>> Go Digital

Language Transfers Handbook
See pages 16–19 for grammatical structures that do not transfer. Hmong, Spanish, Vietnamese, Arabic, Tagalog, Cantonese, and Korean speakers may overuse or omit articles.

Grades 2-3 Foundational Skills Kit
Use Phonics Card 39 to teach variant vowel /ô/ in *saw*; Structural Analysis Card 6 to teach inflectional ending *-ed* (*played*); Routine Card 5 to teach high-frequency words *school, money, ate, used, saw.*

eBook and Games Provide audio support, interaction, and practice with the vocabulary.

LESSON 3: In My New Country

Set Purpose

- Tell students that today they will compare things in their home country with things in the United States. Show page 24 of the Newcomer Cards.

Teach/Model Vocabulary

- Elicit vocabulary from Lessons 1 and 2.
- Lead students through the song/chant on page T7.
- Display the card again and ask: *What does Miguel see and do in his home country?* Partners can discuss the sports, food, celebrations, and money in Mexico.
- Say these sentence frames as you point to Miguel and the pictures: **I am from Mexico. We spoke Spanish there. We used pesos for money.** Cover all of the sentence frames in the sidebar.
- **Talk About It** Have partners talk about where they're from and provide a few details about their life there.
- Repeat the instructional routine using the sentence frames focused on life in the United States: **In the United States, we play ____. We eat ____. We speak ____.** Let volunteers fill in the blanks and eventually say the entire sentences.
- Expand by using present and past tense verbs together: **In the United States, we eat ____. In my home country, we ate ____.** Explain the irregular past tense verb *ate*.

Practice/Apply

INTERPRETIVE

- **Talk About It** Have partners describe the differences between their home country and the United States.
- Have students draw or bring in pictures to create a collage about their home country, using the template on page 153 as a guide. Partners can work together to write labels and practice presenting the collage to the class.

Make Cultural Connections

Ask students to bring in a special souvenir from their home country. Have them talk to a partner about it and then tell the class about the object and their collage. After each presentation, have another student ask a follow-up question.

Name: ______________________________

In My New Country

Use Newcomer Card, page 24

Create a collage of your home country. Label the pictures. Write sentences about your home country and the United States.

SONGS/CHANTS

START SMART: What's Your Name? L1, p. 2

What do you say?
What do you say?
That first letter is little ol' A,
B, C, D, E, F, G, go ahead, say it with me.

H, I, J, K, L, M, it's OK to say it again.

N, O, P, and Q,
R, S, T, and then comes U.

V, W, X, Y and Z. That's the end. It's easy to see.

START SMART: What's Your Name? L2, p. 4

Uppercase A, uppercase A,
Where is the uppercase A?
There it is!
No need to shout.

All you do is point it out!

[Repeat for other uppercase and lowercase letters.]

START SMART: What's Your Name? L3, p. 6

My name is ___________ .
My name is ___________ .
I spell my name ___________ .
Spell it now! Spell it now!

START SMART: Greetings, Lesson 1, p. 8

Hello, hello, hello.
I smile and say hello.
I say my name. You do the same.
Hello, hello, hello.

Goodbye, goodbye, goodbye.
I wave and say goodbye.
I say goodbye. I wave goodbye.
Goodbye, goodbye, goodbye.

START SMART: Greetings, Lesson 2, p. 10

Where do you live?
Where do you live?
I live on Main Street.
That's where I live!

Where on Main Street?
Where do you live?
5 Main Street.
That's where I live!

START SMART: Greetings, Lesson 3, p. 12

[First half of class:] I like bananas. I like bananas.
[Second half of class:] Ewww. Yuck. I don't like bananas.
[First half of class:] Why? Why? What's wrong with bananas?
[Second half of class:] They're soft! I like apples. Crunch!

START SMART: Geometric Shapes, L1, p. 14

Shapes, shapes everywhere.
Circle, triangle, rectangle, square.
Shapes are here, shapes are there.
I can draw one in the air.

START SMART: Geometric Shapes, L2, p. 16

I see the red. I see, see the red.

I see the blue. I see, see the blue.

Colors in rainbows, colors on clothes.
Colors on flowers, colors on toes!

START SMART: Geometric Shapes, L3, p. 18

Green squares for windows.
Blue circles for clocks.
Brown rectangles I see for blocks and blocks.

Yellow carpets.
Orange balls.
Purple diamonds on the walls.

START SMART: Numbers, Lesson 1, p. 20

We like to count from one to ten,
And then we start all over again:
One to ten
Ten to twenty
And up to thirty
That is plenty!

START SMART: Numbers, Lesson 2, p. 22

How old are you?
How old are you?
I'm __________ years old.
I'm __________ years old.
He is __________ .
She is __________ .
But I'm __________ years old.

START SMART: Numbers, Lesson 3, p. 24

How many bananas did you get from the store?
Let's count how many: one, two, three, four.
I got four bananas from the store.

How many puppies followed you home? Plenty!
Let's count how many: five, ten, fifteen, twenty.
Whew! The number of puppies is plenty!

UNIT 1: In the Classroom, Lesson 1, p. 28

Blue pens, green books.

A ruler, one or two.

Two pencils, four markers, and a calculator for you.

Lots of items in my class.

Lots of things to use. My classroom is a busy place

with lots of items to choose.

UNIT 1: In the Classroom, Lesson 2, p. 30

What are you doing?
What are you doing?
Reading and writing
All day long.

What are you doing?
What are you doing?
Talking and listening
Or singing a song.

UNIT 1: In the Classroom, Lesson 3, p. 32

The teacher says and you will hear
These commands throughout the year:
Please sit down.
Raise your hand.
These are the words to understand.
There are other commands to know:
Like Come here. Stop! And Go, go, go!

UNIT 1: Computers, Lesson 1, p. 34

Where is the pen? It is around.
Where is the pen? Let's look around.
Is it above the notebook? No!
Is it under the notebook? Yes! There it is!

Where is the ruler? It should be here.
Do you think it's somewhere near?
Is it between the eraser and pencil? No!
Is it behind the computer? Yes! There it is!

UNIT 1: Computers, Lesson 2, p. 36

I ask for help when I don't know,
for answers to questions or where to go.
Can you help me? Please repeat.
Is this correct? Where do we eat?
I don't understand. Please explain.
Can you show me what to do again?

UNIT 1: Computers, Lesson 3, p. 38

Click, click, click
In the computer lab.
Type, type, type
On the keyboard.
Scroll, scroll, scroll
Searching the Internet.
See what we find today.

UNIT 1: A Day at School, Lesson 1, p. 40

I go to the library,
What do I see?
A lot of books, waiting for me.

I go to the classroom,
What do I see?
A lot of friends, waiting for me.

UNIT 1: A Day at School, Lesson 2, p. 42

School places. Cool places.
The gym is where we play.
We play there every day.

School places. Cool places.
The library has books we read—
Books we love and books we need.

School places. Cool places. (repeat)

UNIT 1: A Day at School, Lesson 3, p. 44

There's the nurse! There's the nurse!
I hurt my finger.
See the nurse!

There's the principal! There's the principal!
I have a question.
See the principal!

UNIT 1: Calendar, Lesson 1, p. 46

Seven days in every week.
It's one day, as we speak
Monday, Tuesday, Wednesday too
Lots of fun on days for you.
Thursday, Friday, Saturday, Sunday
Every day is a day for fun-day!

UNIT 1: Calendar, Lesson 2, p. 48

It's time to get up, get up, get up.
It's time to start the day.

It's time to go to bed, go to bed, go to bed.
There's no more time to read or play.

UNIT 1: Calendar, Lesson 3, p. 50

When morning comes,
We start our day.
Breakfast time is on the way.
By afternoon,
We can have fun.
Reading, singing, run, run, run.
And at night, we go to sleep.
We don't make a sound, not a peep.

UNIT 1: Weather, Lesson 1, p. 52

When it's warm and sunny, I like to play
Outside in the sun all day.
But when it's cold, and it starts to freeze,
Let me in! Please, please, please!

Rain is wet and snow is cold.
Clouds are high and fog is low.
But my favorite time to see my friends
Is when it's warm and sun never ends.

UNIT 1: Weather, Lesson 2, p. 54

There are four seasons every year:
Spring, Summer, Fall, Winter.
Spring is when a flower grows.
In summertime the hot sun shows.
Leaves come down in the fall.
Winter is the coldest of all.

UNIT 1: Weather, Lesson 3, p. 56

It is dark.
It is night.

The moon and stars
Shine so bright.

The sun's so bright
In the sky each day.
It shines down on Earth
and lights our way.

UNIT 2: My Body, Lesson 1, p. 60

What do you look like? What do you see?
I have a face and eyes right here.
What do you look like? What do you see?
This is my nose and these are my ears.

What do you look like? What do you see?
I have fingers I can wiggle around,
And legs and feet that hit the ground.

UNIT 2: My Body, Lesson 2, p. 62

Staying healthy, staying clean.
This is what we call hygiene.
I... brush my hair, brush my hair.
I... brush my teeth, brush my teeth.
I... wash my hands, wash my hands.
I... take a shower, I stay clean.
I stay healthy, I stay clean.

UNIT 2: My Body, Lesson 3, p. 64

I see, I feel, I hear, I taste, I smell
Things around me very well.
I see with my eyes.
I feel with my hands.
The bumpiest rocks and the softest of sands
I taste with my mouth.
I hear with my ears.
I smell with my nose.
The sweet smell of a rose.

UNIT 2: Clothing, Lesson 1, p. 66

What do you like to wear?
This is a shirt
I like to wear shirts.
These are jeans.
I don't like to wear jeans.
These are shorts.
I like to wear shorts.
I like to wear shirts and shorts!

UNIT 2: Clothing, Lesson 2, p. 68

Winter, spring, summer, and fall.
There's special clothing for them all.
Winter's cold, wear a coat.
Spring is warm, wear a tee.
Summer is hot, wear a bathing suit.
Fall can be rainy:
You'll need your boots.

UNIT 2: Clothing, Lesson 3, p. 70

Going swimming?
What to wear?
Wear your bathing suit.

Going hiking?
What to wear?
Wear a t-shirt and some boots.

UNIT 2: Feelings, Lesson 1, p. 72

Am I angry? Am I glad?
Am I afraid, or am I sad?
Look at my face and you can see
How am I feeling? Just look at me.

UNIT 2: Feelings, Lesson 2, p. 74

When I'm with my friends,
We laugh and play
And eat together every day.
We work together all the time.
I am his friend and he's mine.

UNIT 2: Feelings, Lesson 3, p. 76

How do we help a friend?
How do we help a friend?
By listening, talking, sharing, and caring.
That's how we help a friend.
That's how we help a friend.

UNIT 2: My Family, Lesson 1, p. 78

That is his daughter. That is his mother.
Sister, father, son, and brother.
Grandfather and grandmother, too.
Family for me, family for you!

UNIT 2: My Family, Lesson 2, p. 80

She has dark hair and brown eyes.
He has light hair. What a surprise!
I am taller than my mother.
Sister is shorter than her brother.
I have blue eyes. So do you.
We both have short hair. Yup, it's true!

UNIT 2: My Family, Lesson 3, p. 82

We are with family.
We are with family.
What do we do?
What do we do?
We eat out together,
We visit together.
That's what we do.
That's what we do.

UNIT 2: My Home, Lesson 1, p. 84

We live in different places,
We live in different spaces.
Some of us live in apartment buildings
With other people next door.
Some of us live in mobile homes
Which only have one floor.
And some of us live in houses
With two, three rooms or more.

UNIT 2: My Home, Lesson 2, p. 86

Where do we put the couch?
In the living room!
Where do we put the bed?
In the bedroom!
Where do we put the sink?
In the kitchen!
Couch, bed, and sink
We sit, we sleep, and take water to drink!

UNIT 2: My Home, Lesson 3, p. 88

What is the father doing?
Cook, cook, cook.
What is the mother doing?
Clean, clean, clean.
What is the daughter doing?
Sort, sort, sort.
What is the son doing?
Dust, dust, dust.

UNIT 3: My Community, Lesson 1, p. 92

Where's the school?
Help me look!
Next to a bank?
Or across from the park?

Where's the school?
Help me look!
Is it there, next to you?
It's down the street. I see it too!

UNIT 3: My Community, Lesson 2, p. 94

Who works in a hospital?
I'm a nurse.
I sure do, I sure do!

Who works on a bus?
I'm a bus driver.
I sure do, I sure do!

Who carries mail?
I'm a mail carrier.
I sure do, I sure do!

UNIT 3: My Community, Lesson 3, p. 96

What are you doing?
What are you doing?
I'm recycling, recycling.

What are you doing?
What are you doing?
I'm planting flowers, planting flowers.

We can help, we can help. Every day, in every way.

UNIT 3: Technology, Lesson 1, p. 98

Smartphone, smartphone.
You have one, too?
I use a smartphone the whole day through.
Tablet, tablet.
You have one, too?
I use a tablet the whole day through.

UNIT 3: Technology, Lesson 2, p. 100

I take a picture:
Snap, snap, snap.
I send a text:
Chat, chat, chat.
I check my phone:
Swipe, swipe, swipe.
I email mom:
Type, type, type.

UNIT 3: Technology, Lesson 3, p. 102

I need mom.
I need to call.
I need a ride to the mall.

I need information.
I need to look
On the Internet to find a book.

UNIT 3: Transportation, Lesson 1, p. 104

Walk signs, stop signs,
Street signs all around!
Crosswalk, bus stop,
Street signs all around!

Stop or walk?
Come or go?
See the signs
Now you know.

UNIT 3: Transportation, Lesson 2, p. 106

How do we get from here to there?
A car can take us anywhere!
We take a bus around the town.
Going uptown, going down.
To get from Park Street over to Main,
We pay our fare and take the train.

UNIT 3: Transportation, Lesson 3, p. 108

Make a left turn, make a right.
The school is almost right in sight.
Look for the parks, look for the malls,
The school is right between them all!
Cross the street, one block away.
There's the mall. You found the way!

UNIT 3: Food and Meals, Lesson 1, p. 110

I'm hungry, I'm hungry.
Let's order! Let's eat!
I'd like to order something sweet!
Or maybe something salty, too.
A sandwich? A drink? Or thick, rich soup?
The menu will tell us what is there
To crunch or munch or offer to share.

UNIT 3: Food and Meals, Lesson 2, p. 112

Oodles of noodles,
Eggs and cheese,
Carrots, carrots.
I'd like more please.

Yogurt, yogurt,
Rice and peas,
Cereal, cereal.
I'd like more please.

UNIT 3: Food and Meals, Lesson 3, p. 114

Lunch at school, lunch at school.
What are you having?
For lunch at school?

Are you having soup?
I'm having some carrots.
He's having some soup.

Are you having fruit?
I'm having some noodles.
He's having some fruit.

UNIT 3: Shopping, Lesson 1, p. 116

At the store, at the store.
It's time to shop at the grocery store.
I need some bread. Where do I go?
Go to the bakery.
Go, go, go.
I need some apples. Where do I go?
Go to produce.
Go, go, go.

UNIT 3: Shopping, Lesson 2, p. 118

I have a dollar, You have a dime,
What can we buy? We have no time!
Let's get three apples!
We can buy three apples.
I have a quarter, You have a nickel.
What can we buy? What are you thinking?
Let's get one orange!
Or milk for drinking.

UNIT 3: Shopping, Lesson 3, p. 120

At the grocery store, we can
Make a list and have a plan
Of what to buy, what we need.
We need a list, of who we feed.
At the grocery store, we can
Push a cart, with our hand.
We pick up fruit and veggies, too.
It's a good day at the store for you!

UNIT 4: Measurement, Lesson 1, p. 124

If something's long,
We measure the length
With a ruler, tape measure, or yard stick.

If something's heavy
We measure the weight.
A scale is the tool that we pick!

UNIT 4: Measurement, Lesson 2, p. 126

This leaf, that leaf, are they the same?
Let's get a ruler and measure again.

This leaf is taller, that leaf is smaller.

This leaf is yellow, that leaf is red.

Let's look for differences instead!

UNIT 4: Measurement, Lesson 3, p. 128

Is the book longer than the leaf?
Let's measure, inch by inch.
The book is longer, the leaf is shorter.
See?
That was a cinch.

UNIT 4: Animals, Lesson 1, p. 130

Shhh! Watch closely and you'll see
Wild animals and insects roaming free:
There's a bear running: crash, crash, crash.
There's a raccoon crawling: dash, dash, dash.
There's a squirrel jumping: Scratch, scratch, scratch.
And there's a bee flying: buzzzzzzzzzz!

UNIT 4: Animals, Lesson 2, p. 132

Do you have a pet to play with? Some of us do!
Some have a bird that tweets and sings, too.
Some have a dog that likes to catch.
Some have a cat that likes to scratch.
Some have a fish that swims all day.
Some have a hamster that likes to play.
Some have a rabbit that eats for fun.
Some have a turtle that sits in the sun.

UNIT 4: Animals, Lesson 3, p. 134

On the farm, the animals run around,
Eating and jumping up and down.
The chickens cluck, run, and fly.
The cows watch as they go by.
The sheep baa and eat the grass,
And the goats jump as they all pass.

UNIT 4: Growth and Change, Lesson 1, p. 136

First, there is an egg, very small.
Then, a caterpillar that will crawl.
Next, it turns into a pupa and hides.
Finally it turns into a butterfly and flies.

UNIT 4: Growth and Change, Lesson 2, p. 138

First, you plant a seed in the ground
And water until a seedling is found.
Then a budding plant will start to grow.
Finally, a flower will start to show.

UNIT 4: Growth and Change, Lesson 3, p. 140

First you were a baby and cried a lot.
Now you are a child, you like to play.
Next you'll be a teenager, you'll learn a lot.
Then you'll be an adult who works all day.
At every stage--who could guess?
That every stage of life is best!

UNIT 4: United States, Lesson 1, p. 142

Welcome to the United States,
Where your future life awaits.
From the Rocky Mountains, big and bold
To the Appalachians where it's
sometimes cold,
From South to North and East to West,
This is America at its best.
Northwest is here, Southwest is near
Midwest is there, and Northeast over there.

UNIT 4: United States, Lesson 2, p. 144

So many national landmarks.
Which ones do you want to see?
The Statue of Liberty
The Grand Canyon
Or the White House for me!
Mount Rushmore
The Golden Gate Bridge
Or maybe Yosemite!

UNIT 4: United States, Lesson 3, p. 146

I want to live somewhere
Where I can see the water in motion:
Near a river, a lake, or the ocean.

I want to live somewhere
Where there's no one else but me:
Near a mountain, a farm, or a rolling prairie.

UNIT 4: My World, Lesson 1, p. 148

Where are you from?
A big city or a small town?
Did you see pandas all around?
Tell us, tell us, what did you eat?
Was it crunchy? Was it sweet?

UNIT 4: My World, Lesson 2, p. 150

What animals do you see?
Do you see pandas?
I don't see pandas.
Do you see camels?
I don't see camels.
What animals do you see?
I see starfish. I live by the sea.

UNIT 4: My World, Lesson 3, p. 152

Where are you from?
How do you pay?
In the United States we use dollars.
That's how we pay!
Where are you from?
What do you play?
In the United States we play baseball.
That's what we play!

ANSWER KEY

START SMART: What's Your Name?, Lesson 1

Letters of the Alphabet

Use Newcomer Card, page 1

Name: ______

A. Write the missing letters of the alphabet.

A B C D E F G H I
J K L M N O P Q R
S T U V W X Y Z

A B C D E F G H I
J K L M N O P Q R
S T U V W X Y Z

B. List the letters you wrote. Read them to a partner.

Answers will vary.

START SMART: What's Your Name?, Lesson 2

Uppercase and Lowercase

Use Newcomer Card, page 1

Name: ______

A. Match the uppercase letter to its lowercase letter.

B	d
P	a
D	m
A	b
M	p

B. Write the pairs of letters you matched.

Bb, Pp, Dd, Aa, Mm

START SMART: What's Your Name?, Lesson 3

Spelling My Name

Use Newcomer Card, page 1

Name: ______

Match the names from the box to the scrambled letters. Write the name on the line.

Kai Ted Roberto Mina Aisha

1. i k a My name is Kai.
2. o r b t e r o My name is Roberto.
3. a a s h i My name is Aisha.
4. e d t My name is Ted.
5. a m n i My name is Mina.

START SMART: Greetings, Lesson 1

Hello and Goodbye

Use Newcomer Card, page 2

Name: ______

Write other words in the chart that mean "hello" and "goodbye." Tell a partner when we use "hi" and when we use "hello."

hello	goodbye
hi	bye
good morning	good night

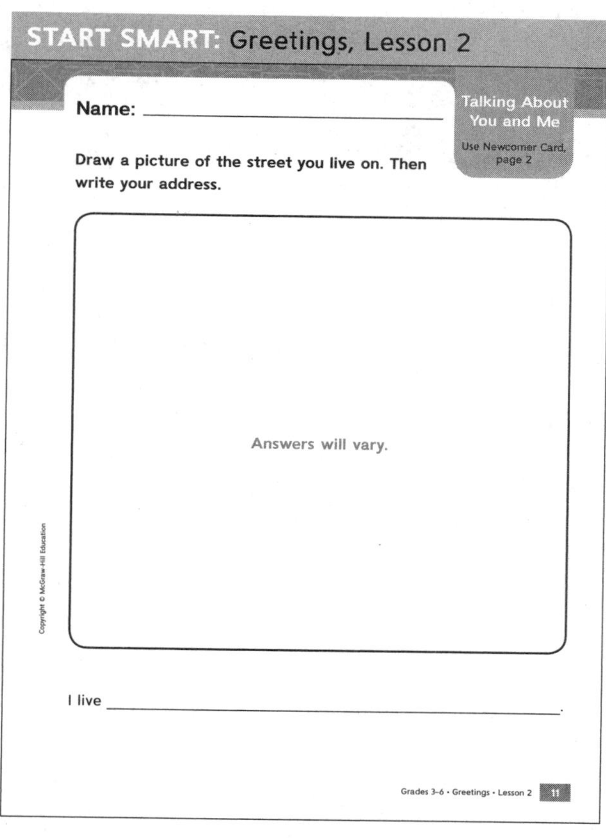

START SMART: Greetings, Lesson 2

Name: ______________________

Talking About You and Me

Use Newcomer Card, page 2

Draw a picture of the street you live on. Then write your address.

Answers will vary.

I live ______________________.

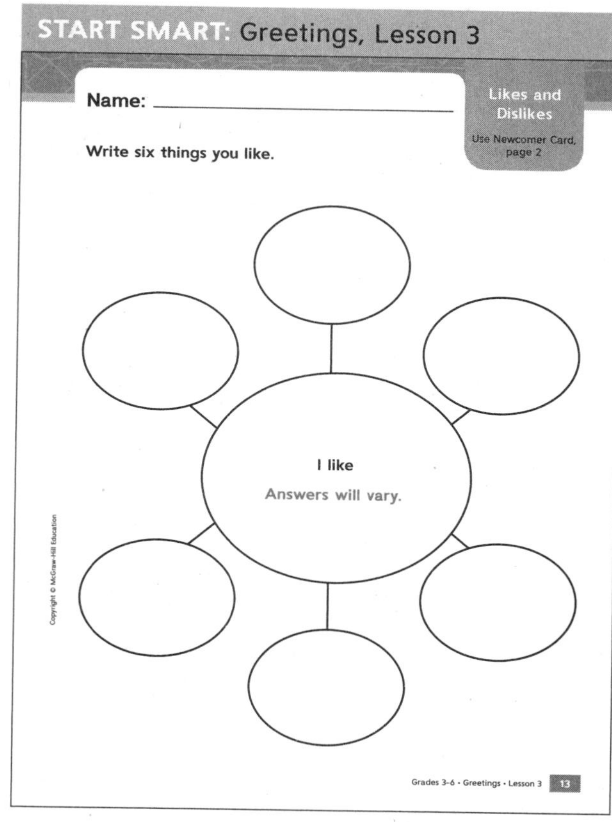

START SMART: Greetings, Lesson 3

Name: ______________________

Likes and Dislikes

Use Newcomer Card, page 2

Write six things you like.

I like

Answers will vary.

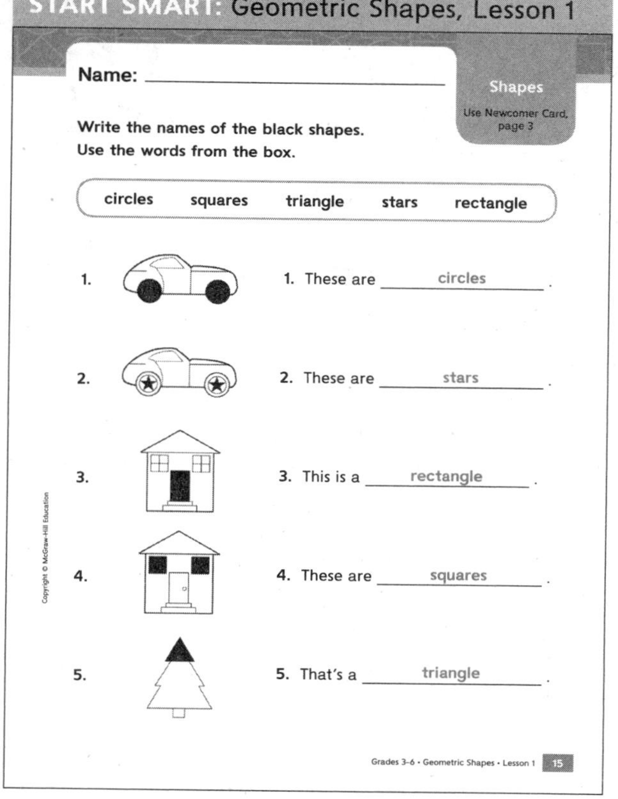

START SMART: Geometric Shapes, Lesson 1

Name: ______________________

Shapes

Use Newcomer Card, page 3

Write the names of the black shapes. Use the words from the box.

circles	squares	triangle	stars	rectangle

1. These are circles.
2. These are stars.
3. This is a rectangle.
4. These are squares.
5. That's a triangle.

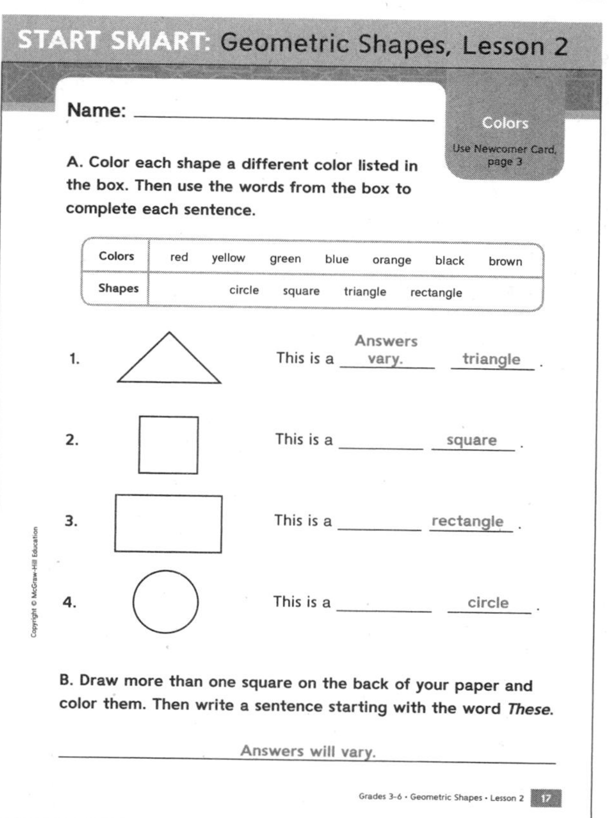

START SMART: Geometric Shapes, Lesson 2

Name: ______________________

Colors

Use Newcomer Card, page 3

A. Color each shape a different color listed in the box. Then use the words from the box to complete each sentence.

Colors	red	yellow	green	blue	orange	black	brown
Shapes	circle	square	triangle	rectangle			

1. This is a Answers vary. triangle.
2. This is a ________ square.
3. This is a ________ rectangle.
4. This is a ________ circle.

B. Draw more than one square on the back of your paper and color them. Then write a sentence starting with the word *These*.

Answers will vary.

ANSWER KEY

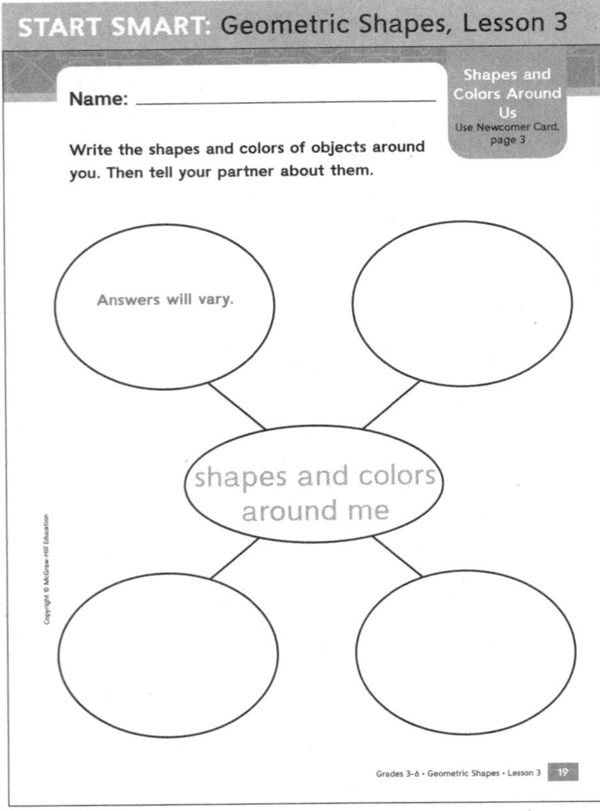

START SMART: Geometric Shapes, Lesson 3

Shapes and Colors Around Us
Use Newcomer Card, page 3

Name: ____________________

Write the shapes and colors of objects around you. Then tell your partner about them.

START SMART: Numbers, Lesson 1

Numbers 1–100
Use Newcomer Card, Page 4

Name: ____________________

A. Read each number in the first box. Find the numbers and circle them in the second box.

1 62 99 50 25 18

45	(1)	16
28	82	(25)
(50)	11	(99)
72	4	51
14	43	8
65	95	(62)
(18)	37	28
21	81	20
30	96	15

B. Choose a number. Write a sentence that names the number.

Answers will vary.

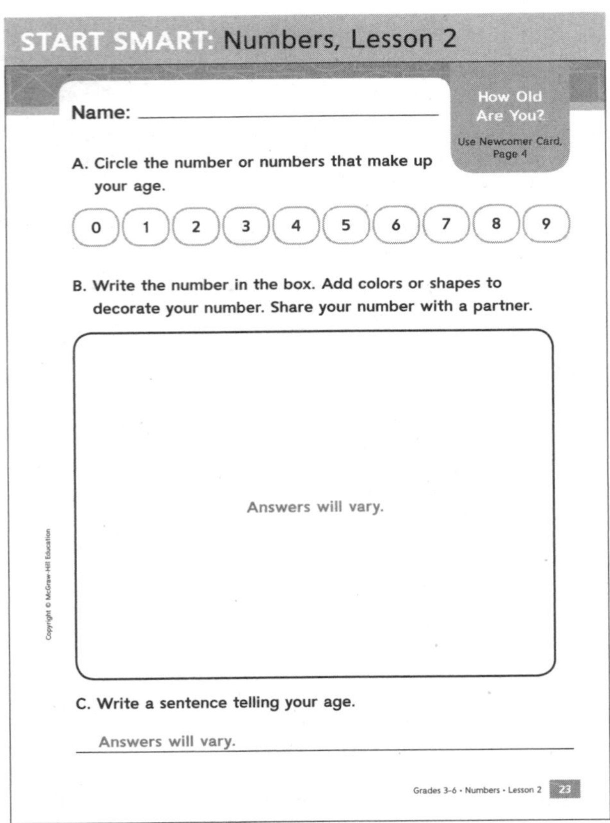

START SMART: Numbers, Lesson 2

How Old Are You?
Use Newcomer Card, Page 4

Name: ____________________

A. Circle the number or numbers that make up your age.

0 1 2 3 4 5 6 7 8 9

B. Write the number in the box. Add colors or shapes to decorate your number. Share your number with a partner.

Answers will vary.

C. Write a sentence telling your age.

Answers will vary.

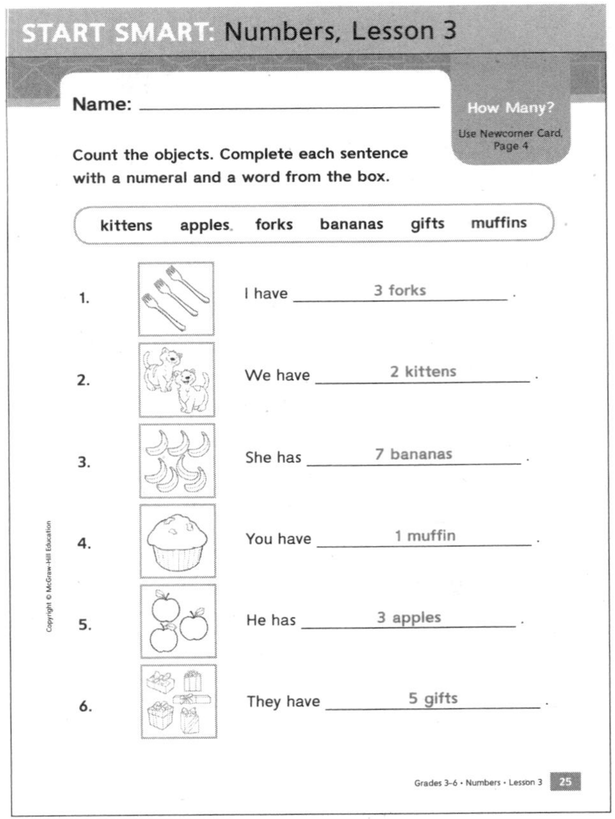

START SMART: Numbers, Lesson 3

How Many?
Use Newcomer Card, Page 4

Name: ____________________

Count the objects. Complete each sentence with a numeral and a word from the box.

kittens apples forks bananas gifts muffins

1. I have 3 forks.
2. We have 2 kittens.
3. She has 7 bananas.
4. You have 1 muffin.
5. He has 3 apples.
6. They have 5 gifts.

UNIT 1: In the Classroom, Lesson 1

Name: ______________________

Classroom Objects

Use Newcomer Card, page 5

A. Match each sentence to the correct picture.

1. He has a backpack. — b.
2. They have notebooks and pens. — a.
3. He has a calculator. — c.
4. She has pens and pencils. — d.

B. Write a sentence about the classroom objects you have.

Answers will vary.

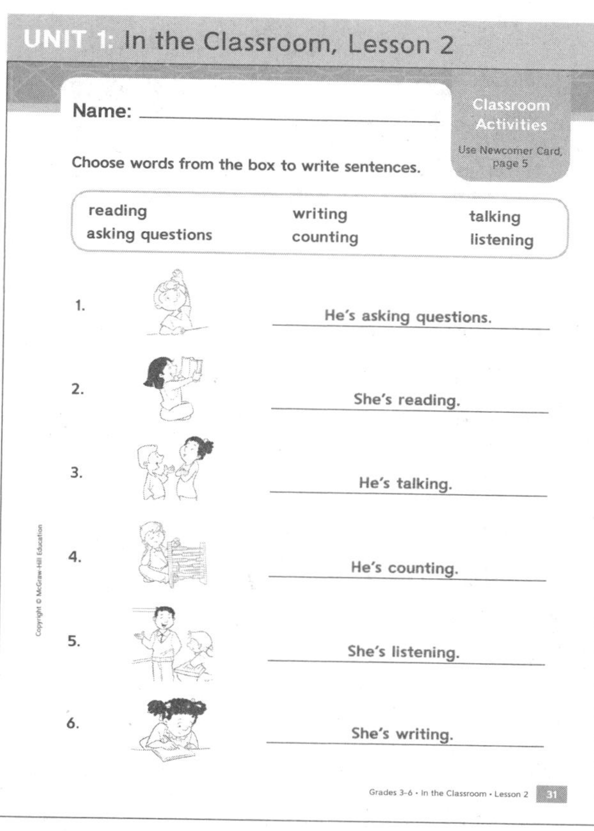

UNIT 1: In the Classroom, Lesson 2

Name: ______________________

Classroom Activities

Use Newcomer Card, page 5

Choose words from the box to write sentences.

reading	writing	talking
asking questions	counting	listening

1. He's asking questions.
2. She's reading.
3. He's talking.
4. He's counting.
5. She's listening.
6. She's writing.

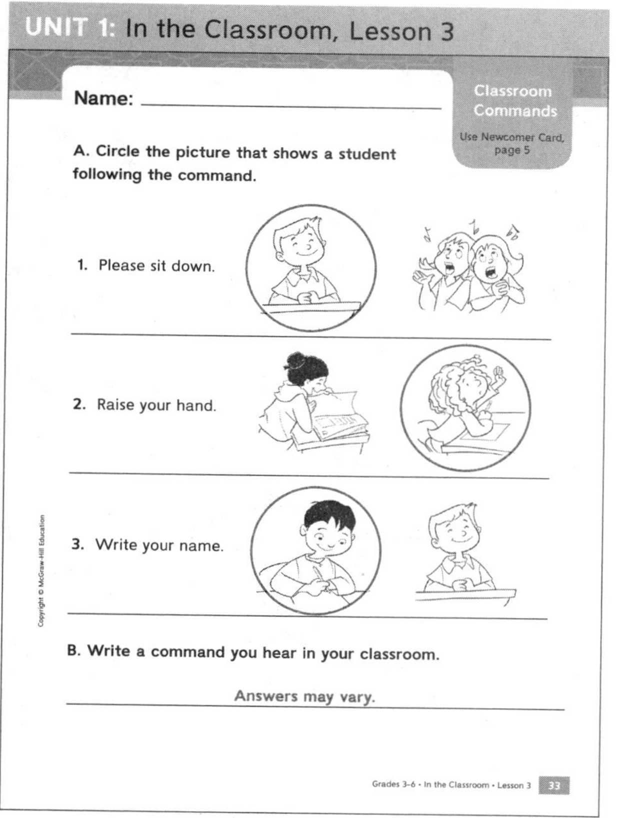

UNIT 1: In the Classroom, Lesson 3

Name: ______________________

Classroom Commands

Use Newcomer Card, page 5

A. Circle the picture that shows a student following the command.

1. Please sit down.
2. Raise your hand.
3. Write your name.

B. Write a command you hear in your classroom.

Answers may vary.

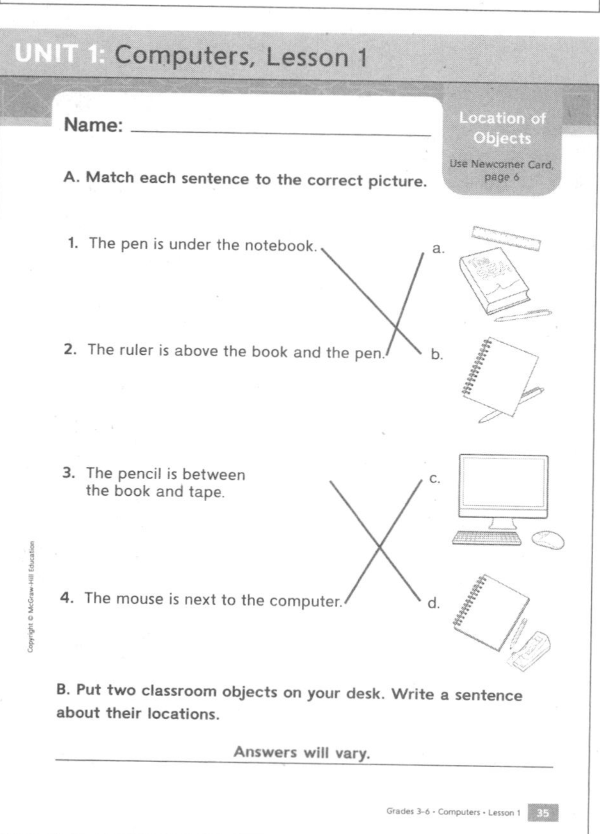

UNIT 1: Computers, Lesson 1

Name: ______________________

Location of Objects

Use Newcomer Card, page 6

A. Match each sentence to the correct picture.

1. The pen is under the notebook. — b.
2. The ruler is above the book and the pen. — a.
3. The pencil is between the book and tape. — d.
4. The mouse is next to the computer. — c.

B. Put two classroom objects on your desk. Write a sentence about their locations.

Answers will vary.

ANSWER KEY

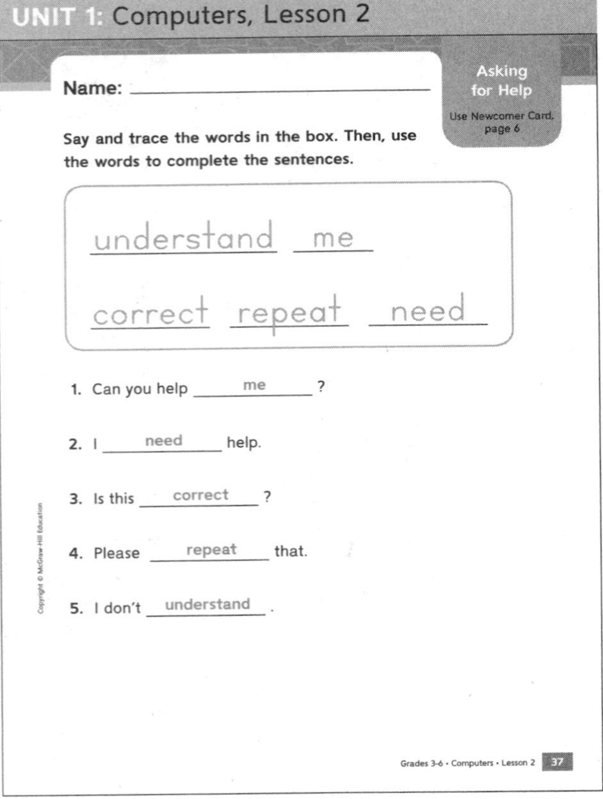
UNIT 1: Computers, Lesson 2
Name:
Asking for Help
Use Newcomer Card, page 6
Say and trace the words in the box. Then, use the words to complete the sentences.
understand me
correct repeat need
1. Can you help me ?
2. I need help.
3. Is this correct ?
4. Please repeat that.
5. I don't understand .
Grades 3-6 • Computers • Lesson 2 37

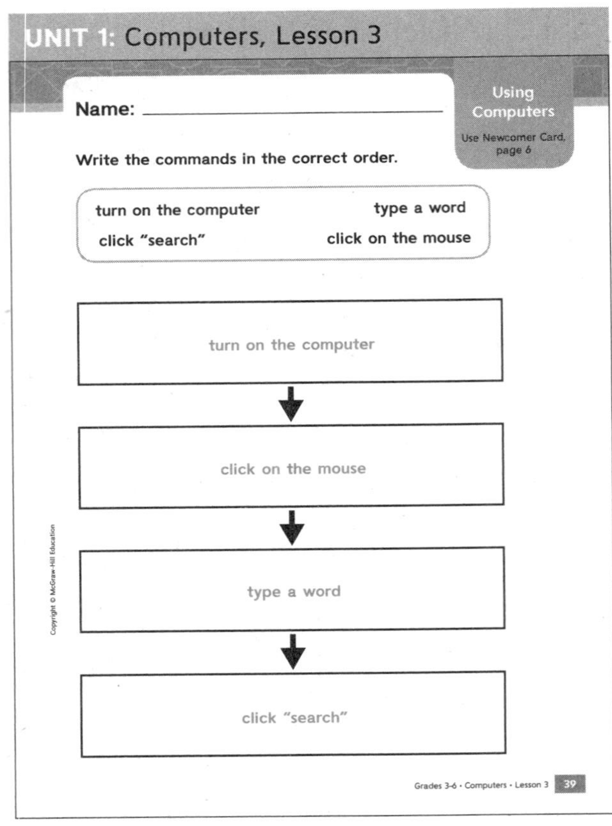
UNIT 1: Computers, Lesson 3
Name:
Using Computers
Use Newcomer Card, page 6
Write the commands in the correct order.
turn on the computer
type a word
click "search"
click on the mouse
turn on the computer
click on the mouse
type a word
click "search"
Grades 3-6 • Computers • Lesson 3 39

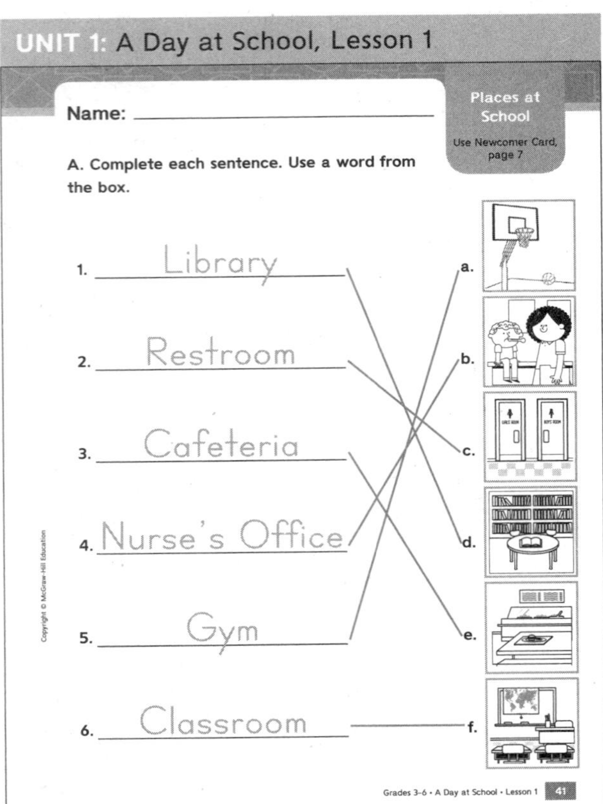
UNIT 1: A Day at School, Lesson 1
Name:
Places at School
Use Newcomer Card, page 7
A. Complete each sentence. Use a word from the box.
1. Library
2. Restroom
3. Cafeteria
4. Nurse's Office
5. Gym
6. Classroom
a.
b.
c.
d.
e.
f.
Grades 3-6 • A Day at School • Lesson 1 41

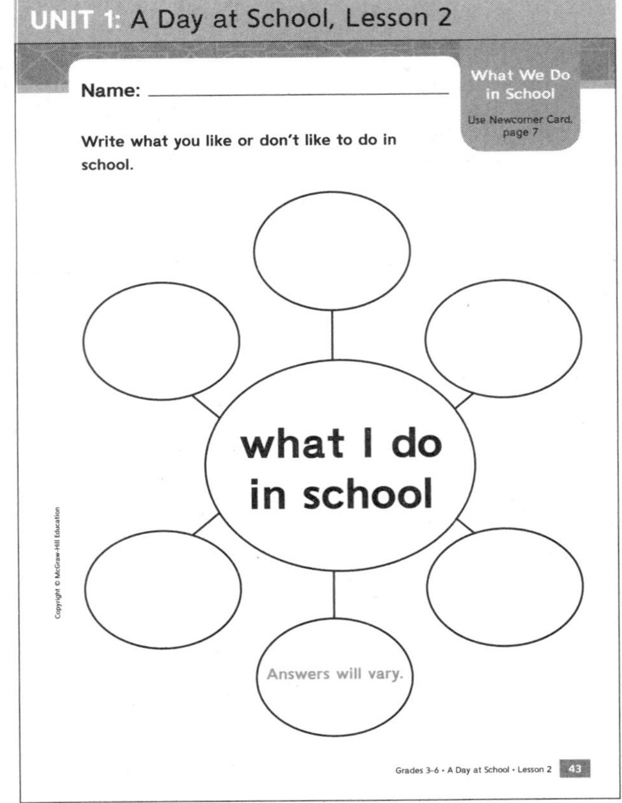
UNIT 1: A Day at School, Lesson 2
Name:
What We Do in School
Use Newcomer Card, page 7
Write what you like or don't like to do in school.
what I do in school
Answers will vary.
Grades 3-6 • A Day at School • Lesson 2 43

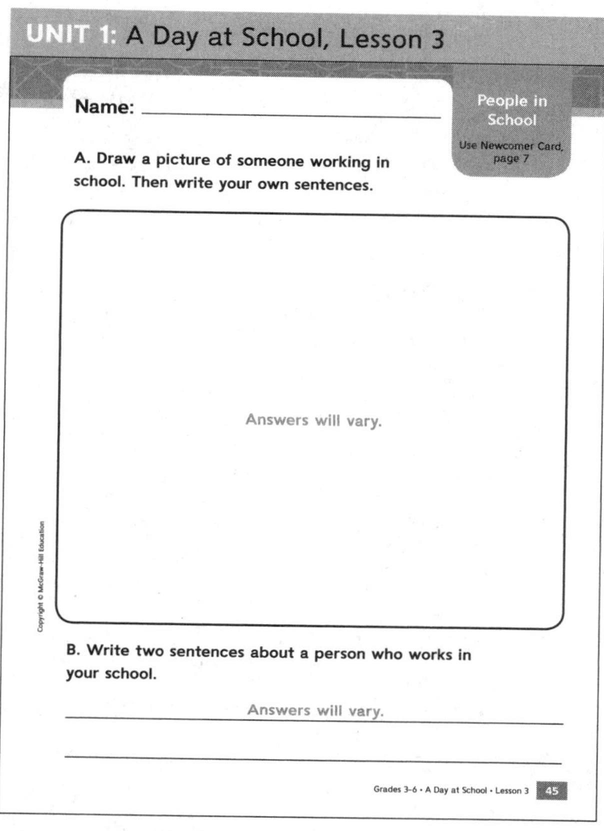

UNIT 1: A Day at School, Lesson 3

People in School
Use Newcomer Card, page 7

Name: ______________________

A. Draw a picture of someone working in school. Then write your own sentences.

Answers will vary.

B. Write two sentences about a person who works in your school.

Answers will vary.

UNIT 1: Calendar, Lesson 1

Days and Months
Use Newcomer Card, page 8

Name: ______________________

Say and trace the days. Then complete the sentences with the correct day.

Sunday Monday Tuesday
Wednesday Thursday
Friday Saturday

1. Today is Answers vary.
2. Yesterday was Answers vary.
3. Tomorrow is Answers vary.
4. The day after tomorrow is Answers vary.

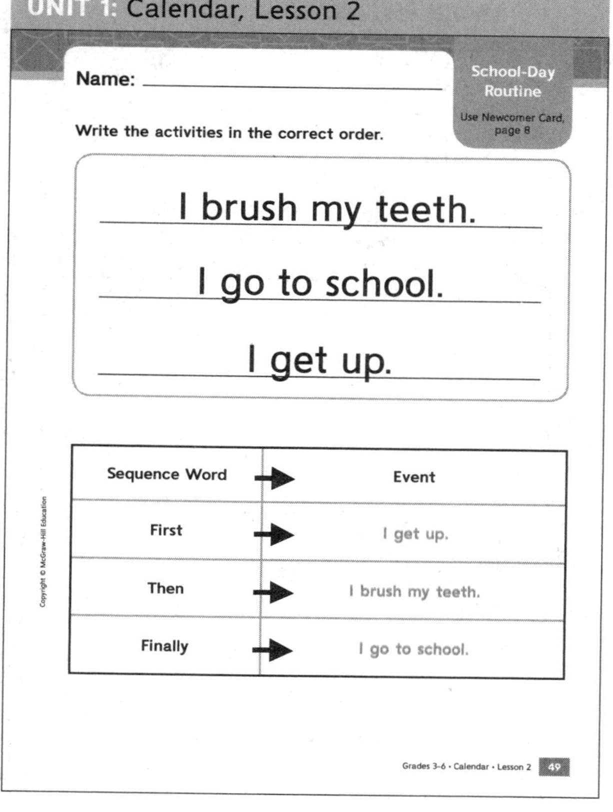

UNIT 1: Calendar, Lesson 2

School-Day Routine
Use Newcomer Card, page 8

Name: ______________________

Write the activities in the correct order.

I brush my teeth.
I go to school.
I get up.

Sequence Word	Event
First →	I get up.
Then →	I brush my teeth.
Finally →	I go to school.

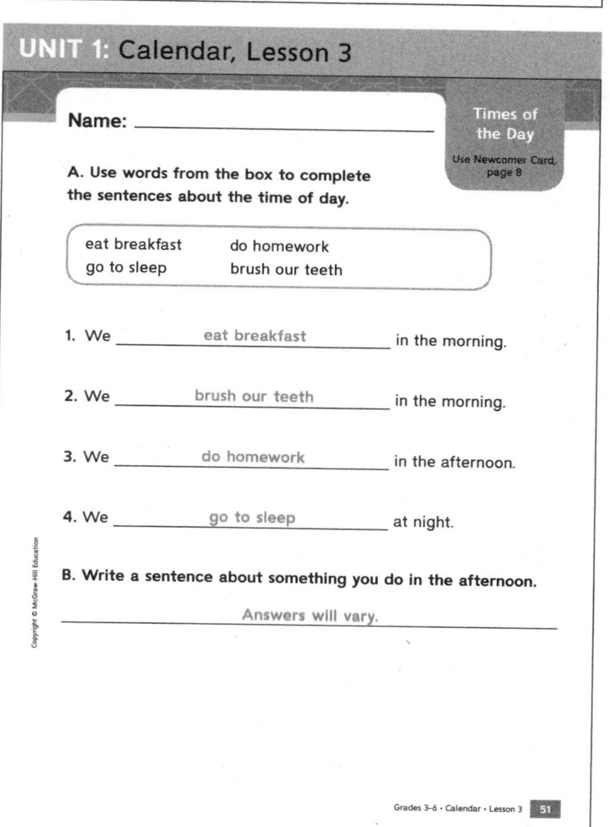

UNIT 1: Calendar, Lesson 3

Times of the Day
Use Newcomer Card, page 8

Name: ______________________

A. Use words from the box to complete the sentences about the time of day.

eat breakfast	do homework
go to sleep	brush our teeth

1. We eat breakfast in the morning.
2. We brush our teeth in the morning.
3. We do homework in the afternoon.
4. We go to sleep at night.

B. Write a sentence about something you do in the afternoon.

Answers will vary.

ANSWER KEY

UNIT 1: Weather, Lesson 1

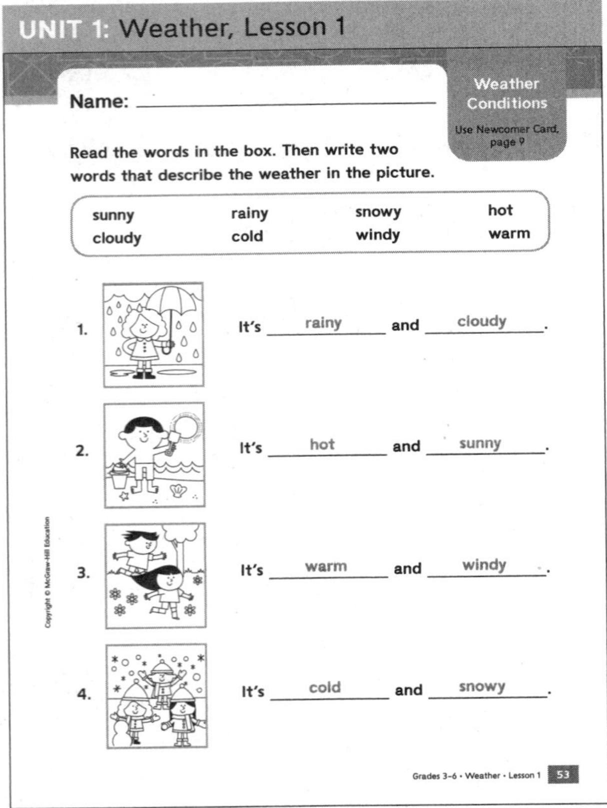

Weather Conditions

Use Newcomer Card, page 9

Name: ______________

Read the words in the box. Then write two words that describe the weather in the picture.

sunny	rainy	snowy	hot
cloudy	cold	windy	warm

1. It's rainy and cloudy.
2. It's hot and sunny.
3. It's warm and windy.
4. It's cold and snowy.

Copyright © McGraw-Hill Education

Grades 3–6 • Weather • Lesson 1 53

UNIT 1: Weather, Lesson 2

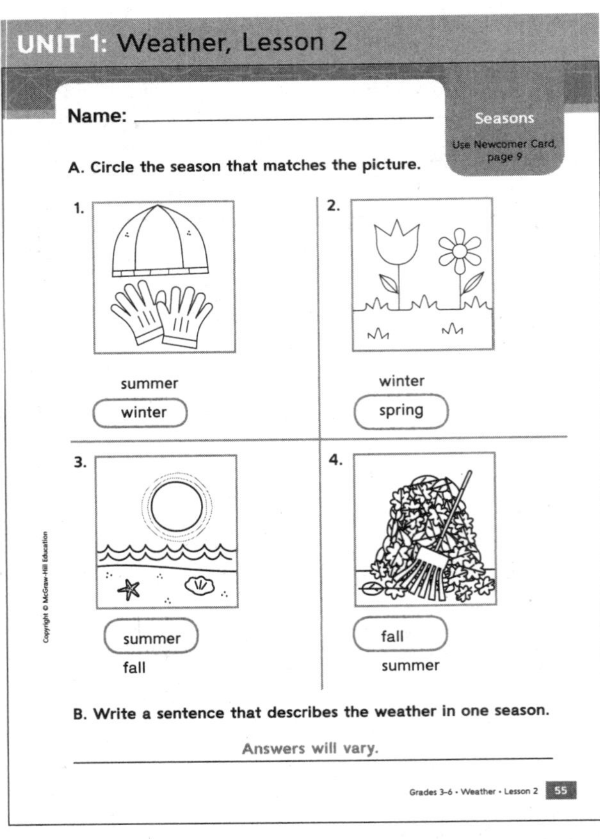

Seasons

Use Newcomer Card, page 9

Name: ______________

A. Circle the season that matches the picture.

1. summer / (winter)
2. winter / (spring)
3. (summer) / fall
4. (fall) / summer

B. Write a sentence that describes the weather in one season.

Answers will vary.

Copyright © McGraw-Hill Education

Grades 3–6 • Weather • Lesson 2 55

UNIT 1: Weather, Lesson 3

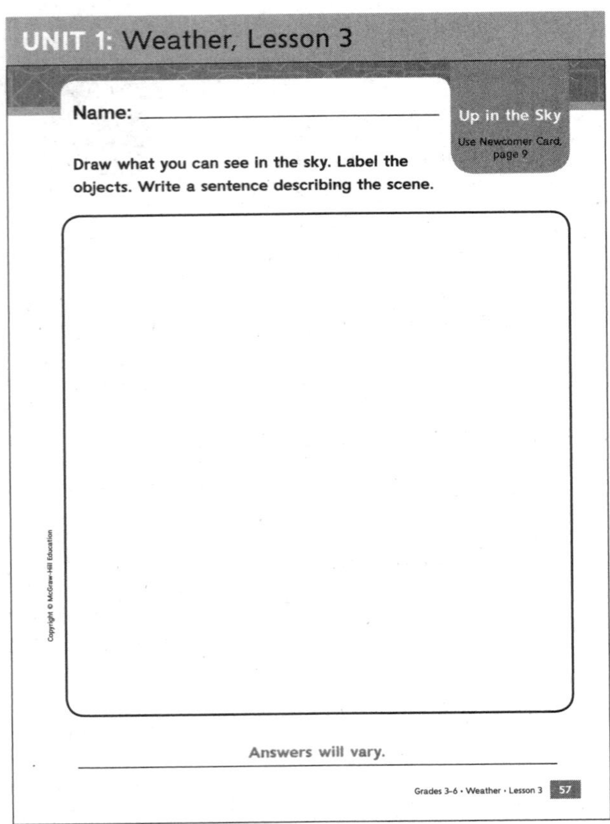

Up in the Sky

Use Newcomer Card, page 9

Name: ______________

Draw what you can see in the sky. Label the objects. Write a sentence describing the scene.

Answers will vary.

Copyright © McGraw-Hill Education

Grades 3–6 • Weather • Lesson 3 57

UNIT 2: My Body, Lesson 1

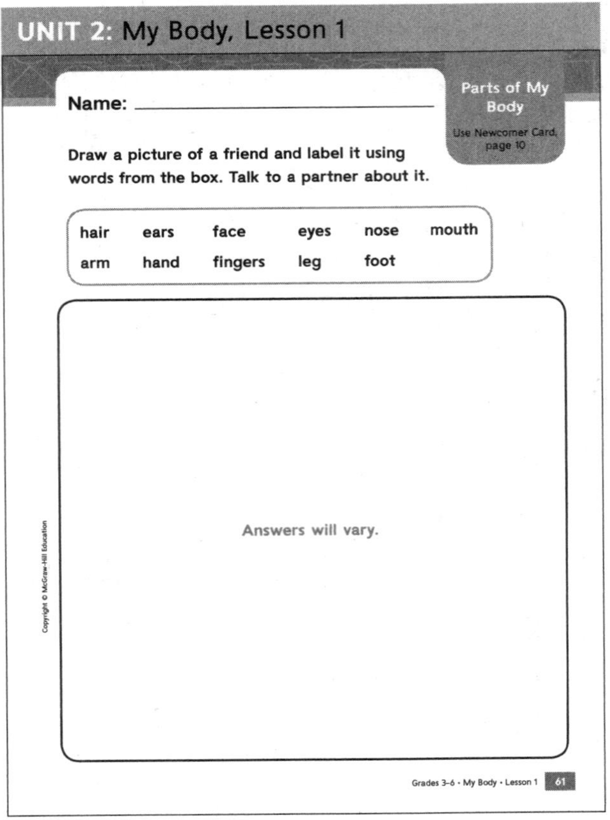

Parts of My Body

Use Newcomer Card, page 10

Name: ______________

Draw a picture of a friend and label it using words from the box. Talk to a partner about it.

hair	ears	face	eyes	nose	mouth
arm	hand	fingers	leg	foot	

Answers will vary.

Copyright © McGraw-Hill Education

Grades 3–6 • My Body • Lesson 1 61

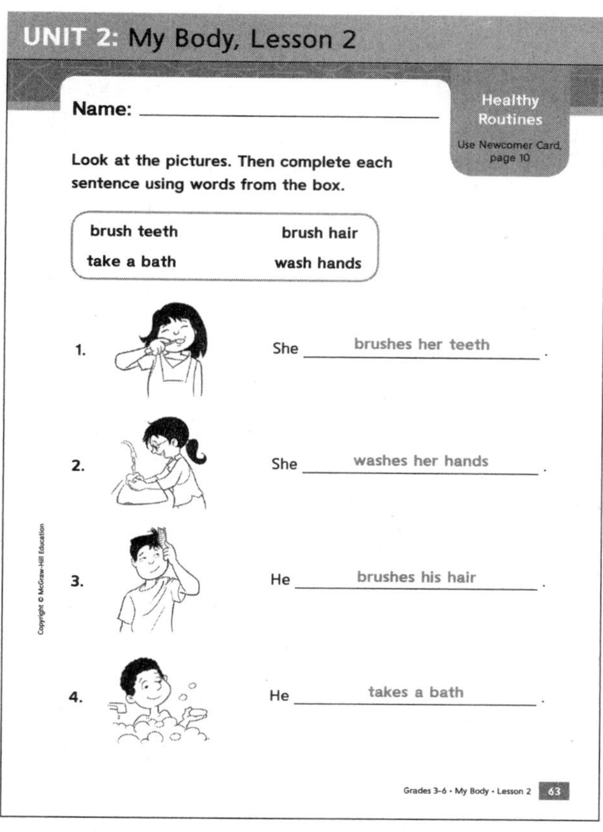
UNIT 2: My Body, Lesson 2

Healthy Routines
Use Newcomer Card, page 10

Name: ____________________

Look at the pictures. Then complete each sentence using words from the box.

brush teeth	brush hair
take a bath	wash hands

1. She brushes her teeth.
2. She washes her hands.
3. He brushes his hair.
4. He takes a bath.

Copyright © McGraw-Hill Education

Grades 3–6 • My Body • Lesson 2 63

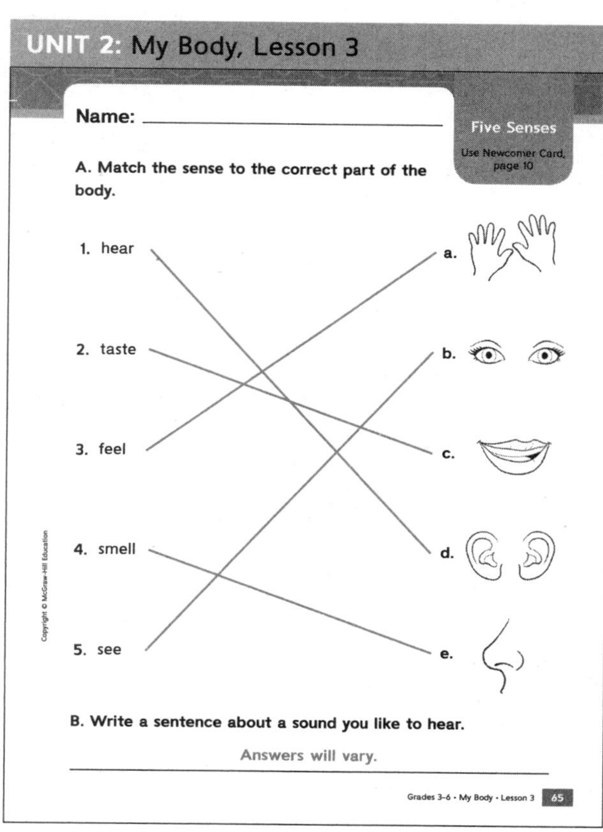
UNIT 2: My Body, Lesson 3

Five Senses
Use Newcomer Card, page 10

Name: ____________________

A. Match the sense to the correct part of the body.

1. hear — d.
2. taste — c.
3. feel — a.
4. smell — e.
5. see — b.

B. Write a sentence about a sound you like to hear.

Answers will vary.

Copyright © McGraw-Hill Education

Grades 3–6 • My Body • Lesson 3 65

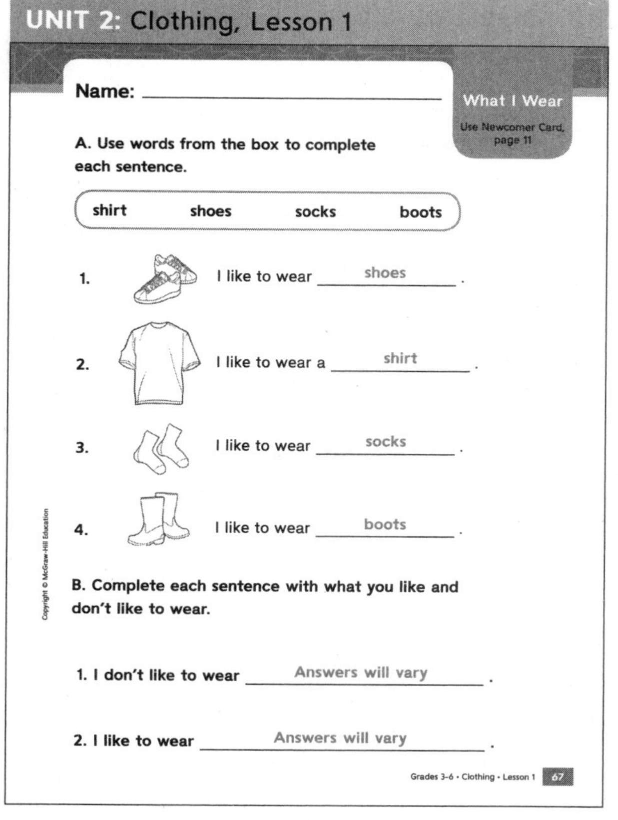
UNIT 2: Clothing, Lesson 1

What I Wear
Use Newcomer Card, page 11

Name: ____________________

A. Use words from the box to complete each sentence.

shirt	shoes	socks	boots

1. I like to wear shoes.
2. I like to wear a shirt.
3. I like to wear socks.
4. I like to wear boots.

B. Complete each sentence with what you like and don't like to wear.

1. I don't like to wear Answers will vary.
2. I like to wear Answers will vary.

Copyright © McGraw-Hill Education

Grades 3–6 • Clothing • Lesson 1 67

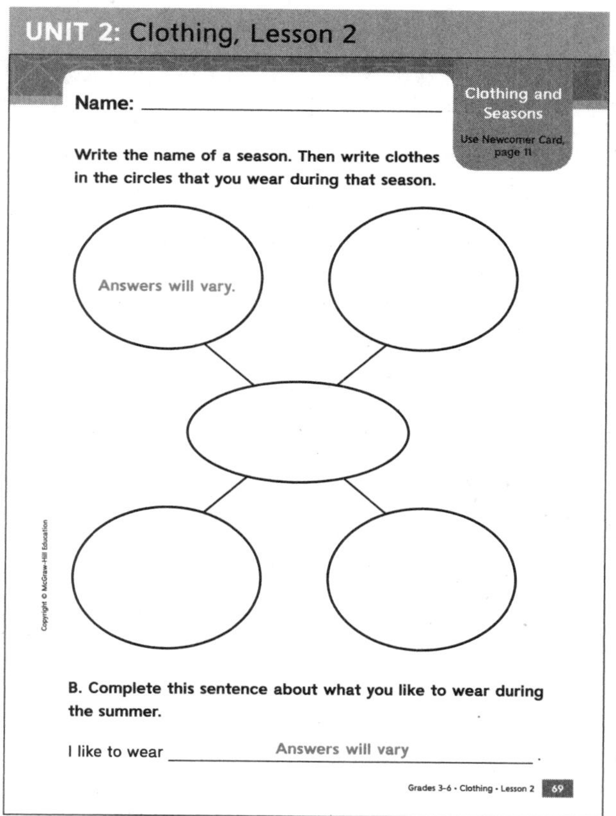
UNIT 2: Clothing, Lesson 2

Clothing and Seasons
Use Newcomer Card, page 11

Name: ____________________

Write the name of a season. Then write clothes in the circles that you wear during that season.

Answers will vary.

B. Complete this sentence about what you like to wear during the summer.

I like to wear Answers will vary.

Copyright © McGraw-Hill Education

Grades 3–6 • Clothing • Lesson 2 69

ANSWER KEY

UNIT 2: Clothing, Lesson 3

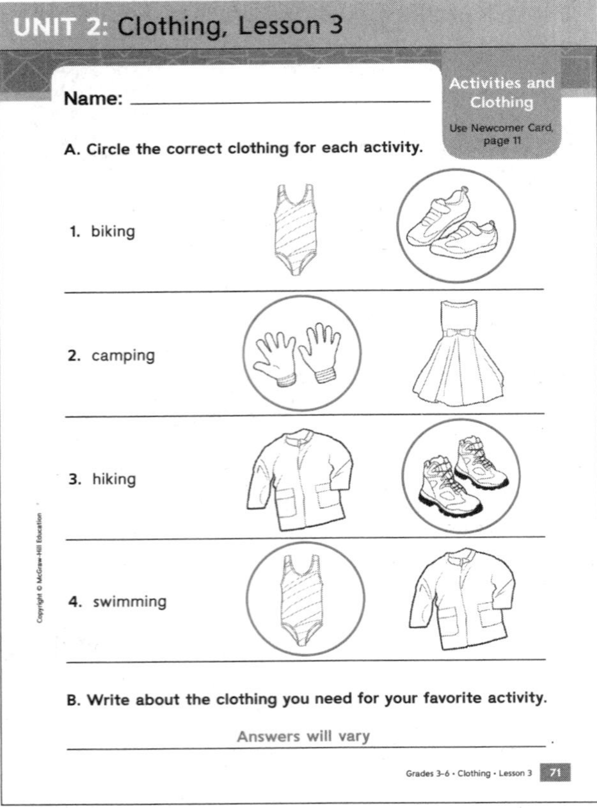

Name: ______

Activities and Clothing

Use Newcomer Card, page 11

A. Circle the correct clothing for each activity.

1. biking
2. camping
3. hiking
4. swimming

B. Write about the clothing you need for your favorite activity.

Answers will vary.

UNIT 2: Feelings, Lesson 1

Name: ______

How I Feel

Use Newcomer Card, page 12

A. Complete each sentence with the correct feeling.

angry confused happy sad

1. I am confused.
2. I am sad.
3. I am happy.
4. I am angry.

B. Describe how you feel when you watch a funny video.

______

UNIT 2: Feelings, Lesson 2

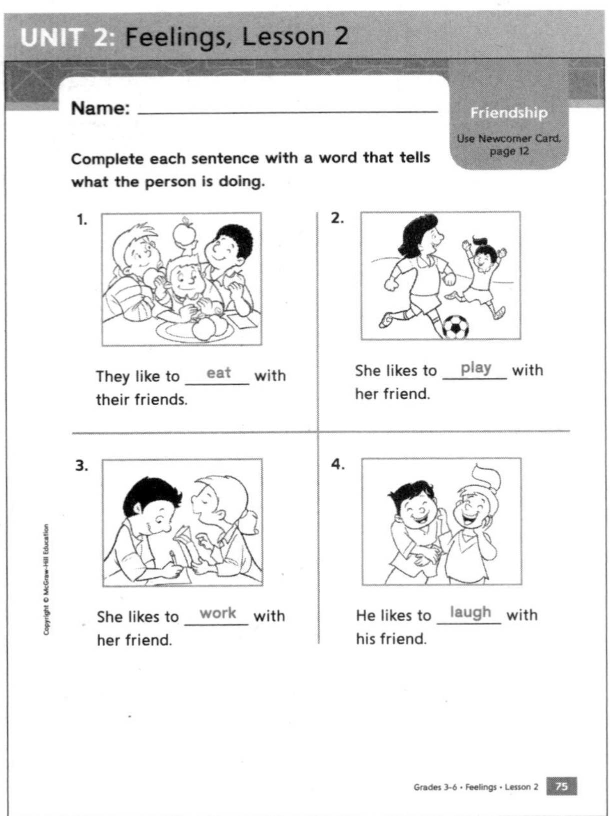

Name: ______

Friendship

Use Newcomer Card, page 12

Complete each sentence with a word that tells what the person is doing.

1. They like to eat with their friends.
2. She likes to play with her friend.
3. She likes to work with her friend.
4. He likes to laugh with his friend.

UNIT 2: Feelings, Lesson 3

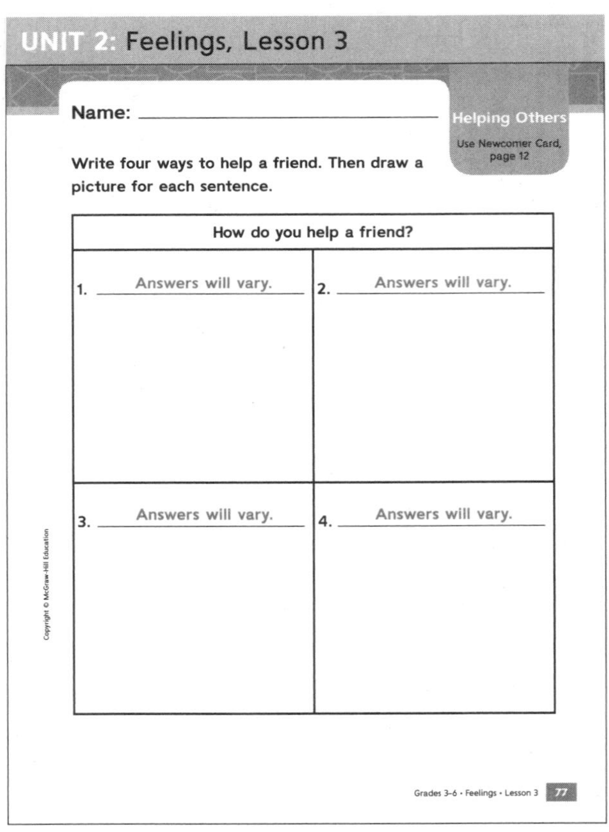

Name: ______

Helping Others

Use Newcomer Card, page 12

Write four ways to help a friend. Then draw a picture for each sentence.

How do you help a friend?	
1. Answers will vary.	2. Answers will vary.
3. Answers will vary.	4. Answers will vary.

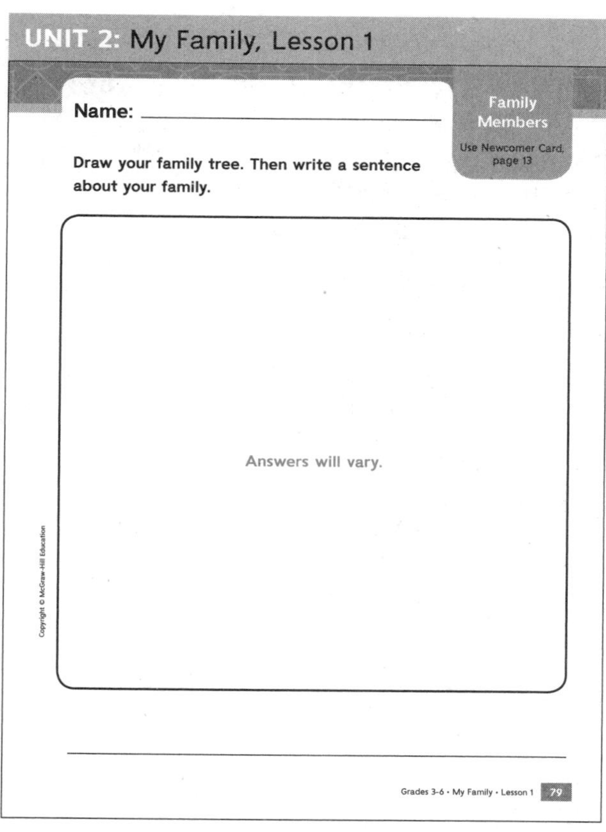

UNIT 2: My Family, Lesson 1

Family Members

Use Newcomer Card, page 13

Name: ____________________

Draw your family tree. Then write a sentence about your family.

Answers will vary.

____

Grades 3-6 • My Family • Lesson 1 79

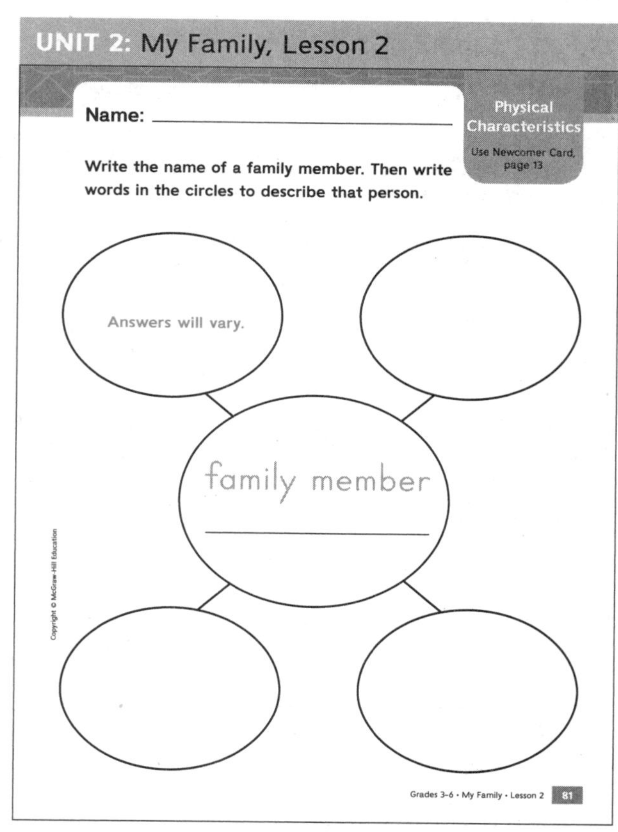

UNIT 2: My Family, Lesson 2

Physical Characteristics

Use Newcomer Card, page 13

Name: ____________________

Write the name of a family member. Then write words in the circles to describe that person.

Answers will vary.

family member

Grades 3-6 • My Family • Lesson 2 81

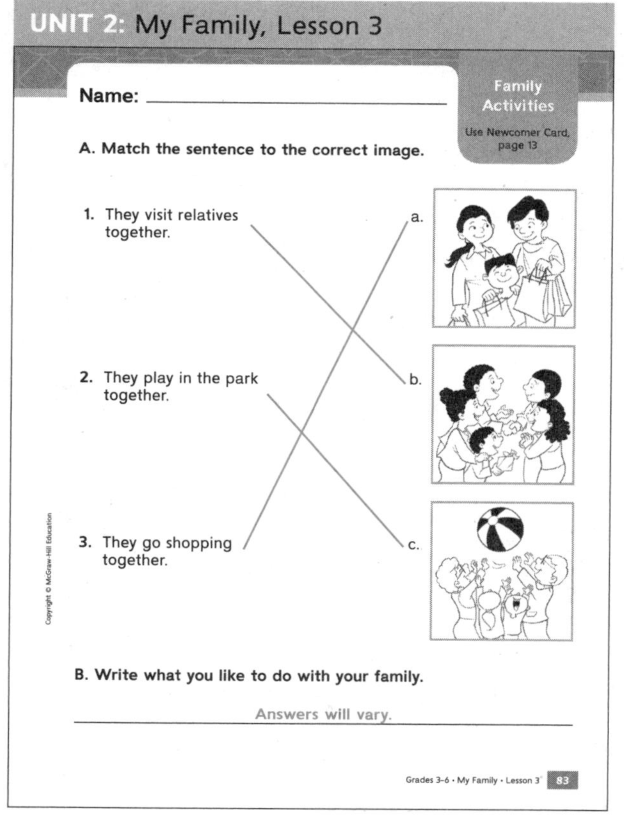

UNIT 2: My Family, Lesson 3

Family Activities

Use Newcomer Card, page 13

Name: ____________________

A. Match the sentence to the correct image.

1. They visit relatives together. — b.
2. They play in the park together. — c.
3. They go shopping together. — a.

B. Write what you like to do with your family.

Answers will vary.

Grades 3-6 • My Family • Lesson 3 83

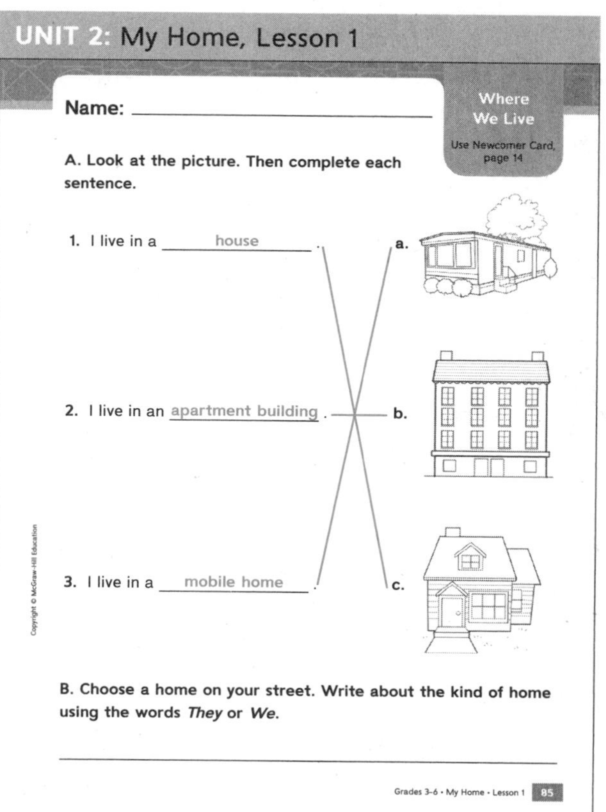

UNIT 2: My Home, Lesson 1

Where We Live

Use Newcomer Card, page 14

Name: ____________________

A. Look at the picture. Then complete each sentence.

1. I live in a house. — c.
2. I live in an apartment building. — b.
3. I live in a mobile home. — a.

B. Choose a home on your street. Write about the kind of home using the words *They* or *We*.

____

Grades 3-6 • My Home • Lesson 1 85

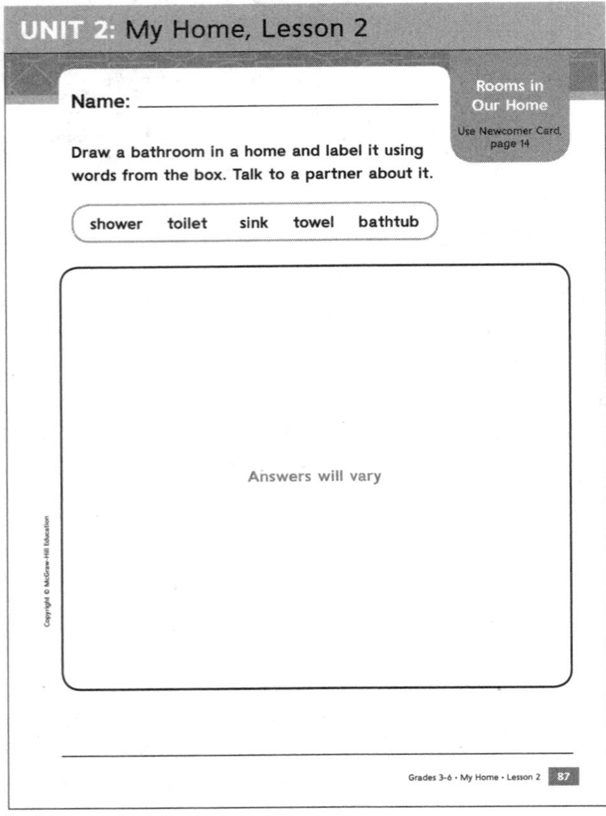

UNIT 2: My Home, Lesson 2

Name: ______________________

Rooms in Our Home

Use Newcomer Card, page 14

Draw a bathroom in a home and label it using words from the box. Talk to a partner about it.

shower toilet sink towel bathtub

Answers will vary

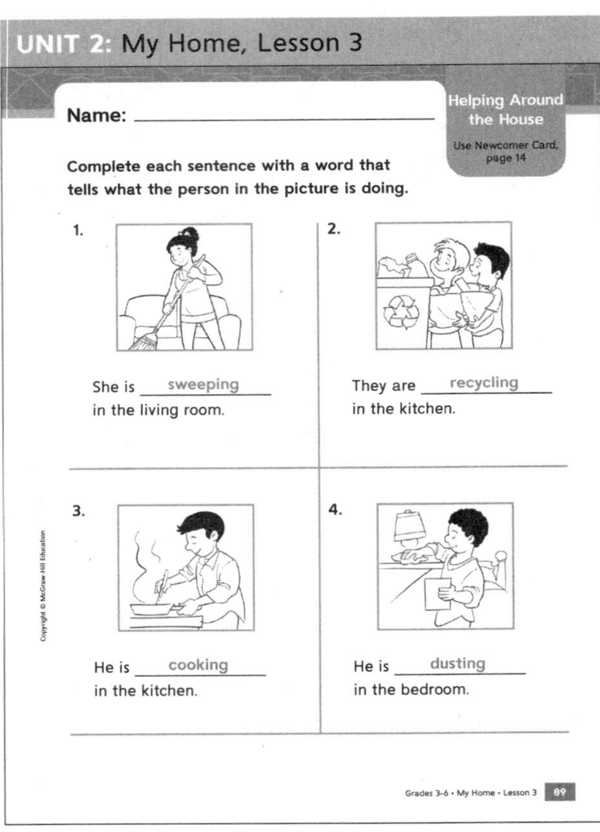

UNIT 2: My Home, Lesson 3

Name: ______________________

Helping Around the House

Use Newcomer Card, page 14

Complete each sentence with a word that tells what the person in the picture is doing.

1. She is sweeping in the living room.
2. They are recycling in the kitchen.
3. He is cooking in the kitchen.
4. He is dusting in the bedroom.

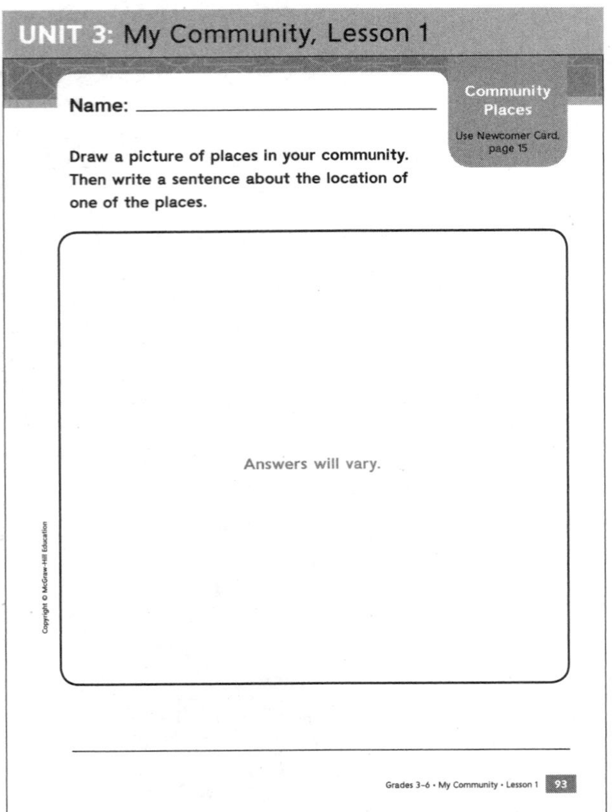

UNIT 3: My Community, Lesson 1

Name: ______________________

Community Places

Use Newcomer Card, page 15

Draw a picture of places in your community. Then write a sentence about the location of one of the places.

Answers will vary.

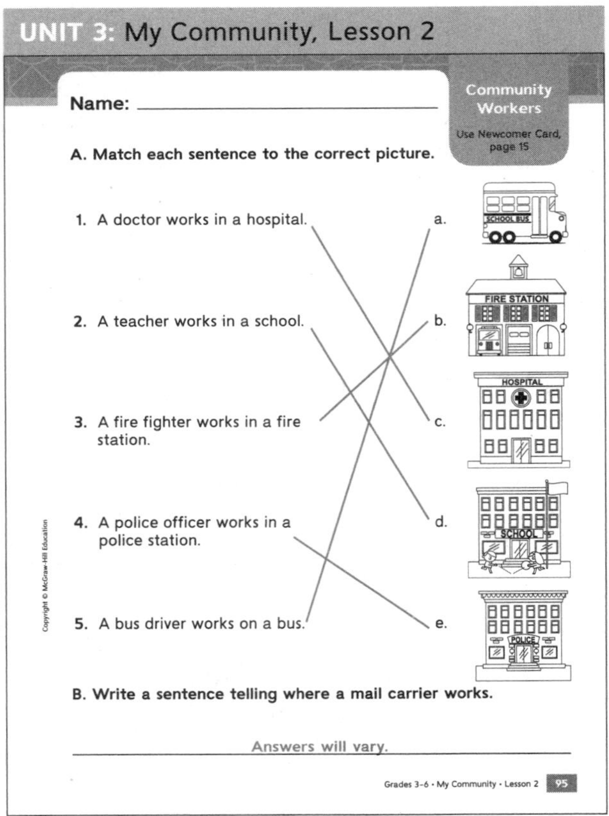

UNIT 3: My Community, Lesson 2

Name: ______________________

Community Workers

Use Newcomer Card, page 15

A. Match each sentence to the correct picture.

1. A doctor works in a hospital.
2. A teacher works in a school.
3. A fire fighter works in a fire station.
4. A police officer works in a police station.
5. A bus driver works on a bus.

a. b. c. d. e.

B. Write a sentence telling where a mail carrier works.

Answers will vary.

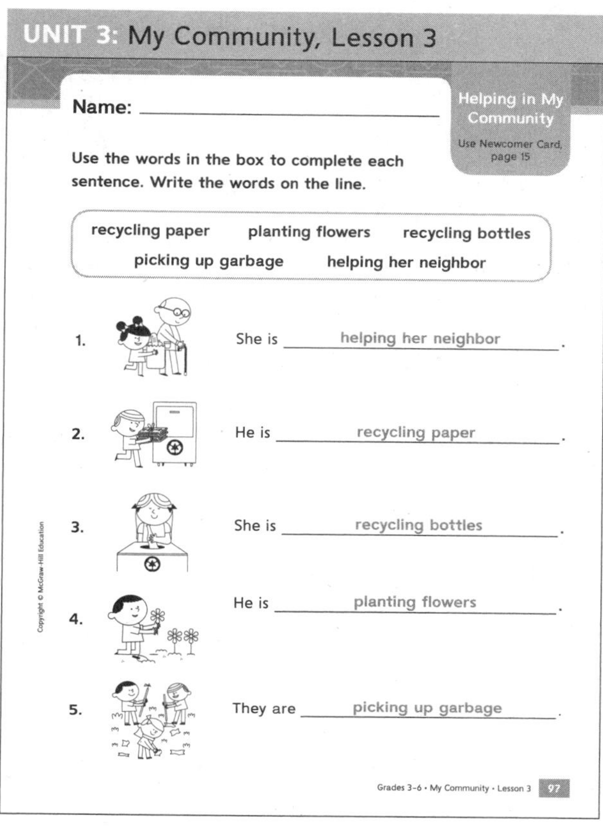
UNIT 3: My Community, Lesson 3

Helping in My Community
Use Newcomer Card, page 15

Name: ____________

Use the words in the box to complete each sentence. Write the words on the line.

recycling paper | planting flowers | recycling bottles | picking up garbage | helping her neighbor

1. She is helping her neighbor.
2. He is recycling paper.
3. She is recycling bottles.
4. He is planting flowers.
5. They are picking up garbage.

Copyright © McGraw-Hill Education

Grades 3–6 • My Community • Lesson 3 97

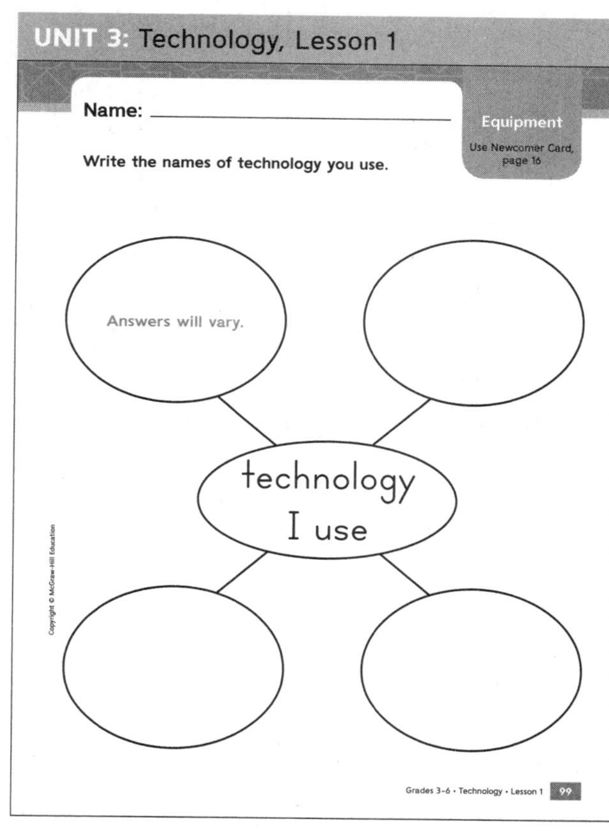
UNIT 3: Technology, Lesson 1

Equipment
Use Newcomer Card, page 16

Name: ____________

Write the names of technology you use.

Copyright © McGraw-Hill Education

Grades 3–6 • Technology • Lesson 1 99

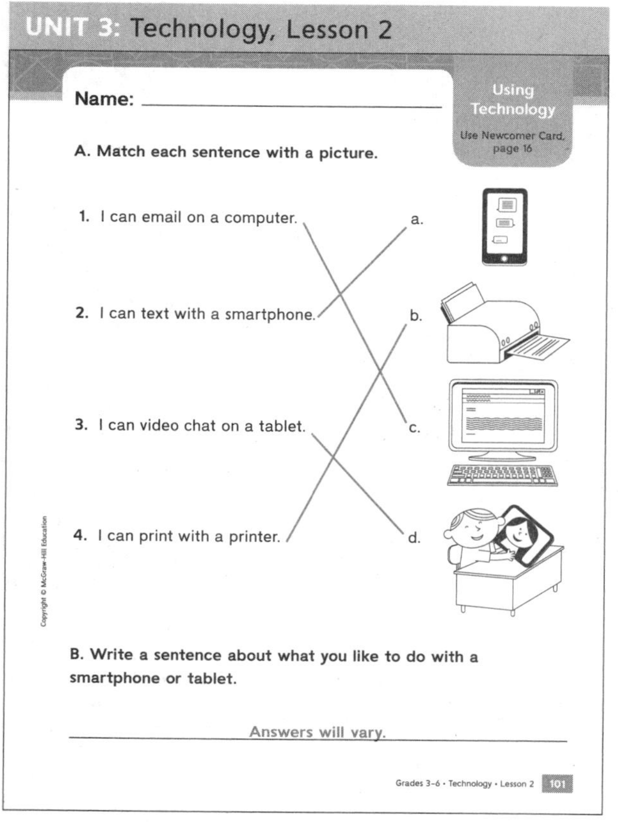
UNIT 3: Technology, Lesson 2

Using Technology
Use Newcomer Card, page 16

Name: ____________

A. Match each sentence with a picture.

1. I can email on a computer. — c.
2. I can text with a smartphone. — a.
3. I can video chat on a tablet. — d.
4. I can print with a printer. — b.

B. Write a sentence about what you like to do with a smartphone or tablet.

Answers will vary.

Copyright © McGraw-Hill Education

Grades 3–6 • Technology • Lesson 2 101

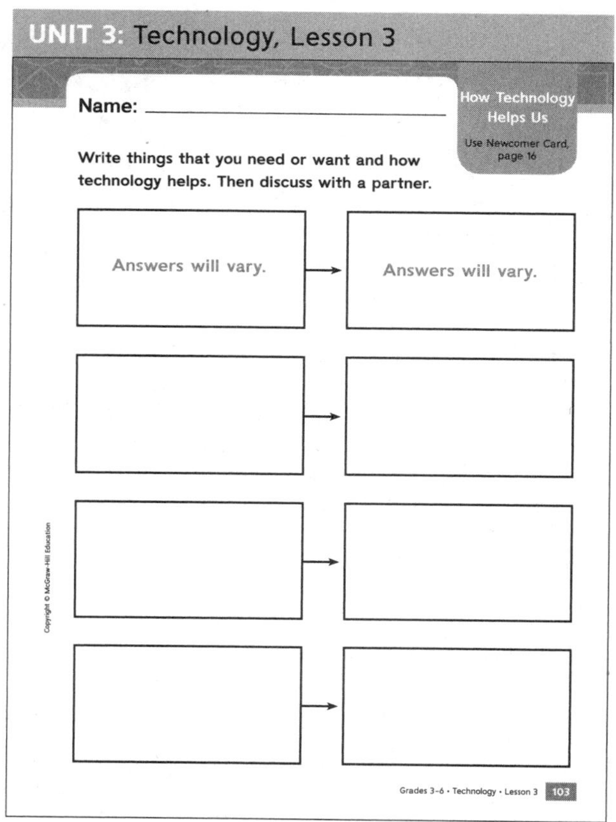
UNIT 3: Technology, Lesson 3

How Technology Helps Us
Use Newcomer Card, page 16

Name: ____________

Write things that you need or want and how technology helps. Then discuss with a partner.

Answers will vary. → Answers will vary.

Copyright © McGraw-Hill Education

Grades 3–6 • Technology • Lesson 3 103

ANSWER KEY

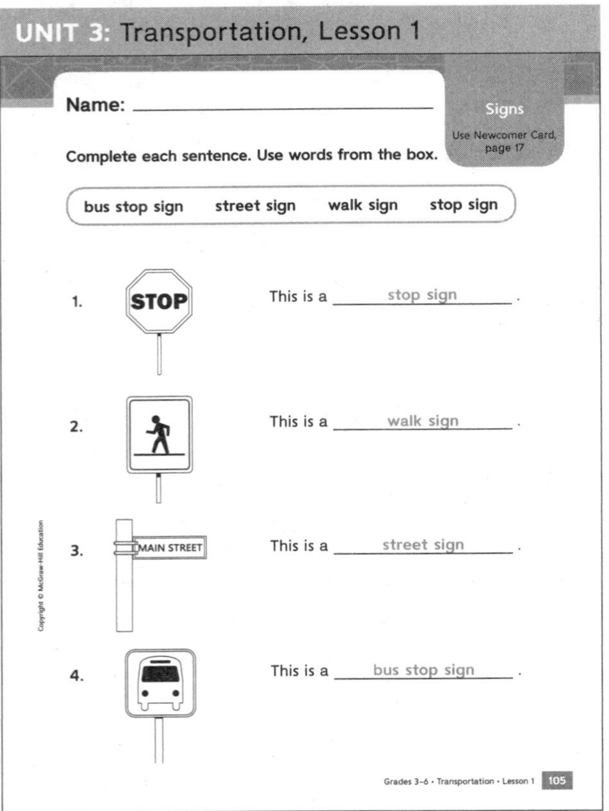

UNIT 3: Transportation, Lesson 1

Name: ______________________

Signs
Use Newcomer Card, page 17

Complete each sentence. Use words from the box.

bus stop sign street sign walk sign stop sign

1. This is a stop sign.
2. This is a walk sign.
3. This is a street sign.
4. This is a bus stop sign.

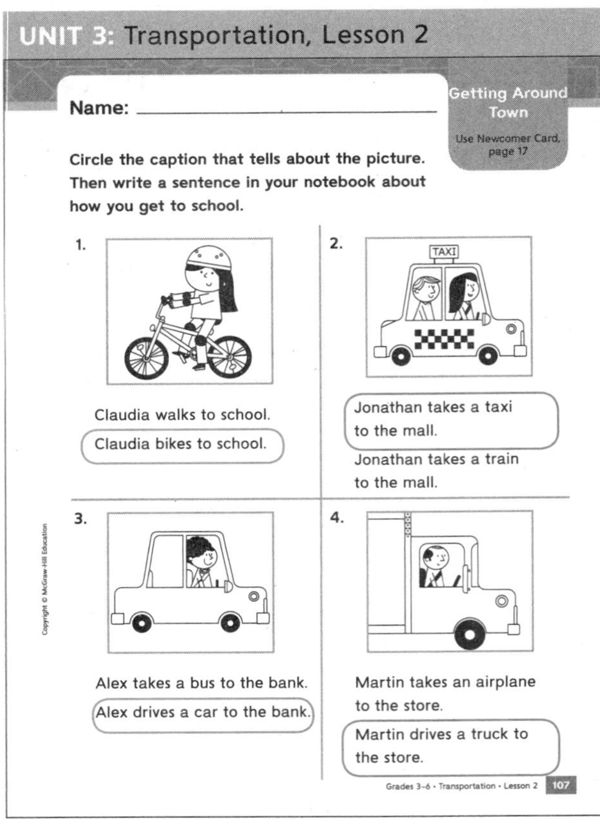

UNIT 3: Transportation, Lesson 2

Name: ______________________

Getting Around Town
Use Newcomer Card, page 17

Circle the caption that tells about the picture. Then write a sentence in your notebook about how you get to school.

1. Claudia walks to school. / **(Claudia bikes to school.)**
2. **(Jonathan takes a taxi to the mall.)** / Jonathan takes a train to the mall.
3. Alex takes a bus to the bank. / **(Alex drives a car to the bank.)**
4. Martin takes an airplane to the store. / **(Martin drives a truck to the store.)**

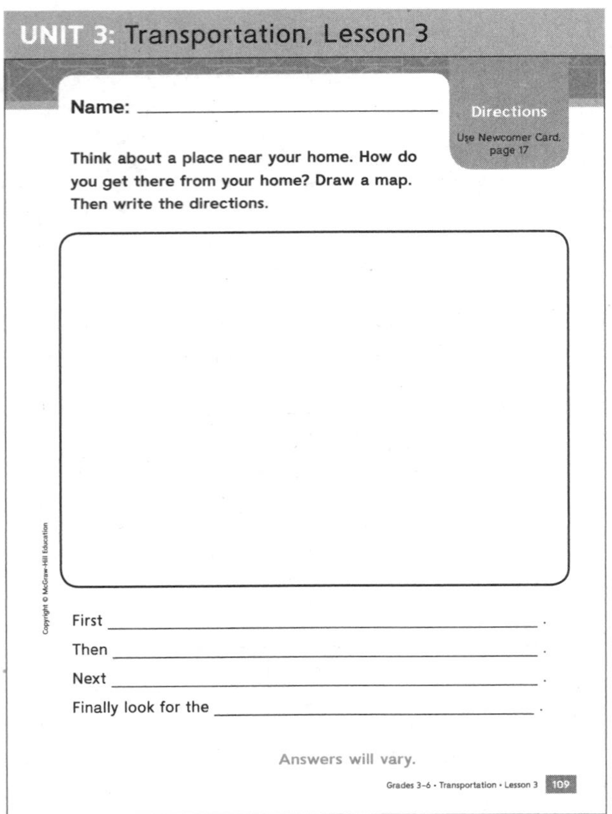

UNIT 3: Transportation, Lesson 3

Name: ______________________

Directions
Use Newcomer Card, page 17

Think about a place near your home. How do you get there from your home? Draw a map. Then write the directions.

First ______________________.
Then ______________________.
Next ______________________.
Finally look for the ______________________.

Answers will vary.

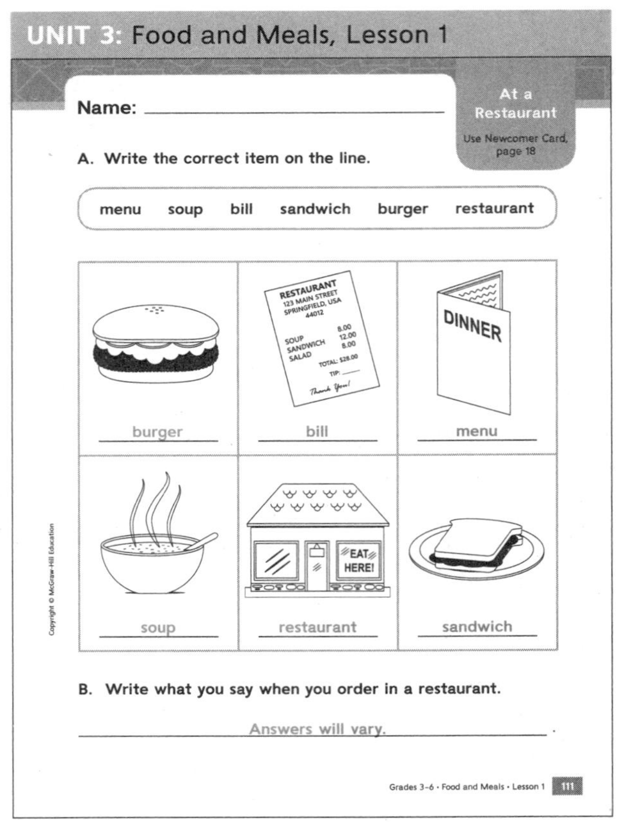

UNIT 3: Food and Meals, Lesson 1

Name: ______________________

At a Restaurant
Use Newcomer Card, page 18

A. Write the correct item on the line.

menu soup bill sandwich burger restaurant

burger	bill	menu
soup	restaurant	sandwich

B. Write what you say when you order in a restaurant.

Answers will vary.

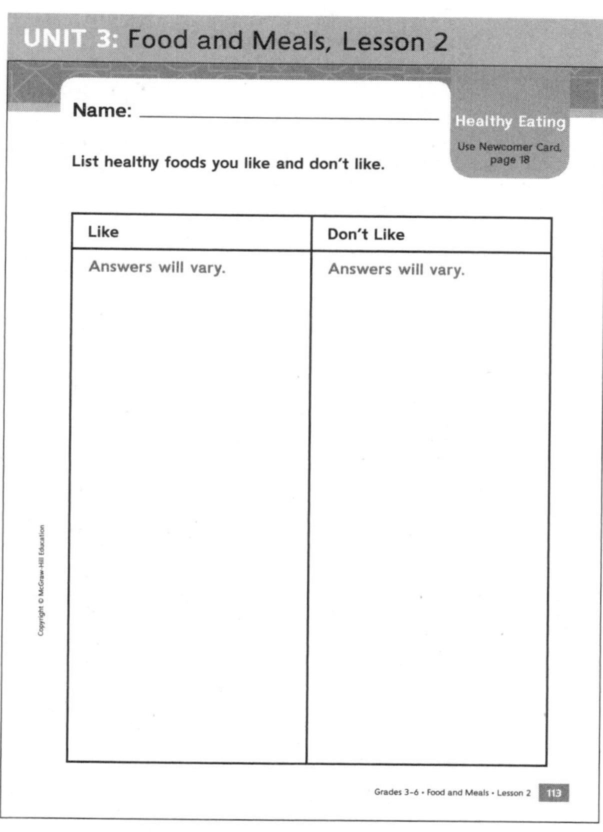
UNIT 3: Food and Meals, Lesson 2

Healthy Eating
Use Newcomer Card, page 18

Name: ______________________

List healthy foods you like and don't like.

Like	Don't Like
Answers will vary.	Answers will vary.

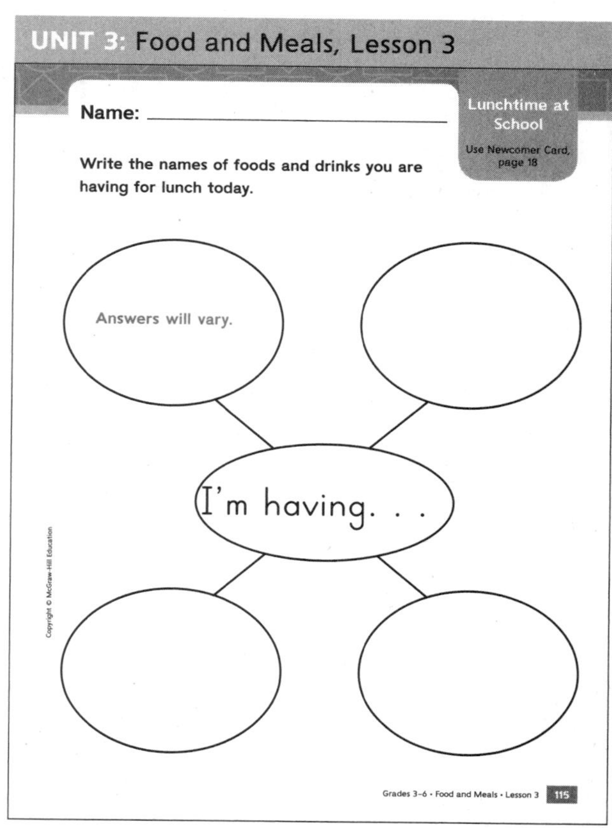
UNIT 3: Food and Meals, Lesson 3

Lunchtime at School
Use Newcomer Card, page 18

Name: ______________________

Write the names of foods and drinks you are having for lunch today.

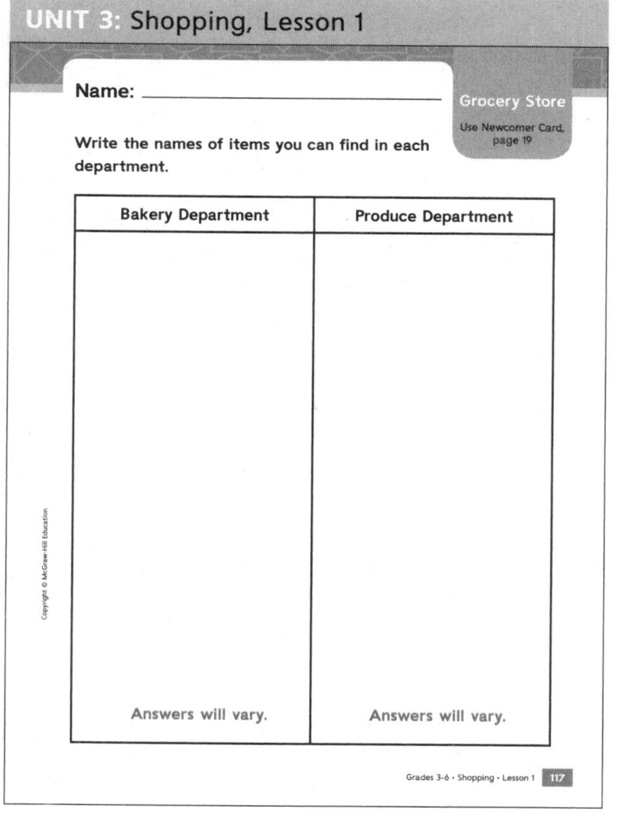
UNIT 3: Shopping, Lesson 1

Grocery Store
Use Newcomer Card, page 19

Name: ______________________

Write the names of items you can find in each department.

Bakery Department	Produce Department
Answers will vary.	Answers will vary.

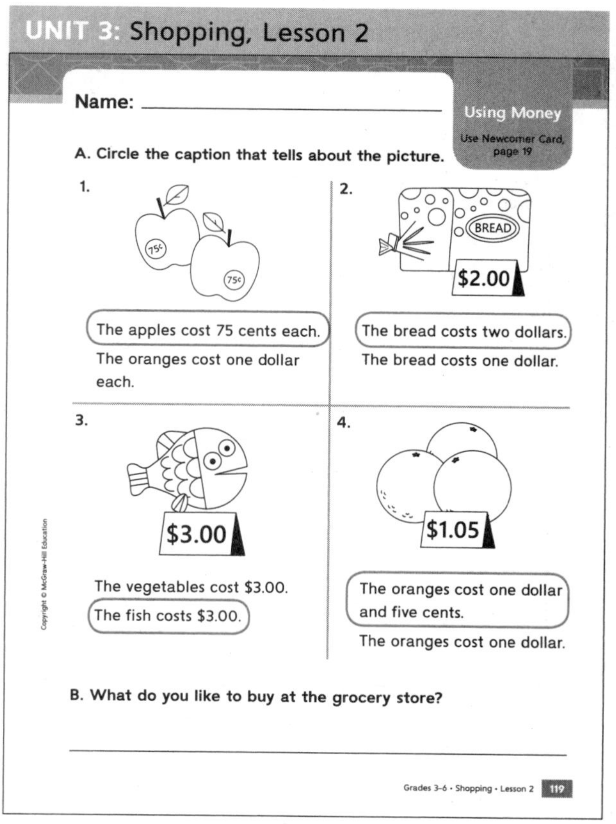
UNIT 3: Shopping, Lesson 2

Using Money
Use Newcomer Card, page 19

Name: ______________________

A. Circle the caption that tells about the picture.

1.

The apples cost 75 cents each.
The oranges cost one dollar each.

2.

The bread costs two dollars.
The bread costs one dollar.

3.

The vegetables cost $3.00.
The fish costs $3.00.

4.

The oranges cost one dollar and five cents.
The oranges cost one dollar.

B. What do you like to buy at the grocery store?

____

ANSWER KEY

UNIT 3: Shopping, Lesson 3

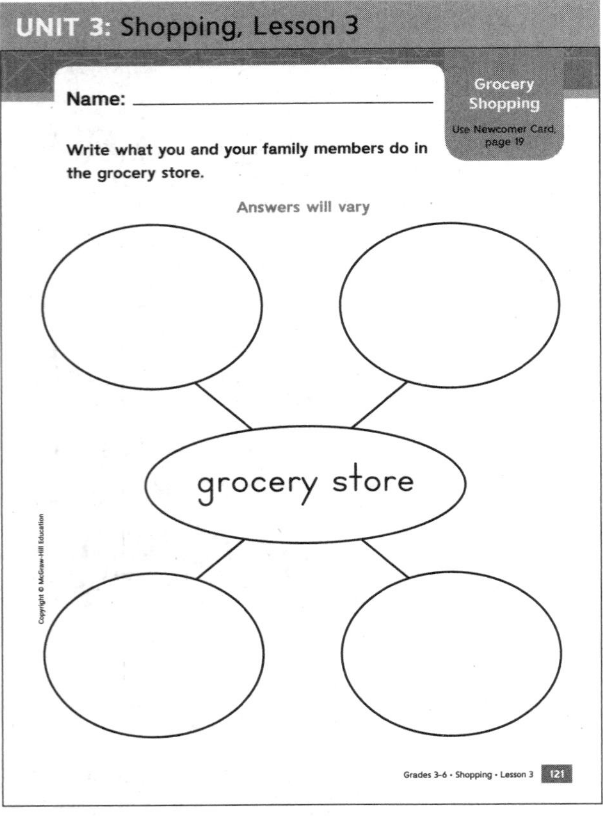

Name: ______

Grocery Shopping

Use Newcomer Card, page 19

Write what you and your family members do in the grocery store.

Answers will vary

grocery store

Copyright © McGraw-Hill Education

Grades 3–6 • Shopping • Lesson 3 121

UNIT 4: Measurement, Lesson 1

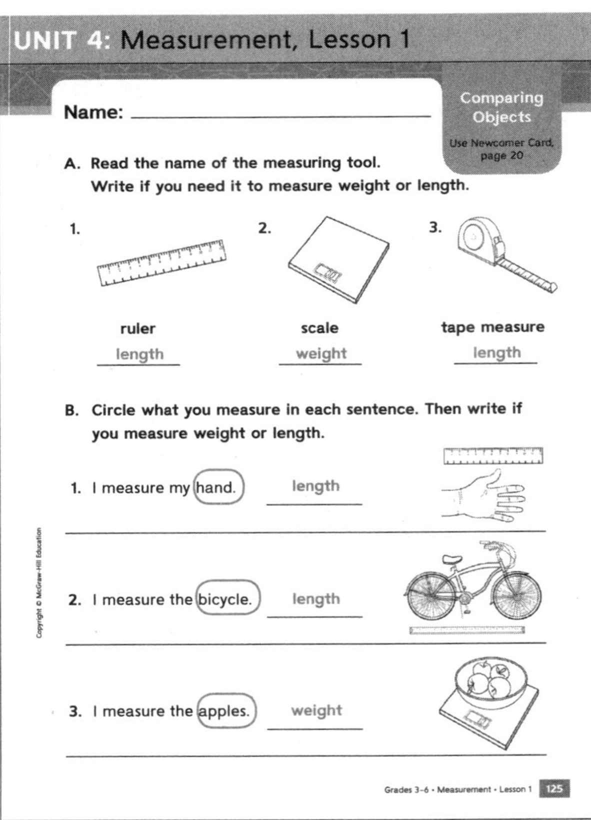

Name: ______

Comparing Objects

Use Newcomer Card, page 20

A. Read the name of the measuring tool. Write if you need it to measure weight or length.

1. ruler — length
2. scale — weight
3. tape measure — length

B. Circle what you measure in each sentence. Then write if you measure weight or length.

1. I measure my (hand.) — length
2. I measure the (bicycle.) — length
3. I measure the (apples.) — weight

Copyright © McGraw-Hill Education

Grades 3–6 • Measurement • Lesson 1 125

UNIT 4: Measurement, Lesson 2

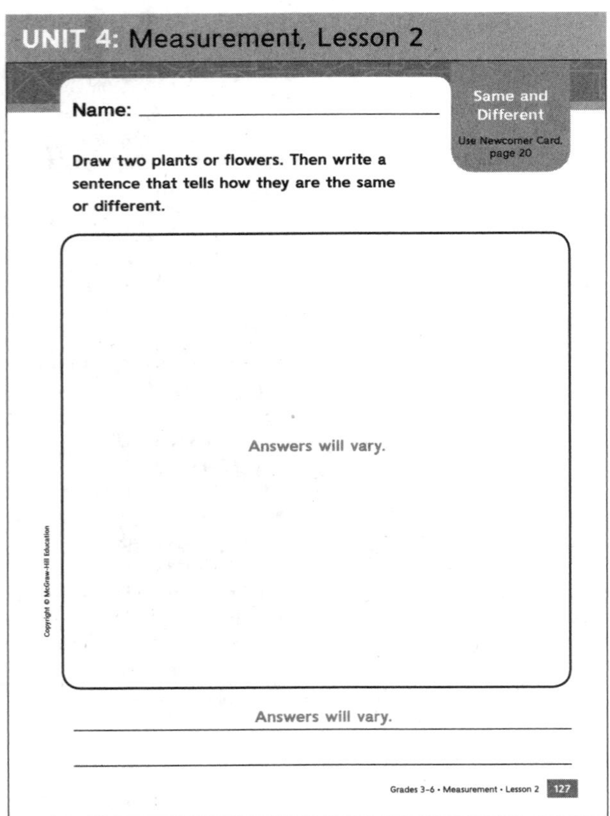

Name: ______

Same and Different

Use Newcomer Card, page 20

Draw two plants or flowers. Then write a sentence that tells how they are the same or different.

Answers will vary.

Answers will vary.

Copyright © McGraw-Hill Education

Grades 3–6 • Measurement • Lesson 2 127

UNIT 4: Measurement, Lesson 3

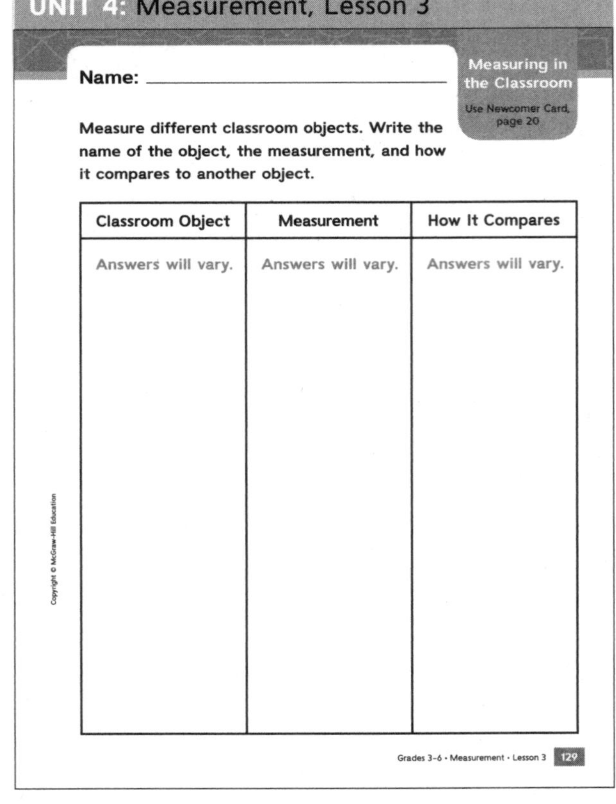

Name: ______

Measuring in the Classroom

Use Newcomer Card, page 20

Measure different classroom objects. Write the name of the object, the measurement, and how it compares to another object.

Classroom Object	Measurement	How It Compares
Answers will vary.	Answers will vary.	Answers will vary.

Copyright © McGraw-Hill Education

Grades 3–6 • Measurement • Lesson 3 129

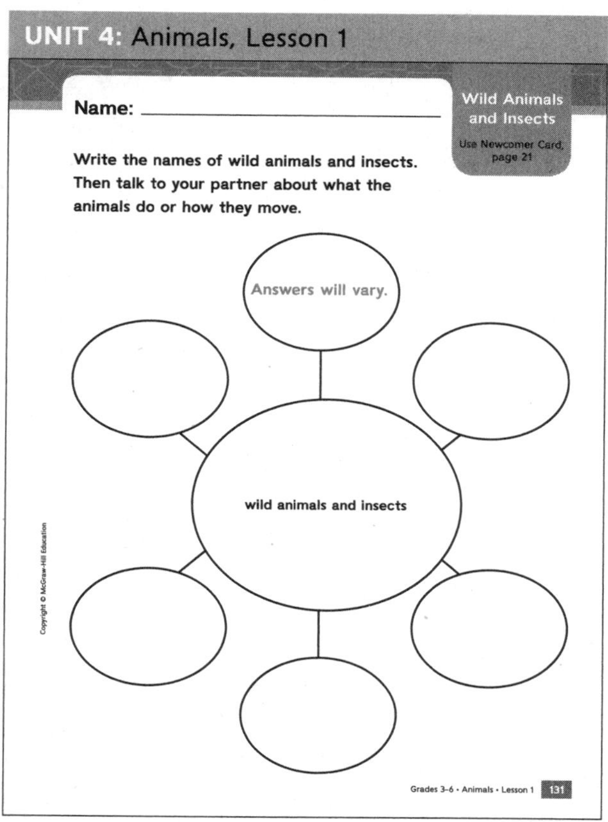
UNIT 4: Animals, Lesson 1
Name:
Wild Animals and Insects
Use Newcomer Card, page 21
Write the names of wild animals and insects. Then talk to your partner about what the animals do or how they move.
Answers will vary.
wild animals and insects
Grades 3–6 • Animals • Lesson 1 131

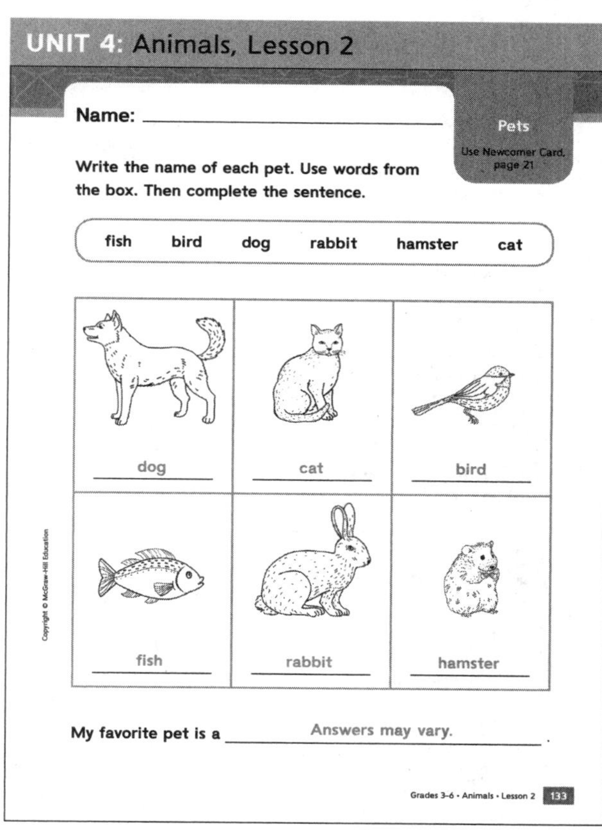
UNIT 4: Animals, Lesson 2
Name:
Pets
Use Newcomer Card, page 21
Write the name of each pet. Use words from the box. Then complete the sentence.
fish bird dog rabbit hamster cat
dog
cat
bird
fish
rabbit
hamster
My favorite pet is a Answers may vary.
Grades 3–6 • Animals • Lesson 2 133

UNIT 4: Animals, Lesson 3
Name:
Farm Animals
Use Newcomer Card, page 21
Complete the sentences with words from the box.
big small
The horse is big.
The pig is small.
bigger biggest smaller smallest
The chicken is the smallest.
The pig is smaller than the sheep.
The sheep is bigger than the pig.
The horse is the biggest.
Grades 3–6 • Animals • Lesson 3 135

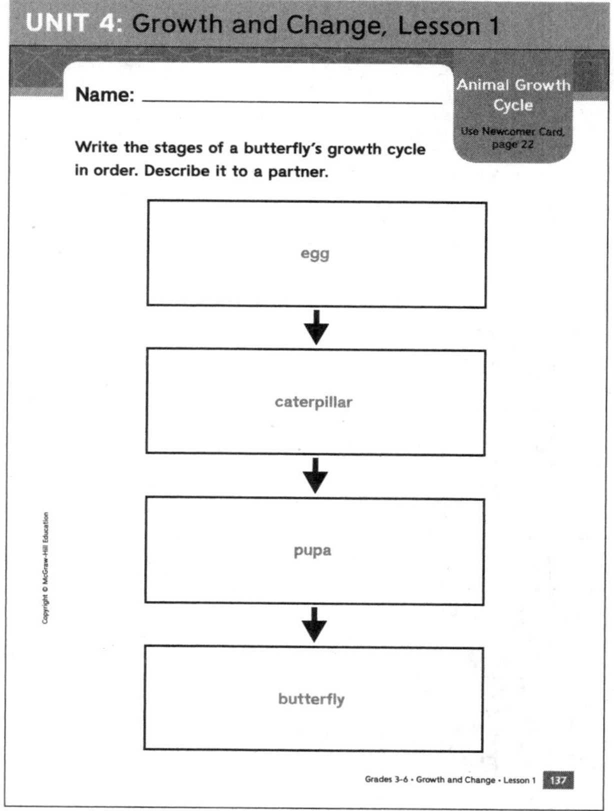
UNIT 4: Growth and Change, Lesson 1
Name:
Animal Growth Cycle
Use Newcomer Card, page 22
Write the stages of a butterfly's growth cycle in order. Describe it to a partner.
egg
caterpillar
pupa
butterfly
Grades 3–6 • Growth and Change • Lesson 1 137

ANSWER KEY

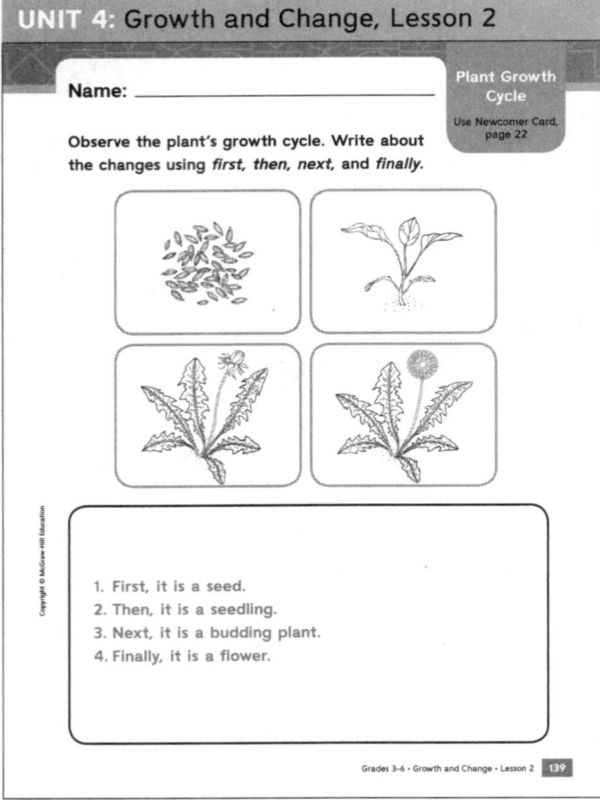
UNIT 4: Growth and Change, Lesson 2
Name:
Plant Growth Cycle
Use Newcomer Card, page 22
Observe the plant's growth cycle. Write about the changes using first, then, next, and finally.
1. First, it is a seed.
2. Then, it is a seedling.
3. Next, it is a budding plant.
4. Finally, it is a flower.
Grades 3–6 • Growth and Change • Lesson 2 139

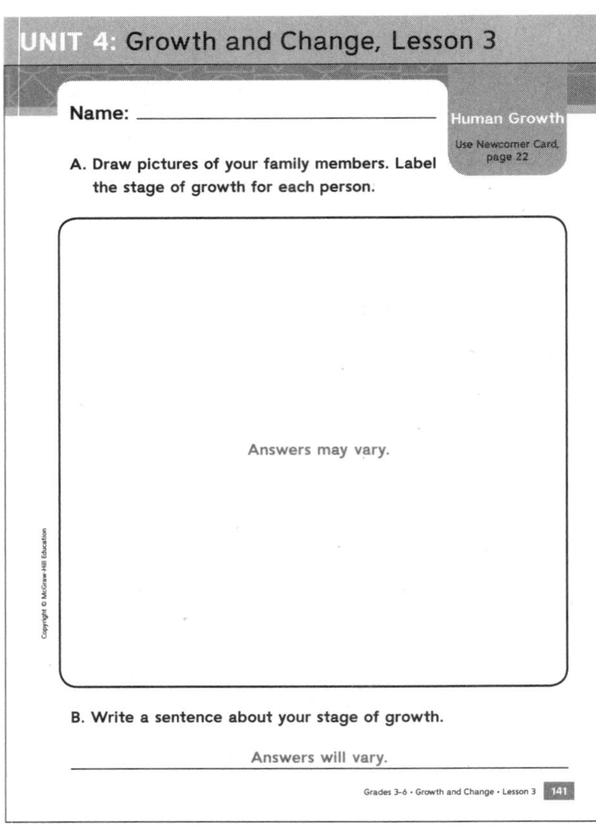
UNIT 4: Growth and Change, Lesson 3
Name:
Human Growth
Use Newcomer Card, page 22
A. Draw pictures of your family members. Label the stage of growth for each person.
Answers may vary.
B. Write a sentence about your stage of growth.
Answers will vary.
Grades 3–6 • Growth and Change • Lesson 3 141

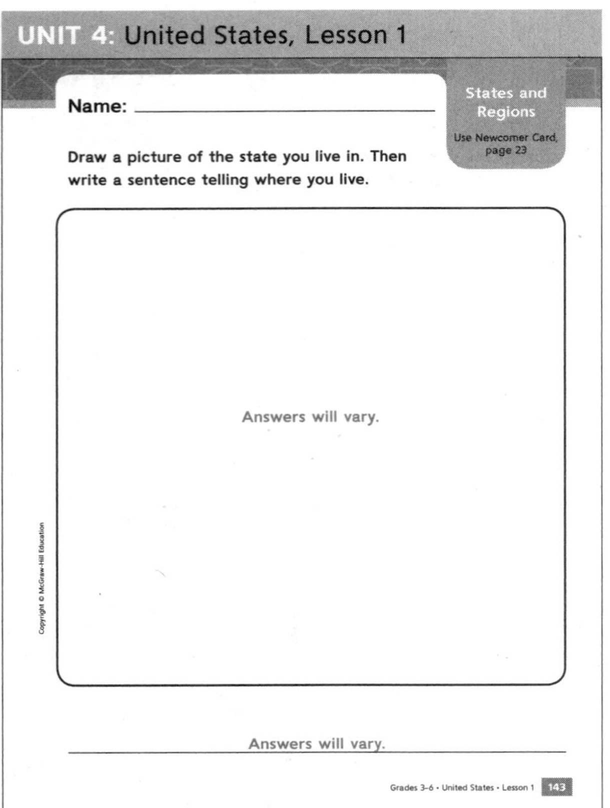
UNIT 4: United States, Lesson 1
Name:
States and Regions
Use Newcomer Card, page 23
Draw a picture of the state you live in. Then write a sentence telling where you live.
Answers will vary.
Answers will vary.
Grades 3–6 • United States • Lesson 1 143

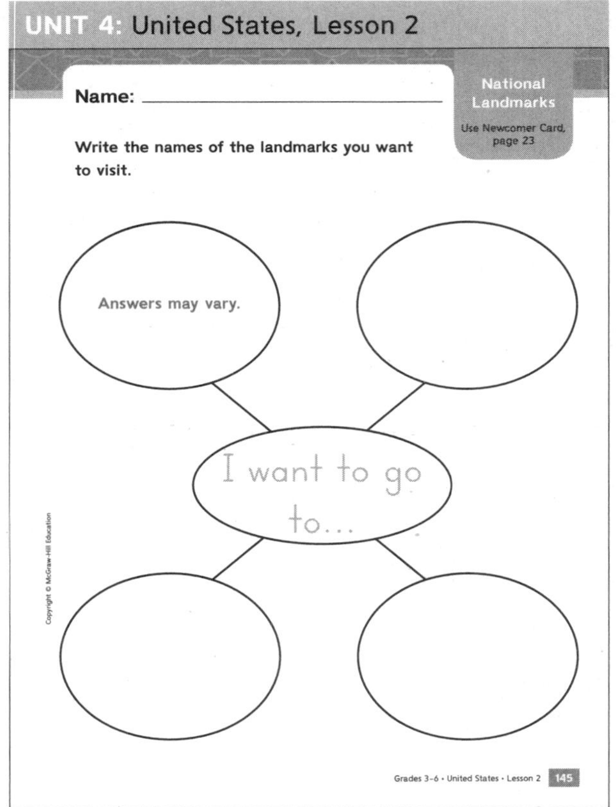
UNIT 4: United States, Lesson 2
Name:
National Landmarks
Use Newcomer Card, page 23
Write the names of the landmarks you want to visit.
Answers may vary.
I want to go to...
Grades 3–6 • United States • Lesson 2 145

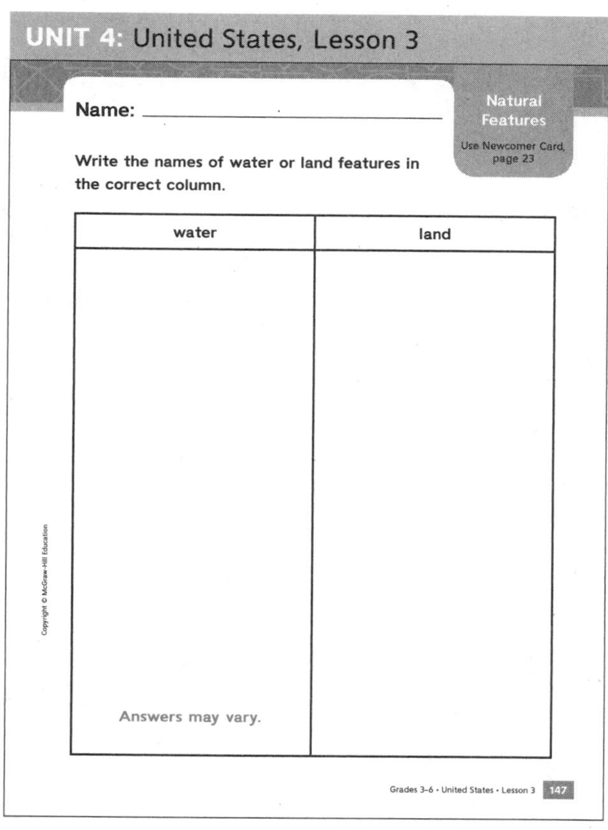
UNIT 4: United States, Lesson 3
Name:
Natural Features
Use Newcomer Card, page 23
Write the names of water or land features in the correct column.
water
land
Answers may vary.
Grades 3–6 • United States • Lesson 3 147

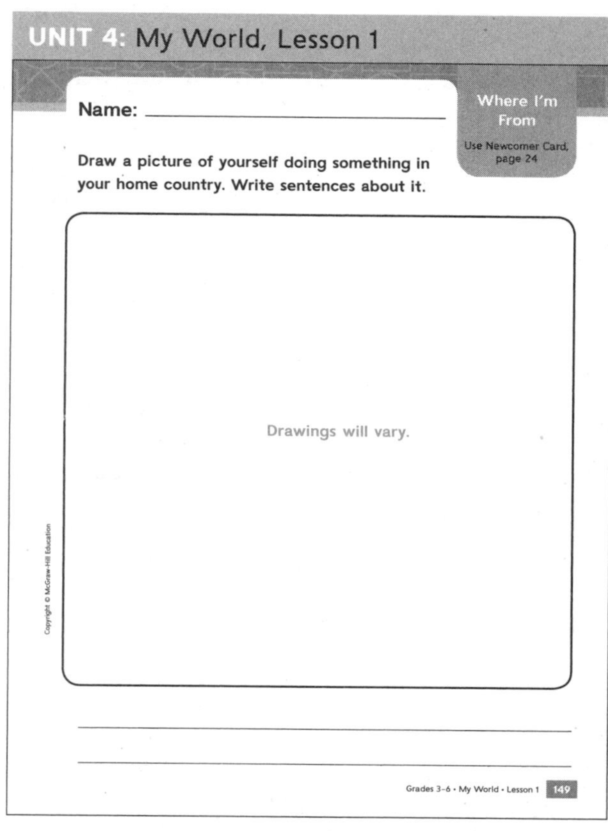
UNIT 4: My World, Lesson 1
Name:
Where I'm From
Use Newcomer Card, page 24
Draw a picture of yourself doing something in your home country. Write sentences about it.
Drawings will vary.
Grades 3–6 • My World • Lesson 1 149

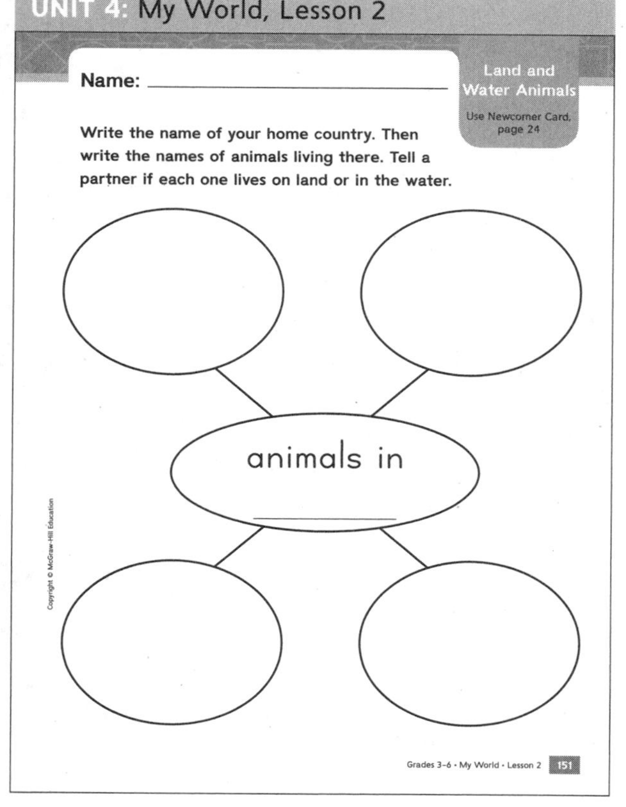
UNIT 4: My World, Lesson 2
Name:
Land and Water Animals
Use Newcomer Card, page 24
Write the name of your home country. Then write the names of animals living there. Tell a partner if each one lives on land or in the water.
animals in
Grades 3–6 • My World • Lesson 2 151

UNIT 4: My World, Lesson 3
Name:
In My New Country
Use Newcomer Card, page 24
Create a collage of your home country. Label the pictures. Write sentences about your home country and the United States.
Grades 3–6 • My World • Lesson 3 153

SPEECH BALLOONS

Name: ______________________________

Name: ______________________

CONVERSATION STARTERS

Hello, I'm

____________________.

What's your name?

What country are you from?

I'm from

____________________.

How old are you?

I'm _______________ years old.

I like _______________ because ___________.

I don't like _________ because ___________.

What are you doing?	I'm ________________ and ________________.
How do you feel?	I'm ________________.
Where do you live?	I live in ____________________.
What's your phone number?	My number is ____________________.

CONVERSATION STARTERS

What are you eating?

I'm eating ________ and ____________.

Do you like ______?

Yes, I like ________.
No, I don't like ______.

What do you need to buy?

I need ________ and ____________.

Where are the _____and_____?

They are ________.

GAMES

These collaborative games will help students practice the language learned and can be used to extend the Practice/Apply section of any lesson.

Save Five and Describe

PURPOSE Students practice *vocabulary* and *commands*.

INSTRUCTIONS Students take turns saying "Say five!" and naming five words they have learned. Students can add words to the command to play more challenging rounds. For example, "Say five things that are heavy and big!" Play two or three rounds. The student who can answer the most "Say Five!" commands wins the game.

EXAMPLES First round: *yellow, fire fighter, house, happy, window*

Second round: (Say five things that are heavy and big) *elephant, desk, door, bed, car*

Who Are You? What Are You Saying?

YOU NEED Index cards with words that name related roles and/or activities from the lesson

PURPOSE Students practice *nouns* that name people and occupations, *verbs* that name activities related to those people and occupations, and modal verbs *can, may,* and *must*.

INSTRUCTIONS Students play in groups of three. Two students decide who they want to be and role-play a conversation, using informal and formal language. When the pair completes their "conversation," the third student guesses who is who in the conversation. Students switch roles and play again.

For a further challenge: Students can role-play the conversation in the past tense.

EXAMPLES Teacher/student, mail carrier/person receiving or sending a letter, brother/sister, buyer/seller, waiter/customer

GAMES

A Phone Call

YOU NEED Index cards with topics (The weather and clothes you wear, What you do at school, etc.)

PURPOSE Students practice talking about *habits* and *likes* and *dislikes.*

INSTRUCTIONS Students play with partners. Pairs take turns role-playing a phone conversation around the topic. Other pairs observe and clap if they like the conversation. The pair that gets the biggest applause wins the game.

EXAMPLES Student says: *I like to play sports at school.* Partner says: *I like to play sports, too. I don't like to draw.*

Put Them in Order

YOU NEED Blank index cards; timer

PURPOSE Students practice *sequence*.

INSTRUCTIONS Students use recently learned vocabulary to make a set of index cards with a sequence of numbers, steps, stages, or activities. Students shuffle their cards and exchange them with a partner. Set a time. Partners put the cards in order. The first student to order the cards describes the sequence and wins the game. Students change partners and play again.

EXAMPLES *A sequence of numbers, times of the day, days of the week, months, seasons, growth cycle stages, or a set of activities that happen first, then, next, last.*

How Many?

YOU NEED Index cards with names of objects, animals, people, and places; number cube

PURPOSE Students practice *numbers.*

INSTRUCTIONS Partners take turns rolling the cube and take that number of cards. Students look at the cards, categorize them, and say complete sentences describing the categories of things they have. Play multiple rounds. The student who has more correct sentences wins the game.

EXAMPLES Student rolls the number 4 and takes four cards: *hamster, elephant, school,* and *eraser.*

Student says: *I have two land animals. I have two school-related things. I have two small things and two large things.*

Say It With Actions

PURPOSE Students practice *gerunds.*

INSTRUCTIONS Students play in groups. One student says an action. The rest of the group acts out the action. Students take turns saying and acting out the actions. Play a second round by having groups decide on an action without saying it aloud. The group acts out the action and students in other groups say the actions.

EXAMPLES First round: *We are walking; We are singing.*

Second round: *They are playing; They are reading.*

Say Something About . . .

YOU NEED Number cube; word cards

PURPOSE Students practice saying *affirmative sentences* in the *present* or *past tense.*

INSTRUCTIONS Groups place cards on the floor in a line and mark the "Start" and "End" of the line. Students take turns rolling the cube and advance that number of cards from "Start." One student says a sentence in the present or past tense using the word on the card where s/he lands. If the sentence is correct, the student rolls the cube again.

EXAMPLES (grapes) *I ate grapes yesterday.* (panda) *The panda is a land animal from China.*

GAMES

Let's Compare

YOU NEED Blank index cards; cards with the following commands: Order from smallest to largest; Order from slowest to fastest; Order from shortest to tallest; Order from lightest to heaviest.

PURPOSE Students practice *comparatives* and *superlatives.*

INSTRUCTIONS Students play in pairs. Each pair takes a card with a command and reads it. Each student writes the name of three vocabulary words on three different index cards. Then they switch cards and see who can put the cards in order as stated on the command card. Students use comparative and superlative words to compare the words seen on the cards. The first student to order and compare the words correctly wins the game.

EXAMPLES *Smallest to largest: eraser, dog, door. The eraser is the smallest. The dog is larger than the eraser. The door is larger than the dog. The door is the largest. Lightest to heaviest: shoe, desk, bed.*

I See, I Like

YOU NEED Index cards with the sentence frames: I see ______. I like _______ because ______.

PURPOSE Students practice the *present tense* of the verbs *to see* and *to like*.

INSTRUCTIONS Students play with a partner. Each partner gets a sentence starter. One student points to or names a thing or place and uses the sentence frame to begin a description. For "I see," the partner adds adjectives or phrases to complete the description. For "I like," the partner adds adjectives and reasons. Partners switch roles. The partner who says the longest sentence wins the round.

EXAMPLES

Student: *I see a big park.*

Partner: *I see a big, green park.*

Student: *I like the red flowers in the park.*

Partner: *I like the tall red flowers in the park because they smell nice.*

Step by Step

YOU NEED Index cards with series of commands; timer

PURPOSE Students practice *saying* and *following commands.*

INSTRUCTIONS Students play in small groups. Each group takes several cards. Set a time. Groups read one card at a time card, discuss the steps, and complete them in order as stated on the card. The group that completes the commands wins the game.

EXAMPLES Find four objects. Point to the objects and count them. Make two groups of two. Talk about your groups.

Spelling Bee

YOU NEED Timer

PURPOSE Students practice *spelling familiar words.*

INSTRUCTIONS Students play in small groups. A group member says a word from the lesson. Group members take turns spelling the word and then saying a sentence with that word.

EXAMPLES *Summer, school, pants, fire station, bathing suit, elephant, bee, walking, hike.*

Play to Compare

YOU NEED Timer

PURPOSE Students practice *describing* and *comparing objects.*

INSTRUCTIONS Students play in small groups. Set a time. Group members look for items or pictures in the classroom that can be compared. When the time is up, students take turns saying sentences that compare their items. The student with the highest number of correct sentences wins the game.

EXAMPLES *The blue book is big and the red book is small.*

The eraser is short. The ruler is longer than the eraser.

The yardstick is the longest.

Summer is hot and winter is cold.

GAMES

True or False

YOU NEED Word cards

PURPOSE Students practice *describing objects* using the verbs *to be* and *to have* and the *pronoun it.*

INSTRUCTIONS Students play in pairs. A student takes a card. The partner says statements about the word on the card. The student answers with *True* or *False* until the partner guesses the word. (Provide support as needed.) Partners switch roles.

EXAMPLES

Nurse

It is an object. False	*It works at a store.* False.
It is a person. True.	*It works at the school.* False.
It works at the hospital. True.	*It's a doctor.* False.
It's a nurse. True!	

Can You?

YOU NEED A ball for each group

PURPOSE Students practice using *affirmative* and *negative sentences* with the verb *can.*

INSTRUCTIONS Students play in small groups. A student takes the ball, says something he or she *can do* and something he or she *can't do,* then throws the ball to another student. Repeat until all students have said what they can and can't do. Encourage them to make silly sentences.

EXAMPLES

S1: *I can fly a kite. I can't play soccer.*

S2: *I can run fast. I can't walk fast.*

S3: *I can play in the afternoon. I can't play at night.*

S4: *I can print with a printer. I can't call with a printer.*

I Can Buy

YOU NEED Word cards that name objects or food items with prices; play money

PURPOSE Students practice verbs in the *present tense* and vocabulary related to *money* and *buying*.

INSTRUCTIONS Students play in small groups. Assign cards and money to each group. Students take turns taking a card and use that word and their money to talk about what they "need" to buy and what they "can" buy. Other group members say if the student is correct. If the student is correct, he or she keeps the card. Students play until all cards are "bought." The student with the most cards wins the game.

EXAMPLES *I need a T-shirt. I have twenty dollars. I can buy a T-shirt.*

Talk About Our Friend

YOU NEED Timer

PURPOSE Students practice using the *present tense, adjectives,* and *conjunctions.*

INSTRUCTIONS Students play in small groups. Set a time. One student is the friend. Group members take turns describing their friend. If a student can't describe the friend, he or she skips a turn and other members continue. Students can play another round by describing their friend's personality and talents or skills.

EXAMPLES First round: *Our friend is a boy. He is 9 years old. He has brown eyes. He is tall. He has blue shorts.*

Second round: *Our friend is smart and nice. He is a good soccer player.*

GAMES

What Is It?

YOU NEED Cards with the words *this, these, that, those*

PURPOSE Students practice *demonstrative pronouns* and *possessive pronouns.*

INSTRUCTIONS Students play in pairs. Partners take turns taking a card and using that word to show an object or a set of objects. Students should use *my, his, her, their,* and *our* in their sentences. The partner who completes all four correct sentences wins the game.

EXAMPLES

These: *These are my shoes.*

That: *That is our teacher.*

This: *This is our classroom.*

Those: *Those are her pencils.*

Here, There, Everywhere!

PURPOSE Students practice asking questions with *where* and using *prepositions.*

INSTRUCTIONS Students play in pairs. Partners take turns. One student asks about the location of an object, place, or person. The partner says where the object, place, or person is located.

EXAMPLES

Where is the teacher? The teacher is here/there/in the classroom/by the door.

Where is the pencil? The pencil is on the table/in the bag/by the computer.

Where is the gym? The gym is next to the library.

Oral Language Proficiency Benchmark Assessment

The Oral Language Proficiency Benchmark Assessment can be given at different points throughout the use of these materials to monitor students' oral language proficiency growth. It is suggested that this assessment be administered twice a year.

How to Administer the Assessment

Work with students individually. Show the illustrations, and use the prompts on page T41. Ask one question at a time, recording the students' answers. The guidelines at the bottom of the prompts page will help you to evaluate each student's oral proficiency. The first time you administer the assessment, you may wish to model the responses after students give their responses. Model how each question could be answered, using complete sentences, restating, rephrasing, or elaborating on students' responses.

Oral Language Proficiency Benchmark Record Sheet

Use the results of this assessment, as well as quick checks, to monitor students' growth and determine areas in which to focus instruction for each student. Note students' progress on the Oral Language Proficiency Benchmark Record Sheet on page T42 to chart their development over time.

Student Profile

Use the Student Profile on pages T43-T44 to record observations throughout the unit.

Self-Assessment

Have students fill out the Self-Assessment on page T45 to evaluate their own progress during the course of each unit and determine areas in which they may need additional practice and support.

1

2

3

4

PROMPTS	STUDENT RESPONSES
Picture 1: Look at this picture. What do you see?	
Picture 1: What are the students looking at? Why?	
Picture 2: Where are the insects? What are the insects doing?	
Picture 3: What happened to the insects? How do you know?	
Picture 3: How do you think the students feel? How do you know?	
Picture 4: What do you see now?	
Picture 4: What can you tell me about how the insect has changed?	
All Pictures: Let's look at all of the pictures together. Tell what happened to the insect using the words *first, then, next,* and *finally.*	

Review students' responses to the prompts. Use the following as a guide to inform instruction:

IF the student is able to use new vocabulary and language structures to respond to questions, **THEN** he or she may be ready for more challenging tasks.

Oral Language Proficiency Benchmark Assessment Record Sheet

STUDENT NAME	AFTER UNIT ______	AFTER UNIT ______

Student Profile

Name ______________________________ **Date** ______________

Unit ____________

Use this chart to record student performance data and inform instruction.

INSTRUCTION	OBSERVATION/NOTES
Language Objectives Student can: • name and describe objects • ask and answer questions • recount events	
Language Structures/Grammar Student can: • use language structures to communicate • use language structures to ask and answer questions	
Vocabulary Student can: • use new vocabulary to ask and answer questions • use new vocabulary during collaborative conversations • use new vocabulary to name and describe things	

Student Profile

Name ______________________ Date ______________

Unit ____________

Use this chart to record student performance data and inform instruction.

INSTRUCTION	OBSERVATION/NOTES
Writing Student can: • write to label objects • write to fill in sentences • write a complete sentence • write multiple complete sentences	
Foundational Skills Student can: • understand the sounds of English letters • understand that some words are made of smaller parts, such as inflectional endings, prefixes, suffixes • recognize and use high-frequency words	
Collaborative Listening Student can: • Demonstrate active listening by answering and asking basic questions with prompting and substantial support	
Collaborative Speaking Student can: • answer yes/no questions during conversations about familiar topics • employ first language and gestures to try to participate more	

Self-Assessment

Write new words you have learned.

____

____

____

____

Mark the boxes.

I became better at:	I want to become better at:
☐ sharing information ☐ listening ☐ writing ☐ adding details	☐ sharing information ☐ listening ☐ writing ☐ adding details

I learned to

____

____

____